MAN WITH A BULL-TONGUE PLOW

MAN WITH A BULL-TONGUE PLOW

A new edition of the
original bestseller by
JESSE STUART

With an Introduction by
John H. Spurlock

JESSE STUART
FOUNDATION
Ashland, Kentucky
2011

Copyright © 2011 by Jesse Stuart Foundation

All rights reserved. Printed in the United States of America. No part of this publication may be reproduced in whole or in part, or utilized in any form or by any means, electronic or mechancial, including photocopying, recording, or by any information or retrieval system, without written permission of the publisher.

ISBN: 978-1-931672-82-5

Published by
Jesse Stuart Foundation
1645 Winchester Avenue
Ashland, Kentucky 41101
(606) 326-1667
jsfbooks.com

FOREWORD

Jesse Stuart's first major work was *Man With a Bull-Tongue Plow*, a collection of 703 sonnets written in 1932 and 1933. The book was published by E.P. Dutton & Company of New York in 1934 and was immediately embraced by the general reading public. It also inspired a wave of critical response that catapulted Stuart to national acclaim. Many reviewers called Stuart a "modern day Robert Burns." The first hardback edition sold out in less than one month and reprints followed.

A second edition, abridged and re-edited by Stuart, was published by E.P. Dutton & Company in 1959 as a 325-page paperback with new frontal material and a new cover. Stuart felt that this second edition was cleaner and less repetitious than the first.

As a continuation of our mission to preserve the legacy of Jesse Stuart and to promote an appreciation for the Appalachian way of life, the Jesse Stuart Foundation is proud to present the book that you hold in your hands, a third edition of *Man With a Bull-Tongue Plow* with a new Introduction by Stuart scholar John Howard Spurlock. This project was made possible by gifts from a network of devoted friends whose names are listed at the end of the book. Their support also enabled us to provide copies of this wonderful book to school and public libraries across Appalachia. While you are examining the list of JSF Friends who contributed to this project, please also note the document that follows. It is a copy of Dutton editor Merton Yewdale's review of the original manuscript and his recommendation for publication. His words of praise have been followed by glowing tributes from many subsequent generations of readers.

Enjoy *Man With a Bull-Tongue Plow*. It is a powerful collection of poems that has played an important role in defining the Appalachian experience.

James M. Gifford
Ashland, Kentucky

INTRODUCTION

The majority of the sonnets in *Man With a Bull-Tongue Plow* were written by Jesse Stuart over an eleven month period, beginning in the spring of 1932, when he was age twenty-five and the nation was in the depths of the Great Depression. Stuart stated a few of the sonnets were written as early as 1930 and that Sonnet 225, "My loves will remain when I have passed," was the first sonnet he ever wrote. The book was first published by E.P. Dutton & Company of New York, a major book publisher of the time, in 1934. It was extremely popular and highly praised by many critics, and it launched Jesse Stuart's career as a writer.

While enrolled in a class of The English Lyric under Professor Donald Davidson in the spring semester of his year of graduate study at Vanderbilt University (1931-32), Stuart began writing his mountain sonnets in the style of the English sonnet. He began seeking Davidson's reaction to his verse and asking for his guidance. Davidson, himself a poet and critic, realized that Jesse had an incredible natural ability to express himself using the sonnet format. He encouraged Stuart to continue writing his poetry in the traditional sonnet form rather than in the more modern free verse style—with its greater emphasis upon literary allusions and abstract symbolism—which Stuart was also attempting at the time. Davidson always advised Stuart to write naturally and in his own way.

The standard English sonnet contains fourteen lines of iambic pentameter arranged in an end-rhyme scheme of four quatrains and a couplet. Most of the sonnets in *Man With a Bull-Tongue Plow* are written in this format, though some have more than fourteen lines, a variation that disturbed some critics but not the youthful author. Because of his unique and self-assured creative skills as an artist, Stuart's readers enter his poetic world unhampered by his variance from the traditional sonnet arrangement.

In May of 1932, the end of his spring semester at Vanderbilt, Stuart returned home to W-Hollow in Greenup County, Kentucky. Over the summer, he tended the crops on his family's farm and continued writing poetry. By summer's end he had completed 152 of the sonnets in this collection. The remainder of the 703 sonnets contained here were written over the fall and spring months of 1932-33, while Stuart was serving as superintendent of the Greenup County school system.

Always the driven and compulsive writer, Stuart often found solitude in the nearby Plum Grove Cemetery in late evening hours as well as on Sunday afternoons, where those who had lived and died in his mountain world could "speak" to him and share their stories. He would then return to his office at Greenup and type the longhand versions of the sonnets he had penned in the silence of the hillside cemetery.

While attempting to find publishers for his rapidly increasing collection of poems, Stuart continued seeking the advice of Donald Davidson, with whom he had bonded as friend and publishing mentor. Davidson suggested Stuart forget the smaller publications and submit his poetry to the nation's major literary magazines. Davidson then wrote letters of introduction on Stuart's behalf. With his guidance, Jesse mailed selected poems to *American Mercury*, *Virginia Quarterly Review*, and *Poetry, a Magazine of Verse*. Thirty-two of his poems were accepted for publication. In the meantime, *Virginia Quarterly* editor, Stringfellow Barr, to whom Davidson had described Stuart as "the first real poet... ever to come out of the southern mountains," was so taken with Stuart's poetry that he suggested to E.P. Dutton that they might wish to consider publishing a book of Stuart's poems. Subsequently, Stuart received a letter from the company inquiring if he had more poems like the ones in *Virginia Quarterly* and *Mercury*. Jesse sent the company the 703 sonnets in this book. The letter he received back included a contract and stated, "This is a great book of poems. It is like a big river with tributaries of life entering in. It is like a symphony of wind." Upon receiving the letter, Jesse "walked in the wind for three days."

The phrase "tributaries of life" is indeed descriptive of the sonnets in *Man With a Bull-Tongue Plow*, which are grouped into four sections entitled "Leaves From a Plum Grove Oak," "Blades From a Field of Corn," "The Enriched Resignations," and "Preface for After Death." The first two sections indicate the promise of a new American poetry firmly rooted in the land. The second two indicate Stuart's personas' acceptance of their mortality and their thoughts regarding eternity.

Sonnets 1, 3, 4, and 337 inform the reader of the poet's identity as a man of the soil, how he is trying to write, of whom he is writing, and how he hopes he and his poetry will be remembered. Stuart greets his reader in Sonnet 1 as "Sir" and introduces himself. He is a poet/farmer singing at his plow on a steep Kentucky hillside, and he sings the songs he knows and loves to sing. He closes the sonnet with a friendly nod, "Yours very respectively [sic], Jesse Stuart."

In Sonnet 3, the poet sings of the men and land he has known and states:

> I speak of men that live in my lifetime,
> And I speak of the men of yesterday.
> I do not care to know if this is art—
> These common words born in a common heart.

In the next sonnet, this earth poet announces his intention to write of life as he knows it, of toiling men plowing rugged soil in a land of crows, hawks, buzzards, and Aprils of blooming flowers blowing in the wind. Later in the book, in Sonnets 675 and 676, the poet describes his unselfconscious artistry arising naturally from his fusion with the land that nourishes his art and has a voice in his poems:

> Why does one write and write and leave one's food?
> The answer is: Why do the stars give light?
> Why does the body's heart keep pumping blood?
> A book is hell—there's nothing to a book;
> But yet one hates to give words to the wind.
> And in a book I never saw a brook,
> I never heard a wind-grass tambourine

❖ ❖ ❖

> The hand that touched the pencil and the brain
> That told the hand to shove the pencil on,
> Did not write this for profit, loss and gain....
> For words are slow to buy a poet bread.

In addition to his use of the land as a running motif, Stuart employs the four distinct seasons of Appalachia to connect the sonnets and give a oneness to his world. The seasons are both inner and outer, temporal and eternal. Spring is the season of planting, summer is the season of work, autumn is the season of harvest, and winter is the season of barren land when families must be sustained by the fruits of their toil.

Many of Stuart's sonnets are apostrophes to spring, and the poet chooses April, among all the months, as his lover because it brings an end to winter and a renewal of the will. It is the poet's beloved month of "the big blue bowl of April wind and sky," and "a light-green month with silver ways" when "dogwoods spread their white sails on the hill." Spring is also the fleeting season of youth and love. In Sonnet 161, the young persona gathers spring flowers for his sweet Elizabeth. Later, in Sonnet 341, the persona cherishes the April nights of loveliness with his dear Wilma O'Shean and hopes memories of their youthful love will keep her forever young, but he also realizes that some day their love will only be recalled in the initials "carved along the cool recesses" of beech trees.

Stuart's poetic season of spring renewal is followed by the heat and toil of Appalachian farmers working in their fields in summer. These hot summer days call forth "tall bronze men beneath wind laps of grain," plowing and hoeing crops of corn, tobacco and cane, and looking at the sky through sweat-dimmed eyes in this season of hard work to produce food to store that will sustain their families through the coming winter.

Summer is also the season for young love. The poet remembers walking with sweet Lydia Doore on summer nights, picking tiger lilies and throwing them into Sandy River and believing their love would last forever. He also recalls night walks with the beautiful Jean Torris with naturally curly auburn hair and eyes bright as dew drops on corn blades in the early morning sun.

Autumns in Appalachia are perhaps the most spectacular in America, and autumn is a season of progressing maturity in various poems of *Man With a Bull-Tongue Plow*. Stuart's autumn poems contain as many different shades of tone and mood as the multi-colored fall leaves. It arrives with the coming of September when the persona welcomes the great solace of the sweet September woods and "white clouds floating in the brook." It is a time when the early autumn moon is "a white disc plowing through the blue-sky dirt." The advancing and deepening tones of an Appalachian autumn turn the pages of *Man With a Bull-Tongue Plow* into multi-colored leaves; lighted by the shifting patterns of autumnal sunlight, they whisper in grieving wind tones. The falling crimson leaves spread upon the frosty ground and become the different colors of autumn's blood. In this season of reflection, the poet recalls the great beauty of Rahoon McCleannahan—her autumn brown skin, black hair falling to her waist, her beautiful curved lips and shapely body—a rich and rare jewel who sleeps in Plum Grove Cemetery.

The poems of autumn are followed by those depicting the barren landscape of an Appalachian winter. Winter is the season of night, of the winter moon—a "bronze disc moon above a barren tree," and of white stars—"lanterns in deep velvet space." It is a time of "birds on barren branches" and of "gray dismal days of gloomy rain." In various winter sonnets, the personas' thoughts often turn to the end of life. The once passionate lovers of Sonnet 238 are asleep beneath the winter snow covering their graves, and the young lovers of Sonnet 272 enjoy the beauty of a winter night walk but realize the brevity of life and that one day they will be dust.

Among the many strengths of *Man With a Bull-Tongue Plow* is Stuart's use of myriad personas to capture the universal truths of human existence. All classes of people are given a voice. They speak from the early days of the American pioneers to the Great Depression years of the 1930s: the good, the bad, the beautiful, the homely, the saints, the sinners, young soldiers, men who drink too much, hard-working farmers, those who barely make a living, good parents, dishonest legal officials, young lovers, those who accept orthodox Christianity and those who do not, those who believe in eternal life and those who do not. All these people and many more speak from the real and mythic worlds of W-Hollow. Anice Bealer's idea of heaven would be to return and work on his farm. The persona of Sonnet 678 believes "Each man's a god and each is crucified." The persona of Sonnet 614 views the grave as a jailhouse and wonders who holds the key to unlock space, time and eternity.

Thus in the poems of *Man With a Bull-Tongue Plow*, the land and the four seasons provide an eternal backdrop where Stuart's mountain personas play out their lives, and the river flowing throughout their world becomes the eternal river of time.

In 1961, following two additional books of poetry and the publication of countless poems in magazines and journals over a period of three decades, Jesse Stuart was recognized by the Academy of American Poets for "distinguished poetic achievement" for his lifework in the genre. He, his wife, Naomi Deane, and their daughter, Jane, traveled to New York City, where Jesse was presented the 1960 Fellowship of the Academy of American Poets—America's highest award for poetry. Stuart was deeply humbled and touched by the honor. Accepting the award at a gathering of Academy members and friends on a memorable November evening, Stuart concluded his remarks by reading the first sonnet from *Man With a Bull-Tongue Plow*, commencing,

"Sir: I am a farmer singing at the plow…"

Following Stuart's reading, John Hall Wheelock, a member of the Board of Chancellors of the Academy, praised Stuart as a great, fine, and sensitive poet, one who "has an almost mystical union with the infinite."

John Howard Spurlock
Professor of English, Emeritus
Western Kentucky University

TABLE OF CONTENTS

Sonnets 1 - 200
Leaves From a Plum Grove Oak
Page 1

Sonnets 201 - 450
Blades From a Field of Corn
Page 103

Sonnets 451 - 650
The Enriched Resignations
Page 231

Sonnets 651 - 703
Preface for After Death
Page 333

Acknowledgments
Page 363

Merton S. Yewdale's Recommendation to Publish
Original Review
Page 365

Leaves

    From a Plum Grove

        Oak

Sir: 1

I am a farmer singing at the plow
And as I take my time to plow along
A steep Kentucky hill, I sing my song—
A one-horse farmer singing at the plow!
I do not sing the songs you love to hear;
My basket songs are woven from the words
Of corn and crickets, trees and men and birds.
I sing the strains I know and love to sing.
And I can sing my lays like singing corn,
And flute them like a fluting gray corn-bird;
And I can pipe them like a hunter's horn—
All of my life these are the songs I've heard.
And these crude strains no critic can call art,
Yours very respectively, Jesse Stuart.

2

And may I pause to sing a corn-field song
Beside my plow between the tall corn rows—
And may I idle my root-plow along
And sing tunes futile as the wind that blows.
There may be some to love the strains that Stuart
Made on Kentucky hills beside his plow—
There may be some to love his rustic art
And keep his futile tunes in brain and heart
When he is quiet and sleeps beneath the clay
And has no thought of his past yesterday.
And we shall hope then for a brighter day
When some young poet guides his plow along
And plows upon the quiet Kentucky clay
Where Stuart plowed and sings a sweeter song!

3

Now I shall take the chance to spin a rhyme
And I shall let the fences go unmended,
I shall not dream of any future time
When strength of hand and power of brain are ended.
I shall consider not the fallow field
But I shall leave it for others to plow.
It is not time to think of plowing now,
For others can do work upon the field—
Now let them do it while I write a rhyme.
I speak of them and color of the clay,
I speak of men that live in my lifetime,
And I speak of the men of yesterday.
I do not care to know if this is art—
These common words born in a common heart

4

Now look, my friends: look to the east and west.
Look anywhere on land I love the best,
Look on this April land I love the best
And you will see the men behind their plows,
And you will see them turn the rugged soil.
Oh, watch them turn the land, these sons of toil!
The crows fly over now to build a nest.
The hawks have built a nest in the pine grove.
The hungry buzzards circle high above,
Must be a calf is dead out in the cove.
Oh, April is the fairest month to us—
White flowers in the silver blowing wind—
And their leaves in the wind hang tremulous,
And wind and leaves play a sweet violin.

5

Across the empty fields winter retreats,
Releasing his high mortgage on the weather—
Then wary Spring trips back on airy feet
And buds and grass and wind all laugh together:
"Where is the mortgage winter held on weather—
Where is the winter desolate and gray?
Gone—Gone—and gone we hope forever."
The wind-flowers nod: 'Yes, gone forever,
And gone we hope forever and a day—'
And that is all the white wind-flowers said,
Standing by last year's stems so cold and dead.
The land is left a scroll for winds to read—
The gray-starved land is used to birth and growth.
The gray-starved land is left to Spring and youth.

6

Ah, we get out to work in early April.
We brave our bodies to the wind and sun.
We swing the plow around the rugged hill
From break of day until the setting sun.
We break the earth to plant in corn and cane.
We canvass burley-beds upon the hill.
And we must work and work in early April.
We plant some corn before late April rain.
We work, for April is the time to work.
And April is the time to plant and sow—
The time to work, for winter days are coming
When over barren earth the winds will blow—
The winds will blow and seeds fall on the snow—
The seeds that fall the birds will eat, I know.
April is here—we work, for night is coming!

7

My land is fair for any eyes to see—
Now look, my friends—look to the east and west!
You see the purple hills far in the west—
Hills lined with pine and gum and black-oak tree—
Now to the east you see the fertile valley!
This land is mine, I sing of it to you—
My land beneath the skies of white and blue.
This land is mine, for I am part of it.
I am the land, for it is part of me—
We are akin and thus our kinship be!
It would make me a brother to the tree!
And far as eyes can see this land is mine.
Not for one foot of it I have a deed—
To own this land I do not need a deed—
They all belong to me—gum, oak, and pine.

8

Oh, I have seen the winter desolate-gray
Hang months and months over the barren lands,
I've heard the winter winds blow through the trees,
Blow through the icy heavens filled with leaves.
We felt secure, housed with fruits of the land—
We felt secure—no one can understand
How fine it is to live close to the land—
To neighbors in distress we lent a hand.
We saw the crows go flying cross the land,
Up in the icy heavens with the leaves,
We saw the crows fly over gray-starved land
When winter winds sighed in the last year leaves.
And cozily we sat by our fireside
And ate of corn and supped of berry-wine;
We sat and let the snow-world drift outside;
We sat and watched through frosted window panes
The snow flakes drifting through green tops of pine.

9

The wind is lazy here—the wind is free,
It blows the cotton from the milk-weed stems.
The wind is lonesome here—one loves to be
Out wandering by a lazy meadow stream.
Sweet summer here with bud and bloom and breeze
And tall bronze men beneath wind-laps of grain—
Sweet summer here with wind among the trees,
With wind among the flowers and honey bees—
Among the flowers—beneath the stars above—
The silver wind plays with the stars above,
With flowers and moonlight on the leafy trees—
Plays with the ferns and trees and clouds above
And summer fields that I have learned to love.
Winds call to me around my mountain shack—
And when I leave I hear their lonesome call,
And when I hear their call I must come back.

10

Hot summer days and we toil in the fields,
We hoe and plow tobacco, corn and cane,
We walk barefooted on mulch in the fields
Until the mulch is made mud by the rain,
When loose earth packs by rain we hoe again,
And when weeds grow we cut the weeds again.
Beneath the sun we watch the drifting skies,
We lift our hoes and look with sweat-dimmed eyes.
We watch the lazy drifting, drifting skies—
Tobacco leaves are pretty in the wind,
When all the weeds are cut around the stalks
And plows have cleaned the weeds well from the balks.
Tobacco plants are pretty in the wind—
Oh, prettier plants are harder now to find.

11

We love the tall corn, for it makes us bread.
Tall corn is pretty on the hill-side rows—
Tall corn is pretty where one hoes and hoes
And leaves weeds wilted in the long corn rows.
When jeweled-dew drips from the blades of corn
It's fine to hear a fresh breeze oozing through,
Filled with the fragrance of the silking corn,
Kissed by the dew a-dripping from the corn—
And this is sweet to smell on August morn
When morning glories vine around the corn.
If one could only understand corn-words,
The corn a-talking to the wind and birds
And leaves—the whispering of the corn
Is fine to hear on any summer morn.

12

I know that Jenny loves the whispering corn.
She loves to skip lark-free across the wheat—
I love to watch Jenny on skipping feet
Run out among wind-waves of blowing wheat.
And Jenny loves the smell of morning corn
And morning glories twined around the corn.
Jenny and I go evenings after cows
And on the grassy hill where cattle browse
We stand to watch the glow of setting sun.
We watch red-evening clouds above green timber
(Red-evening clouds we always shall remember)
Riding at ease above the corn and timber—
Red-evening clouds near setting of the sun.
Jenny cannot forget—I shall remember!

13

Summer is season for the wind and sun.
Summer is season for to gather food
And put away before the summer ends——
To store before the winter has begun.
Summer is time to work, for night is coming.
The grasshopper will pine, the ant will thrive,
The grasshopper did dance and flit and sing
Over the blackberry vine on sputtering wings.
The ant did summer work that he may live
Through winter—and let ants work to live!
And let grasshoppers dance and sing and pine
And flit on summer days across the berry vine!
Do summer work, for winter night is coming!
One time to work—work for the night is coming!

14

When golden leaves begin to shiver down
Among the barren brush beneath the trees,
And scarlet leaves and yellow and light-brown
Begin to play in wind and pepper down
To earth—these clean and frosted leaves drip down.
Then it is time the corn is in the stack,
Potatoes in the hole—hay in the mows.
This is the time rust has grown on the plows;
The time to haul the pumpkins to the shed,
Since frosts have come and pumpkin vines are dead.
And this is time to garner autumn fruit
(Give unto earth the waste—you take the loot)
And time to run the apples through the press
And share the multi-colored loveliness
Of trees that lose shreds from their golden dress!

15

Now you can think of autumn biting cold
When frost is on the ground and on the stack,
And you can think of ragweeds turning black
And how the autumn freely spends her gold.
And these are clean Kentucky scenes, remember,
From tenth of September till late November!
I have lived here my life and I remember!
I've seen the dead leaves start before my eyes
And drift and drift into the windy skies.
And I have heard the crisp-air ring with cries
Of birds now going to the south—I've heard
The lost cries of these migratory birds
Above brown fields, beneath the windy skies—
Sounds far too plaintive for a poet's words.

16

I've heard a sadness in the winds of autumn,
A music sadder than an old refrain,
When winds blew through dead milk-weeds in a bottom
And swept the frosted leaves in swirling train.
I've heard a sadness in the rains of autumn
Beating upon my roof both night and day,
And beating dead weeds down upon the bottom,
Beating them down into a new decay!
I've loved this music in the early autumn,
The sound of wind with leaves and grass at play,
I've loved to hear the rain beat on the bottom,
Beat on the leaves now fallen to decay.
Something of autumn then gets in my blood,
Excites my brain into a dead-leaf mood.

17

The multi-colored leaves are dying now,
Some hang like golden jewels to the bough,
And with the wind the pretty leaves go flying,
Over fields empty and forgotten now.
And in the wind the bare tree-tops are sighing,
Rabbits have found new drifts for sleeping now
Where briars have caught the leaves and held them
    down,
Cattle sleep now beneath the green pine bough
When there is not room in the stack and mow,
And cattle bed on dead leaves drifted down
In briars— And overhead day-drifting skies
Are filled with flying leaves and wild-bird cries.
The birds at night sleep in the shocks of fodder
On rugged hills beside the Sandy water.

18

The horns of plenty now are showing here,
Plenty is in the granary, barn and stack,
Crops have been very bountiful this year,
And labor we have given has come back.
We gave our labor to the fields in time
Of sun and rain and season for plant growth,
We went into the fields and sowed our grain
Just after the last frost and first Spring rain.
We watched the first green leaves a-putting forth,
We worked for winter days in wind and sun,
We worked—the winter days we knew would come!
Then plants would not grow in the frozen earth
And under pallid rays of winter sun.
Our crops have been so bountiful this year
And horns of plenty are a-showing here.

19

Fields will be furrowed time and time again.
They will be furrowed by tall men unborn
As they were furrowed by men now forlorn
In dust— And fences will be built again
By men like me and fields be cleaned of brush
By men like me only to grow again.
Other poets will plow and cut the brush
And earn their bread by the sweat from their brow
Behind two steady mules and turning-plow!
I wonder if new plow boys will take time
To sit down by their plows and spin their rhymes!
Then common folks will read in future times!
What man was this that trailed a cutter plow
And wrote a rhyme about sweat on his brow!

20

How would it be for me to stop the plow
And take an hour to spin a useless rhyme,
Then throw it to the wind for you to find—
Better than kept for any future time!
Better to sing of beauty from the heart
And leave the men for other men to kill.
Better to sing of life from where I start—
From mountain folks and from Kentucky hills.
Better to sing and never ask a dime
For ruggedness I spin into a rhyme,
For I can live—to hell with all your gold.
I know I'm strong enough to work the soil.
My friends, this bard will not be bought and sold
Since he can make his bread by honest toil!

21

"Could I recall but thirty years today
I would return into my sought-for youth.
Now I am fifty-one, my hair is gray,
For me the best of life has long gone forth.
I know how barren fields look in the Spring,
But soon returning leaves give life anew,
Oceans of leaves and winds a-blowing through.
I know how flowers bloom and birds do sing,
And I do know how stars come in the sky
And how the April winds pass with a sigh.
To me this is the Spring of life again—
Those days of mine now lost beyond recall,
There is no turning back to live again—
Days of one's youth—the greatest days of all!"

22

"Why now regret your happy youth, my friend,
Why now regret, for only poets do,
Look you above our heads! Oh, look, my friends,
The leaves are green and winds are blowing through!
Look you, a thousand stars are in the sky,
Green leaves are tremulous in a wind sigh.
Now you should be as happy, friend, as I!
You have lived more, my friend—far more than I.
You have seen many springtimes come and go
When you were free with youth you used to know;
When you were young to love and dance and sing
And free as mating birds upon the wing.
You should have memories of the long ago,
Of merry youth, my friend, you used to know."

23

"The youth I used to know—ah, let me see!
Charlie went west and never did return,
And Sue is sleeping, sleeping on the hill—
The Sue I used to kiss and loved to kiss—
Sue with her pretty lips, dust on the hill!
Her sleeping dust must hear the whippoorwill.
Where are the friends of youth I miss—
Elmer and Bert, Oscar, and Jim and John;
Oh, they are gone, poet—they are all gone.
They sleep like Sue—all on a different hill.
Flowers and brush and briars now grow upon
The covers of the beds where they lie still.
And where are Lizzie, Lute, and Jack and Mack!
They, too, have gone and they will not come back."

24

"Now friend, I see the years come back to you.
You ask: 'Where are the roses of yesterday?
Where are the boys and girls of yesterday?
Rose petals have gone back into decay,
Flowers of yesterday are dust today,
The youth of yesterday are dust today!'
Let them be dust—the crown of years must come
As sunsets come and settle down on you.
There is no chance for any strange escape.
The years are something money cannot change,
The years are something hard and soft and strange.
They come and freely give a crown to you.
They come to you—there is no reason why
They should not come—Someday they'll come to me,
Shall I experience immortality?"

25

"Then, poet, take just this advice from me.
Now you are young and you are strong and free,
Go live your days, for life will soon slip by;
I know, for time is near for me to die.
You are a sturdy poplar in the wind,
Deep-rooted in the soil beneath your skies
You hear the music of the violin,
You see the trees bent down and the trees rise.
You stand so fresh and free under the skies.
The years will come and frosts will bite your leaves
And you will sleep among the barren trees—
You one of them—an icy barren tree.
In Spring you were a tree of paradise
But now you stand beneath the winter skies
A symbol of this immortality."

26

"Since 'Wisdom cometh with the years' to you
I listen to your words, my honest friend—
Your words and mine and winds a-blowing through
The leaves— And I must say to you, my friend,
Since you and I must venture to some end
That what I make—ah, such I'll freely spend.
And I shall live free as the blowing wind—
Why save the gold for kin to get and spend!
Better to throw it to the blowing wind!
My friend, I shall write of your yesterday
While I am young and fresh as leaves and free
As wind and far from immortality
As grass is from the moon and sun and stars."

27

"Man's life is like the season of a flower.
From barren earth in Spring the flower comes forth—
A flower springs to blossom and decay.
The Spring is but the season of its youth
And then it blossoms to the wind and sun.
It blossoms forth and stands in fresh array—
Stands in the pride and beauty of its day.
But soon, too soon, these petals know decay,
When Spring has gone quickly the summer goes.
Then autumn frosts and then the winter snows—
The flower's season is the life of man.
Spring is the season for his youth and growth.
Summer is when maturity puts forth.
Autumn brings ending to his futile dreams.
Winter: he's numbered with the dead-leaf stems."

28

He did not write with calculating eye
For cash nor did he write for futile fame,
But he just wrote and never questioned why
Some folks did love and some did curse his name.
What are they after all—failure and fame!
Each in its place can only leave a name!
What is it if men love or if they hate
When words are said—all said—and life is done
And all corn-blades have withered that he won
And strewn on bare fields gray and desolate—
Gray shadows in the yellow winter sun!
Not lines of verse and cash will matter then,
Nor anything will matter that he said,
Him lowly in a world of living men
And ordinary in a world of dead!

29

Perhaps as years drift (for the years do drift)
By the wood fireside in some country place,
A man grown old enough to die will lift
A book of mine and read—perhaps he'll read
With solemnity upon his wrinkled face
The things I have to say about the dead.
And he may read by candle-light my page,
And he may love my words, this white-haired sage.
And if he loves my words he is my friend
And I do wish him to a fruitful end.
And if he hates my words—he's still my friend,
That is, if to my friendship he'll attend.
And since he has grown old enough to die
I pray my words to him will satisfy.

30

When other youth have read the lines I write
And spun into a common cobweb rhyme,
Some will say this: "Yes, once upon a time
We went together on a starry night—
We went: He with his love and I with mine—
Under the trees where wind sang like a rhyme
We went with our dear loves and had one time,
And he sat down and put it in a rhyme—"
Oh, yes, my friend, youth's stars are beautiful,
More beautiful in youth than anytime.
Go out together when the sky is full
Of swarming stars—go out and spin a rhyme.
My friend, this youth is time to write and rhyme,
Oh, Youth, no one can live a greater time!

31

Let the child sleep—oh, do not break its sleep.
Let the child sleep—too soon the child must wake,
And know of life—Oh, let the small child sleep!
There lies the furrow that small child must break,
And while he sleeps this is unknown to him.
Then let him sleep, for he will wake too soon
And sow the seeds on fields unknown to him—
Unknown just now, but he will know them soon.
There he lies and he's a small boy sleeping.
What does he know of all this world around him?
What does he know? I ask. He does not know!
What do you know—you old with years a-creeping
Away—away from you—what do you know?
Oh, you could say, my friend: "The years go slow.
Don't wake the child, leave him where you found him.'

32

Let the child sleep—his infant brain needs rest.
Let the child sleep—why do you want to wake him!
Now let him breathe the air into his lungs,
Let him lie there at rest—it is the best,
Let the child sleep—it's not the time to wake him.
Let him have rest, for he will need some rest.
Tomorrow he must be son of the soil,
His sleep must break and he will learn of toil.
But now he lies and dreams and let him dream.
He is too young—a child too young to wake.
Now let him sleep, soil-man, and you go break
The furrow now—for soon the dawn will gleam
When he shall go to meet life unafraid.
Roll up his sleeves and say: "This must be done
If I must work from dawn till set of sun,
He'll run the truest furrows ever made."

33

Oh, do not wake the child but let him sleep,
For he is small and earth is great in size.
Life is so slight—eternity so deep
And long and dark under the dirt and skies.
Now turn the latch against the creaking door
And pull the shutters down—the rustling shutters,
The child must sleep when night wind mutters,
Mutters, and howls about the shutters and the door,
And blows a little dust upon the floor.
The child must sleep, sleep, for the child will need it.
Yes sleep, my friend—yes sleep—you failed to heed it.
You're old, my friend, and turning down the hill,
Let the child sleep—it has no pulse nor will
While it lies there, breathes there breathlessly still.

34

What is the use, my child, of waking one
Not yet conformed to furrow and the plow—
Better to leave the furrow for an older one,
Better to leave the furrow yet undone
Than wake your child and have him do it now.
If you could see these limbs with opened eyes,
If you could see these limbs and body too,
But, sleeping child, you would not realize—
You lying there asleep with blinded eyes—
The things these limbs and body have gone through.
The howling wind came down against our shutters,
The shutters of the unlearned and the poor—
Against this wind I woke to bar the door.
The lone night wind that mutters, mutters,
Lone wind of thirst and hunger for the poor.

35

Ah, sleep, you child, and let the wind howl round you.
You are too young to listen to the howls.
Lie still my child and sleep where winds have found you,
Lie there and do not wake to threatening scowls.
Do not the heavens often threaten rain,
The thunder peals and yet no rain does fall,
And from a peaceful heaven comes a sudden rain
When one did not dream of a rain at all.
What does it matter what will happen, child?
When you are old as I you'll understand.
But while you can lie there and sleep, my child,
And let men strong as I furrow the land,
Now do not open, child, your blinded eyes,
You'll find the world will take you by surprise!

36

These are my people and I sing of them.
I know these people I am singing of.
I live with them and I was born of them
Where high hills shoulder to the skies above.
I sing of them and will you listen, please,
To the dead-grass lines of my futile song.
Oh, listen to the wind among the trees,
And it is futile as my wind-grass song.
I sing from common heart of common clay,
Of people that I live among today,
And I sing of the men of yesterday.
Tonight I sing: If you would only listen
Where moonlight on the green leaves glistens—
Listen to words like wind among the trees,
Like winds beneath the stars and in green leaves,
I wonder if you'd say: "Stop singing please!"

37

Her arms around her Leonard and she leans
Against his body while the whippoorwill
Sings in the moonlight on the green-briar hill;
And on them falls a golden light and green,
Shadows are falling round them on the briars.
And there entwined they stand beneath the moon
And listen to the whippoorwill and spoon,
When winds are shaking brush and rusty wires.
Nine months and Sadie Williams lifts the shawl
To show the girls her little Leonard's face.
She hates to show her face and that's not all—
Two years: Her baby'd tugging at her breast;
Leonard, they say, is somewhere in the west.

38

The neighbors thought too much of Katherine Darter.
She was the flower of their common lot.
But wonder why the neighbors have forgot
Young Katherine Darter—listen, I'll tell you why
The neighbors have forgot sweet Katherine Darter.
A certain young man asked to tie her garter
And after that Katherine was not the same—
The neighbors said Dick Hailey was to blame.
Nine days before she gave her baby birth
Her Papa marched Dick in before his gun
And Dick Hailey was sure afraid to run.
Then Katherine gave her baby legitimate birth.
Now Dick lives in the house with old man Finn,
The way he works Dick Hailey is a sin.
And he has taught Dick how to work and save
And he has taught Dick Hailey to behave!

39

It's hard for me to think that Hughes is dead.
So full of life I saw him yesterday—
Short of stature, grumbling, brown curly head;
So short among the careless boys at play,
And that was when the college grounds were green
And clouds went floating over lazily,
And apple blossoms showed among green-green;
Green twilight Spring-time in east Tennessee.
It's hard for me to think that Hughes knows night.
Once we were lads and talked far in the night
About the glorious days ahead of us,
And how we planned and things we planned to write.
Now Worley Hughes is sleeping on the hill,
And I am here—I'm plowing on the hill.

40

When his rich earth is amalgamated well
With yellow clay where he was born and raised,
I think a sturdy oak will rise to tell
It sprang from Hughes—a youth of yesterdays.
And through the bark-eyes of the oak he'll look at us
And we shall look at him so unconfused
At his green leaves that hang wind-tremulous
In yellow sunlight and the silver wind.
We'll look at leaves not knowing they are Hughes.
But that will be when years are stacked behind
And we are leaves decaying in the wind;
Our own lone autumn wind in our gray days.
And Hughes shall speak to us in his own tongue
And we shall think it is leaves in the wind
Saying: "It is not best to die so young!"

41

He lives quite humbly in this mountain shack.
He lives unlettered, scanty-clad and poor.
He is known by his neighbors, "Happy Jack,"
It's hard for him to keep wolves from his door—
Those hungry wolves that keep watch for the poor.
He once lived dangerously and he lived wild
Until he married Jane and her first child
Was born—then Happy Jack said he was through
With women, dance, and drink, and fight, and gun,
Then Happy Jack said his rough life was done.
I do not know if he has broken vows,
I seldom hear him swearing vicious oaths
Like once he swore, and I do know Jack loathes
The smell of powder and the taste of gin,
For I have been with company Jack was in.

42

Here is the Crown Prince of the neighborhood—
Plenty of bad in him and little good.
And like wild weeds that spring, his lies are sown.
There is no fight in him—he's just a bluff,
Cowards have made him say he had enough.
His children are victims of circumstance,
But Lum leaves them and goes to the square dance—
Uninvited he goes there and shows his worth.
His wife is in condition now for birth.
And men will say: "Ah, hell, I wouldn't have come
If I had known you were to have old Lum."
Lum always goes the uninvited guest—
He leaves his wife at home to do her best,
His wife near to a birth should now take rest.

43

A slender child, she gathers flowers today,
She gathers blue sweet-williams from the woods
Where trees are still unleafed and woods are gray.
She gathers wild flowers from these solitudes,
Wind-flowers and blue sweet-williams while she may.
The clouds roll over in the sky above
And winds are blowing cross the poplar cove,
And Mae Marberry picks the flowers she loves.
The wind and skies are big, big things to her,
Of wind and fallen trees she has no fear,
White blood-root flowers are a joy to her.
And soon white blood-root petals will be gone
Back to the earth the stems are growing on,
And soon the child will come a woman grown
And gather petals in a silver gown.

44

He stays close to the land and tills the land,
His flesh is brown, his hands are calloused by
The handles of the plow, the ax and spade.
Gleen Hylton is as rugged as his land,
He sees years come and ripen and roll by,
He does not laugh at them nor does he sigh,
But solemnly he stands as years roll by.
No finer hill farmer has ever made
Furrows in earth than Gleen Hylton has made—
A man of earth, he lives close to the earth,
And such has been Gleen Hylton's heritage.
And he has lived among these hills since birth,
Though young in years hard work has made him age.
Gleen Hylton is as honest as the day,
His metal is as true as native clay.

45

Oh, Quadroon is the fairest of this lot,
A maid she is to love the stars and trees,
The wind, the moon, the sun, and birds, and bees,
A lover of these is dear Quadroon Mott.
Sometimes she tries to spin a little rhyme,
Wherein she speaks of hills and phlox and thyme.
Now I have kissed the lips of Quadroon Mott
And crossed the meadows with her in the sun.
I've walked with Quadroon after day was done
And white stars swarmed into the evening sky.
Together we have listened to winds sigh,
And watched the white night clouds float cross the sky.
And we have listened to the water's cry—
Death cadences of water flowing by,
And happy were sweet Quadroon Mott and I.

46

Here is a man dishonest with his neighbors.
He steals from them and tells them horrible lies.
He is a man his neighbors do despise,
Has weakness in his chin, cheat in his eyes.
He does not live by fruits of his own labors.
And when he comes to us and tries to borrow,
We never have and we express our sorrow.
And thus he runs and tries to borrow clothes,
To every house in the neighborhood he goes—
Clothes for his body and shoes for his feet—
And then he tries to borrow food to eat;
And clean clothes hanging to the line and palings,
And glass jars leaning on the worm-fence railings—
Stick to those hands of one I shall not name.

47

I shall not speak soft words for her—my mother.
I shall not praise her to the lofty skies,
But I shall leave her on the earth—my mother
Would choose the earth in preference to the skies.
I say the strength of oak is in my mother;
Color of autumn leaves is in her skin.
The solidness of hills is in my mother
And in her is the courage of the wind.
And in her is the rain's cool sympathy.
I hope she gives me strength of the oak tree;
I hope she gives me solidness of hills—
This with the strength of twisted grape-vine will.
I hope she gives me courage of the wind
And backbone that is hard as stone to bend—
I need these things to serve me to the end.

48

I shall not speak soft words with stilted phrase
To one who has worked all her live-long days
In furrowed fields and in the open spaces,
But I shall sing of her in plowman's phrase.
The blood that flows in her now flows in me,
Like sap, two seasons, flows in the same tree.
And I am proud to have her blood in me.
I pray for more her solidness in me,
I pray for more of her philosophy,
I want a heart as free as hers to give,
I want a love like hers to see men live
And women live—her love to help the sick.
I want her meekness—never wanting praise,
And for this rugged mother of the hills—
I sing for her in rugged plowman phrase.

49

And you, my mother, who will stack by you?
In beauty—yes—others are beautiful
And you are not in flesh and fancy guise.
But you have lived a life so rich and full,
Few worldly beauties stack beside of you.
If they'd gone through with all you have gone through,
Their eyes would blear and blue fade from the blue,
Their flesh would be as rugged as yours too.
You've asked no man the odds of work to do,
You've done your share—you've done it with a will,
You've done it with the solidness of hill.
And unafraid you've met your life, my mother—
Now unafraid, I say there is no other
That after all can stack beside of you—
The tree in you, flower in you, the hill,
Color of autumn leaf, the twisted grape-vine will.

50

The hills are dear to you, my mountain mother.
Corn-fields are dear to you—green in the sun,
The touch of wind is dear to you, my mother,
The rock ribs of the hills are dear to you.
White rain that falls on leaves is dear to you.
The lightning-storm will make no fear to you.
One of the elements, you surely are,
With power to love, a child, a stone, a star,
A will to work—one unafraid of life—
One that loves life and gave her seven life.
An autumn tree, my mother, now you are.
The gold of age is hanging to your boughs.
And unafraid you stand to meet new life,
Beneath white glistening beauty of a star.

For M. S.

51

I've seen him go among his corn at night
After his day was done— By lantern light
He went, unless it was light of the moon,
And a bright moon was up—He's broken soon;
Lines are grooved on his face at fifty-two.
The work he does would get the best of you.
And now his love is wind among the corn;
His love is whispering, talking, green corn blades.
His love is cornfields when the summer fades,
Oak leaves to red and fodder blades to brown.
His love is autumn raining dead leaves down
And going out on autumn morns to salt the stock.
He loves his mules and whispering corn at night—
Buff-colored corn in full autumn moonlight.

52

And is he of the hills? He's of their dirt
And all this hill-man knows is work and work.
The color of the sun is in his face,
The pick and adz have calloused his bare hands,
The weights of loads he lifts have curved his back.
But by hardships of life he understands
How fine it is to own his humble shack,
His hundred acres and his mules and plows—
"This is a place to live, a place to die."
Depository for him in the end,
The earth at last becomes his bosom friend,
He's of the dirt and he'll go back to dirt.
His life will ripen like weeds on the hill
When they are sickled by untimely frost,
And when his work is done he will lie still,
Though his dust to the earth will not be lost.

53

With money that he earns he buys the land.
He clears the fields of brush and sows in grass,
And men will note his small farm when they pass.
He does not hurt the land—he loves the land.
If you knew him, then you would understand
The words I say are facts as stars are facts.
This man can use a cutter plow and ax,
A mattock, spade, pitch-fork and scythe and hoe—
This pioneer left over from the long ago—
This man has ripened slowly with the years
And now he stands an autumn stalk of corn.
This man goes on, the winter brings no fears
To him—the winter desolate and forlorn.
He meets his winter now—a stalk of corn,
A ripened stalk of small buff-colored corn.

54

This man has gone through mud and rain and sleet
And drank of whiskey, applejack and gin,
Lived in log shacks when winter winds blew in,
When seasons failed, had half enough to eat.
But did he shrink from this? And did he fear?
"I'll bet I'll get good cropping this next year!"
With spirit such as this he met the years.
There are no lands for him to conquer now,
To clear of brush, to wield the cutter plow,
There are no fields of game for him to squander,
No trails left for this pioneer to follow
Through hazel thicket, pawpaw bank and hollow.
There is no place for his wild blood to wander.
He can't adjust himself to paths through air,
And people and new houses everywhere.

Bill Powers 55

Ah, there he goes—a basket on his arm,
Sickle in hand—a bottle on his hip—
He's going now to cut weeds for his hogs.
Tobacco juice runs down his bearded lip.
And who is he? You know old Whisker-Bill?
Says he: "I've never shaved and never will
Until I see my woman dead and kickin,
Then of all pretty girls, I'll have my pickin."
Old Bill and his two daughters take their sprees
On brew and apple-jack, under the trees.
But one day Sallie hit Bill with a sickle,
For three days and three nights his mind was fickle.
And Libbie snapped a gun on her pap, Bill,
And Libbie aimed it at his heart to kill.
Now his two daughters live upon the hill,
Live in a smoke-house there away from Bill.

Lief McCowan 56

He could march proudly to a drum and fife,
March out to give his life or take a life,
He has no fear of war, no prize for life.
His kin that marched before him sleep in clay.
If he were older he'd sleep there today
Perhaps— He would sleep there beside his kin.
Today he dances to the violin,
This handsome mountain youth of six-feet-two,
His face is classic mold—his eyes, sky-blue.
Better that he now walks above the earth,
And plows the earth, than hear the call of fife
And drum—the call to give and take a life—
Better to dance to a wicked violin
Than now be sleeping by some fighting kin.

Don Colley   57

He loved his whiskey, wine and apple-jack;
He loved his women and his fruitless land;
His barn, his meadows and his clapboard shack;
He loved his sweet-potato bottom sand.
These were the loves of his that men could see,
He lived most of his life so inwardly.
After his young wife died, he took to wine,
Whiskey, hard-cider and sweet-apple-jack.
He lived with his aged mother in her shack.
After his mother died old Don grew worse,
Each breath was spiked and tempered with a curse.
He sold his timber, then he sold his land,
And failed to grow potatoes in his sand.
And men would drive up to his house and say:
"They are all gone—yes, they're all gone away,
This is a house where weeds now have their way."

Charles Stafford   58

Here is a dreamer—tries to spin a rhyme,
He looks beyond to see a future time.
Now men won't listen to his artless lays,
They say: "W'y we've had better in our days.
We've read Longfellow, Whittier, Burns and Poe—
The golden singers of the long ago."
Here is a dreamer and he sits and dreams,
His words are futile chips he throws in streams
To see them drift—to drift away forever.
Though no one hears nor lends an ear to hear,
He sings of soil and seasons of the year,
He sings of people down among the poor,
Unlettered sincere men among the poor.
He cannot drive the wolf from his own door.
And will this dreamer rise and go beyond?

Jet Fillson 59

A shame the way her daughters have turned out,
But who's to blame?—no one's to blame but Jet.
When they were young she let them skip about—
Young Jet, Florine, and Maud, and Margaret,
And Billie Joe, Lucy, and Mary Ann.
Jet urged each one, they say, to find a man.
A man found each I'm sure and married none.
Jet pays in sorrow for her daughters' fun.
Go to the Bingham courthouse and you'll find
(When court is on) Jet's daughters with the men.
They ride with them and laugh and talk and then
Go listen to an obscene trial for rape.
Sometimes Jet's daughters get into a shape
They stay at home and have their bastard babies.
Jet cares for them till they go free as ladies!

Greene Taylor 60

No man is closer to the soil than Greene.
He works day in, day out, a man of power,
He is the hardest worker I have seen—
From sun till sun he does not waste an hour.
What does he have? Not good clothes for his back.
Greene Taylor does not have shoes for his feet.
He does not have beds for his rough plank shack,
Half-time he does not have enough to eat.
And does he care to be so scanty-clad?
Greene Taylor does not care, he is half-glad.
He lets tomorrow come—scant food or plenty!
He lets debts roll—he cannot pay a penny!
"I give myself to work—this is old Greene,
For in the end Death will wipe the slate clean."

Charlie Splean 61

I work like hell, I hate the goddamn law.
I have been drunk and I have laid in jail.
But I had friends enough to go my bail
And get me out. Once I cold-cocked the Law
When the jailer let me out. They put me back.
Pap has paid fines enough for me to buy
A hundred-acre farm. I hate to cause
My Pap this trouble—cause him lose his farm.
But we have got too goddamn many laws.
I've never tried to do my neighbors harm,
And yet I've laid behind stone walls and bars.
I'm going to settle down—get me a wife;
Buy me a farm and live a peaceful life.
I'm going to get prepared to meet my God;
I'm going to trod the path my fathers trod.

Sib Kales 62

I am Sib Kales, my man and me is old,
And we set by the fire—I smoke my pipe.
And Tom, my man, he chaws his home-made twist.
Now we are old and soon we must be cold,
For Tom, my man, is near too old to wipe
Terbacker from his lips—them lips I kissed
Nigh forty years ago when Tom was young
And I was young—now Tom and me is old.
And we set by the fire and dream tonight—
Tom's eyes, once blue, is dimmed, his hair is white.
My hair has turned, there's white among the gold,
And Tom and me's together growing old.
I bore for him ten children—eight are married,
And two of them by Pap and Ma lay buried.

Tom Kales 63

I am Tom Kales—the fire in me is out.
I'm stiff—my legs won't let me get about.
But Sib and me—we set together here
And dream back over many a buried year.
We talk sometimes about our children married,
We talk about the girl and boy we buried,
We talk about the days when we was young,
And Sib, she says terbacker bites her tongue,
Them twists the children buys for her to smoke.
Terbacker from the stores, w'y it's a joke—
It loses strength—w'y it's no count to smoke.
Now Sib and me has spent our life together
And now we're old and helping one another.
We'll keep this house out here and live alone,
For Sib and me's contented to the bone.

Mart Shelton 64

Here is Mart Shelton, not afraid of hell.
He has three daughters and five tall straight sons.
By looking at a Shelton one can tell
By keen black eyes if he's one of Mart's sons.
Mart Shelton is as honest as the day;
His Sires before him sleeping in the clay
Were honest and they taught Mart that away.
Contrary Mart builds his ideas like walls.
He proudly lays each stone in these high walls
Till other men's strong hammers cannot fall
The stone ideas he puts into the wall.
And Mart makes his five sons step fast and high,
Observes his daughters with a careful eye.
Old English Mart is not afraid of hell;
He's raised his family and he's raised it well.

Fred Sowards

65

He heard the guns at Verdun and at Aisne;
He heard the guns at Metz and Belleau Wood
Till guns became a menace to his brain.
Fred Sowards lives now in our neighborhood.
And what is Metz to him? What is the Aisne?
What is Verdun and what is Belleau Wood?
The roar of thunder brings to him again
Old days of rain, and blood, and Flemish mud.
He speaks of France sometimes and wishes for
His sons to never have to serve in war.
This is the wish he makes each budding Spring
When he trails furrows under blooming trees.
He says he'd rather his son would trail these
Than be forced to shoot men he never sees.

66

I aint got much—this fifty acre farm;
A horse, three cows, and mattocks, plows and hoes.
I have a house to keep my children warm,
I sell moonshine and 'backer for their clothes.
I've fourteen kids a-livin and two dead,
Here are the names I think the way they read:
Sylvester, Tronnie, and Silas and Min—
Oscar, Tommy, and Mitch and Dan and Quinn;
Toe Head, and Scout, Will, Mary Ann and Ned,
And Little Tess and one unnamed are dead.
And men, these children never begged for bread.
My family works in fields from sun till sun,
My children play after their work is done.
Beside my bed at night I kneel and pray,
The hunger-wolf's gone from my door to stay.

Walker Blair 67

This song is in my heart enough to sing,
A little song to fit this pasture world.
And now I sit beneath a new-leafed tree
And watch the low black clouds now drifting over.
The birds are fluting from the tall green trees,
Must be the Spring has brought new blood to them
And they cry out: "We want to live forever!"
One corn-bird hovers her brood on the bough,
While one corn-bird is carrying food to them.
"Corn-birds, you have not lived enough to know
This is the season for to sing your songs.
Soon these green hills will be under a snow.
Where will you gather then to sing your songs?
Earth will be desolate—the skies be black,
And you'll begin your days of looking back!"

Wade Fillson 68

Something stirs in my heart enough to sing,
And like a bird I flute it to this world
Where robes of poplar trees are first unfurled
And white blood-roots are first to bloom in Spring.
Once I walked here with my sweet Annie Lee,
We walked beneath the trees, looked at the stars.
I was in love with my sweet Annie Lee
And she and I sat on our pasture bars
And heard the whippoorwill sing to his love.
We heard the wind sigh in the pines above,
And Annie Lee and I spoke of our love.
But where is my sweet Annie Lee today?
Ye faithful ties, I ask—ah, where is she?
Somewhere she sits—a baby on her knee—
I'm cockeyed sure it don't belong to me!

Amanda Church   69

My season will be gone and you will ask
Yourself: "Why was she such a foolish thing?
She had her chance to sing and didn't sing.
For her to flute a song it was no task
In woods as pretty as the woods she knew,
Where idle winds were always blowing through."
And when my season's gone it shall be late,
Too late for me to mourn my helpless fate.
I say the summer birds are foolish things,
For they should flute when blooms are on the bough.
Soon skies turn gray and fields grow desolate
And winter comes—It is too late to sing.
Birds hop on frozen feet and drooping wing,
With empty craws and half-afraid to sing.
Remember, corn-bird, sing in your blithe season,
Then if you fail, there's no regretful reason!

Lowry McClellan   70

I am afraid the curtain will be drawn
And leave me to return to grass and stone.
I am afraid I'll never get beyond
These hills and hollows that I call my own.
I've called these hills my own since I could speak,
For I have known no other land like I
Have known this land—the stars, the evening sky;
The moon and trees and white clouds drifting by.
And I have written verse no man will read—
Just little rhymes—I love to play with words.
I love to flute my songs like fluting birds,
I want to speak before my season's over,
I want to speak about the wind and clover,
To speak before the best in me is over!

Georgia Greene 71

How many know her—this is Georgia Greene!
She chews tobacco—drinks her kerosene!
She goes to church and I have heard her pray
From Three Mile hill—a mile or so away
Beneath the flickering lanterns on the wall,
Georgia Greene has prayed for seedy sinners;
Georgia has helped pray through some new beginners.
She chewed red-horse tobacco—drank her kerosene—
She stood a woman-giant above the crowd;
Her voice was thunder there among the loud—
She told the sinners that they must come clean;
Get in an honest way and talk with God.
Now Georgia Greene has long, long been away;
We wonder where her prayers rise today.

Sam Rankin 72

The old men said he preached the word of God.
Some doubted if the word of God were there
The way he shouted and his thin white hair
Toyed with wind that seeped through broken panes.
No one will ever see Sam's like again.
Now where is he? "It does not matter where."
Time has gone on for many, many a-year
And no one knows just where he is today,
But at the time he left a girl went away,
And no one knows just where they are today.
Heaven for him was steal a girl sixteen
And take her far away to be his bride—
If not his bride, a girl to sleep beside!

Bert Skaggs   73

I raise terbacker and I work like hell,
From time in March I sow terbacker beds
Until I haul my burley off to sell.
But them Pin-Hooks they rob me of my crop.
A poor man has no chance here anymore
Among the hills—he has to work like hell,
And then he has a time a-tryin to sell
Terbacker and his lasses and his corn.
It seems them Big Men try to rob the poor,
For when we ask for credit from the store
They take a lien on our terbacker crop,
Before the crop is done we have to stop
A-drawin, for the Big Men have our crops.
We have no way to make these rascals stop,
The times keeps gettin harder for the poor.

Moll Weston   74

I said she'd better keep my man away;
I told my man he'd better stay at home—
Now Bill got cut there at old Fannie Spry's.
And—Bill—I wouldn't care much if he dies.
He goes down there and then he tells me lies.
I went down to old Fannie Spry's last night;
I beat the mortal hell outten Fannie Spry;
My Bill, he was a-standing close thereby—
He just looked on when we begin to fight,
Then turned and said: "I guess I'd better go."
I stopped and said: "Look here, now Bill Winslow,
If I catch you again with Fannie Spry,
Remember now, I say, you both will die—"
I hear old Fannie has a shore-blacked eye!

Juanita Aimsworth 75

I am in love with life in these quiet woods.
I love to hear the wind blow through the trees
And hear the laughing and the talking leaves.
I am in love with these deep solitudes.
The bee comes here to kiss the wild red rose;
The birds come here for this green paradise,
The air is clean and clear—blue water flows,
And clouds of green are soothing to the eyes.
Poplars are pretty kissing skies of blue
When skies of blue are kissing poplars too.
The mirror in the brook will show you this;
I've looked into the mirror, saw them kiss!
I say I am in love with solitudes;
I live here quietly in these warm sweet woods!

Julian Meeks 76

The poets rave about the mockingbirds;
I've seen them fly above my fields of oats—
I've heard them sing—I did not like their songs—
Not half as pretty as my grunting shoats!
I've heard the mockingbirds trill on the bough.
And listen, men! I never stopped my plow!
But when them old Kentucky red birds sing,
I stop my plow and say: "Ah, this is Spring!"
I'm always glad to hear a red bird sing.
And when the cow-birds chase along my plow,
I never hear the mockingbirds somehow,
Although they're fluting from the woodland boughs.
And when it comes to tell about the birds,
My words sound like the fluting mockingbirds.

Loretta Aims 77

I've done the best I could to make my bread,
To keep shelter and raise my children right—
When I want bread sometimes I get instead
An invitation to a bachelor's bed.
When I refuse I get a curse instead.
I've tried to live a clean, an honest life,
I am disgusted now enough to die—
One must fight hard to live an honest life;
One must fight hard to be a decent wife
When Nature gives appeal to lustful eyes.
Men know flesh-madness, then they soon forget,
When lustful love rebukes the heart and mind—
A woman's love is like the wind, and blind.
I loved one man and he is gone—and yet,
I love him still—I've walked the streets to find
Just any kind of honest work to do,
Not knowing day to day how we'd pull through.

Lance Stevens 78

The cold-white stars show beautifully tonight;
The horse-shoe moon hangs over in the west—
I walk beside the girl I love the best—
I bring sweet Jenny home in white starlight.
The maple leaves turn silver in the wind.
There's talk among leaves on the sycamore,
Winds play through leaf-tops like a violin
And Sandy waters kissed her pebbled shore.
I think I'll marry Jenny in the fall
When I have sold my burley and my cane.
"You'll never marry Jenny Holt at all,
For she'll wed her true lover in the fall—
And her true lover is young Albert Payne."

Harvey Hillman   79

I sit beside a mountain creek today.
I hear the water laughing over stones,
I think of youthful days with Polly Jones
When we came here and threw in sticks and stones.
The stones would thug—the sticks would float away.
You stream, now where is Polly Jones, I ask?
"Somewhere out west I heard the Jones's say,
And they said she was sleeping under clay."
Now I sit here beside this creek today,
I throw in sticks and watch them float away.
I see a dove's nest on a hickory snag,
Two cardinals sit upon a tree and brag,
A larkspur-scented wind is blowing over,
The bees are working on the creek-bank clover.

Leonard Keny   80

I got in trouble with Louella Finn;
The way I did Louella was a sin,
I know the baby that she bore was mine,
And I went west and stayed till it was nine,
Then I returned to see this child of mine.
Louella sleeps today beneath a pine,
Louella Finn is in her grave today.
Louella Finn sleeps soundly under clay.
I wish she knew that I'm not married yet
And in my bosom is a deep regret
That I left her and went far in the west.
She is the woman that I've loved the best,
I wouldn't give Louella for the rest.
If she were up above the ground today
And pretty as she was and young and gay,
I'd give the heavens for Louella Finn—
The way I'd love her it would be a sin.

Kent Saxon

81

I heard the fife and drum—I loved the sound
And for eight years I marched to drum and fife.
Then I came back unto these hills and found
A hill-woman—I took her for my wife.
Now she has borne eight tall strong sons for me;
The last she bore for me was a strong daughter;
And we're contented here as we can be—
My wife and me, my eight sons and my daughter.
I shall not march to beat of drum again,
Nor shall my blood thrill to the trilling fife;
Nor shall my brain grow mad to kill again,
I live to give and not to take a life,
I give for good of man my tall eight sons,
They are not targets for your mighty guns.

82

Now if my native country has to fight,
And war's the only path for them to choose,
If we are ridden down and dared to fight,
Then my tall sons will have no time to lose.
They shall march forward for to face and fight.
But hell with war when there's a path around,
Boys are too hard to raise to be shot down.
Think of the youth who gave mortality
And sleep beneath the stone, the cross, the tree!
They gave their lives and now they sleep full sound,
They should be here instead of underground.
They gave to earth a rich posterity—
But if the country calls and needs their fight
(No rich man's fight—no way to go around)
I want my sons to go and face the night,
No matter if they're left to sleep full sound!

Mary Tongs 83

My shack is here among the scrubby pines
And soap-stone oaks— My man works at the mines.
He stays away from home months at the time.
Sometimes he stays a year— It's lonesome here
For me to stay alone and milk the cows
And tend the same truck patches every year.
I wish we had money so John could stay
And be with me— John is so far away!
He's working under a West Virginia hill.
I got uneasy when a whippoorwill
Came on the porch last night. That is a sign
Death takes one of the house—and that coal mine
Where John is working bears so on my mind.
We could search everywhere and never find
A better place to live than this shack here,
But it's so lonely, lonely, and John not here.

Lute Halley 84

Here is the girl who vamped one hundred men,
A portion of the hundred vamped this Miss.
Now Lute, do you remember boys you kissed?
We know the baby that you had is dead,
Buried out on the hill—little was said.
Now you go out to kiss and kiss again.
Better not let your kisses cause you pain.
Cy Spradling said that you would come to this.
Cy Spradling said that this was in your blood.
Maybe it is the way you greet the men,
And Lute, they love your passion for an hour
Then they move on to some unwilted flower—
After they find you once they leave you then.
But, Lute Halley, go on and vamp the men!

Jim Long   85

I have been lonesome for the winds at home,
I have been lonesome for the fields at home,
Tobacco fields and smell of new ground loam,
The smell of oat fields in the harvest haze,
The smell of tall Spring wheat and waves of rye,
The picture of a white cloud floating by—
Over the meadows and the tall green trees.
To hell with all these penitentiaries!
I am so homesick for the hills at home.
Why is it wrong for men to run a still?
Now Uncle Sam's stool-pigeons sell and buy,
And money is their God—their only cry!
Sam Hix got fifty bucks to spy on me!
Sam Hix, the dirty bastard, found my still.
When I leave here—he is one man I kill!

Millard Artis   86

He has a shanty on this Seaton Hill,
His health is bad—he lives among the pines,
Where early morning sun is first to shine.
His shanty's in a place where all is still,
Save sounds of katydids and whippoorwill
And winds that play among the pines at night.
Sometimes his oxen low before the dawn
And rise from beds of leaves they're sleeping on.
These are the sounds that Millard Artis hears,
These are the sounds he loves and never fears.
The lone life in the shack—the red fox howls,
The wind in trees at night, the bull-bat scowls.
The oxen and the log chain and the cart
Have cut lines in the depths of Millard's heart.

Kim Sperry 87

I rent this farm—I give one-half each year.
My landlord calls it: "Renting on the shear."
He owns the land is all, I do the work—
I clear the brush—I plow the land and sow
The grain—cow-peas, terbacker, corn and cane.
Each year I do these same old things again.
Terbacker's hard to sell—the price is low.
I try but cannot get enough ahead
To keep my children clothes and shoes and bread.
If I could get enough ahead I'd buy
A piece of land and then a span of mules.
I'd dress and send my children off to school,
But now I can't get anything ahead.
I barely keep my children clothes and shoes and bread.

Milton Sloan 88

I saw the sun sink in the golden west,
It lingered there awhile but sank to rest.
I thought: "Here are the hills I love the best,
And here among these hills I leave my past.
My past—and what is it? No one should know.
But it still hovers like the sunset glow
Above these hills—The sun sinks in the west
And leaves a golden radiance where it sinks—
Clouds tinted like wild honey in the sun,
Clouds colored like the scarlet autumn leaves.
I want to leave such when my day is done—
A radiance burning like the autumn leaves,
A golden radiance on the evening sky.
I want my life to hover like a sound,
Above this hallowed golden-leaf strewn ground,
Then I'll not be one half-afraid to die!

Warren Winslow   89

Roll on! Roll on—you skies forever blue!
Roll on! Roll on—white clouds forever too!
Roll on above the loose green clouds of leaves!
Roll on above wind blowing through the trees!
The streams look up to you, you rolling skies,
As you go drifting over paradise!
A paradise of ferns and blue blue water,
A paradise of birds and bees and grass,
A paradise the tired-of-life are after,
That's why I've come to let my decades pass.
Roll on! Roll on—you skies forever blue!
Roll on! Roll on—white clouds forever too!
I have grown strong again—I've lost my fears!
Roll on, you clouds—keep drifting like the years.

Charlie Thombs   90

I heard Tom Murphey said I was afraid
Of him—W'y hell, I'd make Tom eat his dung.
Tom should remember days when we was young.
Tom should remember I was never made
To do a thing—once at Bert Haley's brawl
I cut Squire Hawkins to the hollow twice.
Squire said that I was using loaded dice.
Now if Tom Murphey wants to fight, he can.
I'll go with Tom and fight it man to man.
I'll knife it out with Tom or use a gun.
He must stop blowin round that I'm afraid;
I'll show him how to make him eat his dung.
I'm now a better man than when I's young.
I'll make Tom Murphey swallow threats he's made.

Limp Snodgrass 91

His are all dreams—he never does a thing
But plan his small-farm dreams from Spring to Spring.
There is one hill of timber he must cut;
There is an orchard scarred by yellow rut
He's going to smooth and sow it in sweet-clover.
There is a pasture field he must scythe over
And get the sprouts and tall blackberry briars—
Fences need mending—he must splice some wires
The rust has eaten at the water-gate.
These are his dreams, but he gets nothing done,
Though he gets out and works from sun till sun.
He does his other work and lets dreams wait.
He is a dreamer and he'll be that way
Until he's gone to sleep beneath the clay!

Jim Fox 92

He drives the oxen over the timber road,
The ox cart's creaking with a heavy load.
The logs sweep round the curves and skin the trees
And deposit drifts of old last year's leaves.
"Get up there, Logan—woah, back, Berry!
That off-bull never gets in any hurry!"
Over the trail they go—Jim Fox can drive
Just any bull or steer that is alive
And taught to work—a driver of the ox,
No better ever lived than old Jim Fox.
He steers them well among the stumps and rocks.
And now his cattle have been turned on grass.
Ox teams are things that now have come to pass.
There are no more logs for Jim Fox to haul.
Jim Fox will hate to see the turn of leaf,
This fall his oxen will be sold for beef.

Ike Mullins   93

I've been a timber cutter all my days.
I've helped to cut the timber from these hills.
I can remember the old cord-wood days
When we cut cords and cords of wood to fill
Old Pennsylvania, Hunnewell, Raccoon—
We lived in little shacks—slept on the leaves.
We left before daybreak—came in at noon
Nigh starved to death—we cooked the grub we eat.
And we took off our shoes to rest our feet
At night—I'll bet I've cut a million trees.
Never again I'll cut a million trees—
You see, my boy, your Grand Pap's getting stiff.
I had brute-strength—now I can hardly lift
My feet to drag about.
                    The fire in me is out.

Martin Woodberry   94

I wish that I could live and live forever,
For I do love to live— I hate for age
To creep on me— my hair is turning white.
It can't be long until I meet my night.
I wish that I could live and live forever.
I wish there were no such a-thing as death—
A moment here and we must go forever.
At first we breathe—at last we give our breath.
What is this gold we love to place in banks?
What are these things we own and cannot keep
After the curtain's drawn and we take sleep?
Better to leave them with a card of thanks!
Why do we cheat and kill for things that fade?
Better for us if they were never made.

Lemuel Potter 95

They say that we are children of the night.
My wife and me can't nuther read ner write—
Though my son Paul—he's going off to school,
I don't want my son Paul to be a fool—
I want my Paul to learn to read and write.
I want my boy to learn to figure some—
I don't want him to be a child of night.
No one can steal his education from him,
I'd leave as give Paul this as give him money,
He can't spend this, but he can spend his money.
I guess my son will be ashamed of me
When he grows up and learns a lot from books.
I guess he'll be ashamed of my poor looks.
But I want him to git some learning, see,
So he can figure land and crops fer me.

Johnson Hailstrap 96

I am a farmer and my cutter plow
Makes furrows round the steep Kentucky hill;
I make my living by sweat from my brow.
Sometimes when I am plowing on the hill
I listen to them mockingbirds that trill,
And corn-birds fluting from the black-oak bough.
Life has been very kind to me, indeed.
In Spring these hands go forth to sow the seeds,
Through summer days they cultivate its needs.
In autumn they go out and garner crops—
These hands were made for work—they never stop
From time they plant until they gather crop.
I am a farmer and I love the plow.
I make my bread by hot sweat on my brow.

97

When Little Judd and his tall wife Min Moore
Set their Kentucky burley on the hill;
They set deep in their woods a moonshine still
And nine daughters carried to the store
Whiskey and eggs and bartered them for grub.
That was much easier than using a wash tub.
They had a mortgage on their farm to pay—
One thousand bucks at fifty cents per day!
One hates to work for such a little pay.
The Law got Judd—four years in Federal pen.
Judd's daughters now are sleeping with the men.
The mortgage holder lies in bed with Min,
And now a different life for tall Min Moore—
No outdoor work—she has a younger face—
The mortgage holder deeded Min the place.

98

Tom Friend is the good Shepherd of the hills.
I see him totter with his hickory stick
To part a path through briars across the hills,
For he's a-going now to see the sick.
I know Tom is good Shepherd of the hills.
I know he is good Shepherd for the sick,
For he will sit night-long by one in bed,
And he waits on the sick and helps to dig
The graves and make the coffins for the dead.
And I remember once these words he said:
"I do all I can do for the unjust
And for the just—rain falls on both alike
And in the end they both return to dust."
A chew of homemade and his hickory stick,
The Shepherd's going now to see the sick.

99

Farewell to winter I shall see no more!
Farewell to winter! Welcome early Spring!
How soft the velvet carpet on the floor,
How blithesome are the songs the robins sing!
This winter ice was on the big-room floor
And birds flew hither on their tousled wings,
Alighting here and there half-cheered to sing.
Farewell to winter with her barren store!
For all of us these days shall come no more
Though bitter winter days still lie in store.
But I shall keep this winter in my mind—
The icy earth, the barren trees, the wind,
And birds on barren branches still I hold
And sunsets gleaming through bare trees like gold—
These things of winter last I hope to hold!

100

Let us be fair with one another, friends,
And may I ask you, friends, what do you keep
Of all the winter past that lies asleep?
Do you remember any bitter winds
That chilled the blood in you and numbed your hands?
Do you remember any gray-starved winter lands
And frozen pasture hills with gleaming rocks?
Do you remember things like these, my friends?
The winter sunset gold, the bitter winds,
Would it be better if you would forget
And not allow these scenes to enter mind?
For you hereafter, what are gold and wind!
Do you remember wind-woven sedge-grass locks
And desolate corn-fields with fodder shocks!

101

Farewell to winter and the long black train
Of crows that crying cross the empty fields,
Farewell gray gloomy days of dismal rain
That in their gloom kept valley trees concealed.
Oh, I have seen some winters in my day
With winter days so desolate and gray
When cloudy skies obscured the yellow sun,
I've loved the yellow sunlight on the ground
And I have loved to hear the waters run
At night and winds blow loud with lonesome sound,
I've loved to walk among the hills at night
When cloudy skies rolled over land so gray,
I've loved dank winter gloom and white starlight
Both hanging over barren trees and yellow clay.

102

Farewell to winter and a long farewell,
Farewell to barren poplars in the wind,
Farewell to empty fields and gloomy dell
And dry sedge grass the wind is blowing in.
Farewell to yellow sunlight on the fields
And wasted winter sunlight on the fields
Where roots of fern and phlox now lie concealed.
Farewell to crows that fly above these fields.
And may I say to you: Green leafless briars,
Here is a long farewell, for you shall bloom
After you put your dead leaves in the tomb.
Among your blossoms white the birds shall sing
And humming birds will park on whirring wings
To drink of fragrance from your tiny flower—
This will be Spring-time and a gayer hour.

103

Farewell to winter, for we now depart.
As dead leaves print their likeness on the ground
You print your barren likeness on my heart
And on my heart it leaves a fresher wound—
Now I have said farewell so many times.
Many of these farewells I said in rhymes—
But when I close my eyes at night to see
The bronze-disc moon above a barren tree
(It is the winter moon I love to see)
The bronze-disc smiling frowning down on me—
Blood running in my veins is poetry!
Farewell to winter, for March thaws are over
And blotches of green grass have sprung again.
Around manure piles are tints of clover
And this is one sure sign that winter's over.

104

When winter left I waved my hand to her
And with the other hand I welcomed Spring.
Something to Spring about the whip and stir—
Green blotches on the pasture and the blur
Of soft green leaves in a slow blowing wind.
Something in Spring has caused the birds to sing.
The corn-bird now has put away all care.
Something to Spring makes restlessness in me.
Something to Spring that keeps my blood astir
Like April sap stirs in the veins of tree.
Now desolation with the winter goes
Like a slick black-snake lost its winter skin,
Like a young man that lost his winter clothes
And into his Spring suit is to step in.

105

"Listen, my boy, I know I seed my God
The other night and he was great to see.
Yes-sir—he walked around the timber road
Behind the teamsters a-takin their last load.
Yes, it was great to see God on the sod.
And did my God Almighty smoke a pipe!
I wot my God Almighty smoked a pipe,
And with his boney fingers combed and wiped
The backer ashes from his long white beard.
God Almighty was a little man, I heerd—
But it's a lie—he's bigger than Kit James.
He's bigger than all the lumber-jacks out here.
I was afraid of God—I had a fear
Of stepping in his tracks or a-goin near."

106

"No, Pa—you never seed the living God,
For he's in Heaven settin on his throne.
And men like you are leavin God alone,
Most men like you are sleepin under sod.
No, Pa—you never seed the living God.
Besides I don't believe God smokes a pipe.
I don't believe his fingers comb and wipe
The backer ashes from his long white beard.
You say God smokes a pipe because you smoke.
You say a pipe because you smoke a pipe.
Pa, you're a-tryin for to tell a joke.
Is that gin on your breath, Pa, that I smell—
A-lyin on God and you as drunk as hell!"

107

"Now Charlie, go and leave your Pa alone.
Your Pa has things a-bearin on his mind.
I've lived with him nigh fifty years and know.
Your Pa once had a heart as hard as stone.
He once said things about God to the wind
And that has been nigh forty years ago.
Charlie, your Pa kilt one man in cold blood
And now he drinks his gin to drown his care—
And gin and licker put him in a mood
That he sees God Almighty everywhere.
And ever since your Pa has kilt a man
He reads his chapter in the Bible every-day
And prays forgiveness for the man he kilt—
Each night he kneels beside the bed and prays.

108

I watch the clouds sail over to the west—
Gold-flecked and fleece-clouds float across the sky.
And I have stood and watched them floating by—
Float down beyond the dark hills in the west.
And then into the air I breathed a sigh:
"Where do things go forever drifting by!
The clouds and wind—I wish that it were I
Going beyond the dark hills in the west—
Going beyond the sunset rim of gold—
I wish that it were I now drifting by—
Instead of wind and cloud and sunset gold."
Now what is it that does not hear my cry,
For I can see wind bending down the clover
And I can see the white clouds drifting over.

109

Who said that gold was all there was in life—
If you believe these words walk out with me
And listen to the wind blow through a tree,
Come out and see a different gold with me.
Peach blossoms in the silver wind are gold,
And when frosts come and winds are getting cold
You'll find, my friend, the leaves will turn to gold.
But this is gold you cannot use to buy,
And this is gold, my friend, hard to be bought;
It is that useless gold poets have sought—
But you are not a poet, are you friend?
And peach-leaf gold is not means to an end.
Therefore, my friends, you do not see my gold.
What does gold matter when we both lie cold?

110

The green is now among the April hills
And there is green twilight among these hills.
The wind has smell and dampness of the green.
And here upon green carpet may be seen
Old rabbits mating and young ones at play,
And lapwings come enjoying light of day.
The green is here—an April tender green—
And the lapwings are flitting through the sheen
Of soft-green twilight and wood-leaves soft-green.
And now I stand beside a cross-road tree.
It does not matter if she is with me.
And lapwings, if you know one thing on me,
(If I am wrong her beauty is to blame)
Now keep it silenced till eternity.

111

Peace be to you—my native hills and skies!
Peace be to you—white rivers there among!
Peace to your winds with lonely mocking cries
Over the earth where the gray landscape lies.
Peace be with you—you blithesome Plum Grove young,
The Law is after me—I leave tonight.
I think that I shall travel in the west.
I shall walk country paths under the starlight
To miss the guarded roads and ambush fight,
Escape without a hole torn in my breast—
The night is dark and sparse are stars now out.
I fear footsteps when winds blow leaves about,
I look to see gun blazes from the trees—
The thugs—the deafening sounds the last of me.

112

Under bare poplars where dead leaves are strewn
A man was found next morning stiff and dead,
A white sand-stone was pillow for his head
And yellow leaves a blanket where he laid—
And one brave lad from Plum Grove hills was gone.
An ambush man sent bullets to his breast—
Returning fire to many trees, he fled.
They could not track him by steps where he bled.
He held two holes of spurting blood and fled
Until he found thick leaves to lie upon
And pillow for his head of white sand-stone.
He died before he went behind the bars,
He died with sallow face upturned to stars.
Next day country newspapers thus read:
"Murderer Escapes Left Two Policemen Dead."

113

And now, my friend, these hills would love to say:
"Comrade, we drink your blood—your glorious clay
We take into our arms at last to rest.
We take you back, our son—gray-place in death,
You gave unto the wind your fleeting breath.
You stood out in the open—shot two fair.
How did you do it when these men stood there
Behind the trees? No one will ever know.
But thus, my friend, it happened—happened so!
Peace be to him, we welcome to our clay,
Peace be to him where leaves drift and wind blows.
Peace be to him forever and one day—
Since he lies by where Sandy water flows
Where on his grave grow thyme and woodland rose.

114

The blossoms hang snow-white on cherry boughs,
Italian honey bees work there among,
There Jean and I walk under cherry boughs,
Oh, for that privilege of being young!
For me the merry lapwing flits unseen,
For me winds sigh through cherry leaves in vain,
For I am busy whispering to my Jean,
Knowing that this youth will not come again.
Surely the lapwing loves the cherry blossom;
Surely he sees them drifting, drifting down;
Surely he sees the drifting shriveled blossom—
White cherry blossom—a-wafting, wafting down,
From cherry-tops through bright winds to the
    ground—
White blossoms drifting, drifting without a sound.

115

I love this little world so clean and white
So utterly now filled with raw perfume,
It is an April world bathed in moonlight,
An apple orchard now in fullest bloom.
The scent of wind from apple blooms tonight
Is good to breathe—the taste is sweet as wine.
The white tops of the trees are fair to see.
White tops of trees are fancies such as mine
When they spread like white sails in white moonlight.
I do not blame rabbits for coming here
And mating here and giving birth to young,
And staying here beneath these trees the year
Around— This is the place one loves to be
Beneath these bounds of blooming orchard world
Where blossoms to the April moon are furled
And life now cries: "Why can't we live eternally!"

116

Some say a man is crazy when he goes
Out on an April hill when the wind blows
Under the red-buds and their mouse-ear leaves.
Some hear no music when the wind laments,
No drum-beats when it hoarsely boasts and grieves.
The wind incurs no feeling of discontent
In them nor mirth—incurs in them no moods.
One is no poet then if these red-buds
Are vain to him—bending in the wind's play.
But if one hears gods in the wind and prays
And sees white islands float across the sky
Then this one has a poet's moods and ways
And not the little ways of those that cry
To God from corners on the dirty street
Expecting money from the passers-by.

117

Of all the towns I've seen upon this earth
Corkscrew I hate, and one I would pass by,
I'm sorry that my mother gave me birth
In high Kentucky hills so close there-by.
For Corkscrew has a score of rascal dens—
Of dirty rascals Corkscrew has five-score,
(At least this many—possibly has more)
I've stood there-by and saw those rascal men
Welcome the county ikes into their dens
And ruefully take their good cash and grin.
They say these Corkscrew men have pots of gold,
This profit on the goods to ikes they sold.
Of all the towns on earth gladly would I
Rather pass this thieving, thieving Corkscrew by.

Greenup, Kentucky 118

Winter has kept this town so oddly sleeping.
Winter has made its face death-colored gray.
Winter has kept its towering trees a-sleeping
And creeper vines now lifelessly a-creeping,
Winter has sent upon the pavements gray
Dead leaves to hither, thither, blow their way.
And over where the good folks meet to pray
I see one spire among the tops of trees—
Skyward there-by the winds are drifting leaves.
And here above this town so oddly sleeping,
I've seen gray mists obscure the winter sun.
At dusk I've seen the trees together run.
This is one town I always shall remember
Death-colored sleeping in the gray December.

But Spring awakens this old town now sleeping.
Spring has returned with new blood for each vein
And very little death-colored pallors remain.
Green leaves spring forth from creeper vines a-creeping.
And over where the good folks meet to pray
I see one spire among the tops of trees—
A spire part hidden by a leaf-green spray,
And everywhere the children run and play
Under the green shades where the pavements lay.
The girls trip by on neatly slippered feet
Where dead leaves used to drift upon the street.
And where December mists hung in the air
A fleet of swallows are a-coasting there,
Each cutting circles in the bright-blue air.
Spring has brought back new life unto this town
Peacefully under blue heavens flecking down.

This is the tumbling shack where I was born.
The strength of earth around is in my blood.
And here the morning glories wrap the corn
Behind these palings where my mother worked
And sang away the precious hours she worked.
The winds and waters made in me a mood—
I still can hear the music of the flood
Come sounding from the valley from afar
Over green-fields—under the glittering star.
I still can hear the surging of the wind
(Wind playing like a lonesome violin)
Among the shoe-make leaves and stems of grass,
And I can say I learned to love the wind
When it played marches for my days to pass.

121

And I would love to speak unto this house.
Since I was born therein my parents say:
"This is the place, my son, you first saw light."
I'd love to speak unto this house and say:
"Your rooms are empty to the brown wood mouse.
The room upstairs is left to bats and birds.
Wall plates are empty to the writhing snakes
And you're too deaf to catch my empty words.
I stand before you now and my heart aches
To see you growing, growing desolate—
Fence posts now rotting at the broken gate,
Tall weeds now growing at the broken gate—
I stand before you and I cannot say,
Old logs and stones, the things I'd like to say."

122

I ask where are the ramble rose vines now?
Where are the petals they shed on the ground?
I ask where are the coal picks and the plow?
They are all gone—they're gone forever now.
Where is the strength to hoe my mother gave
When she worked in the corn-fields like a slave?
Like petals from the rose these are decay.
My mother gave her precious strength away
Fed seven babys' mouths including mine.
And she, too, heard the music of the flood
And she, too, heard the music in the wind
In shoe-makes playing like a violin.
The wind and flood gave her a yearning mood
To go beyond dark hills with blowing wind,
To go beyond the music of their flood.

123

The house is silent now—the folks have gone.
Where have they gone—these folks of yesterday?
The house they left has weathered to decay.
The kitchen boards have turned to dun and gray.
The weeds grow tall—the old house slumbers on
Slowly but surely to positive decay.
I wonder if the people once living here
(The merry party of the long ago)
Were to return after many a year,
If this would be the house they used to know.
The mossy boards are curling to the sun.
The gable ends have weathered to a black,
Over the paneless windows creepers run
And something seems to say: "Will they come back?"

124

My boy, stand here beneath the August skies.
Survey this mountain shack both log and stone.
Observe it closely with blue steady eyes,
Observe it closely for it is your own,
One quarter of one century ago
You were born in this tumbling mountain shack.
The weather then had never turned it black
And hollyhocks then grew beside the door
And waved a-nod in dew and white moonlight—
Pink hollyhocks and blue and cream and white,
A ramble rose-vine climbed above the door
And round the wall and through a broken pane
It bloomed and shed its petals on the floor.

125

The wind beat high up here when autumn came
And shoe-make leaves glowed like a burning flame,
The wind beat high and hard and strew the leaves
Among dead stems of grass beside your shack,
The winds sighed lonesome in the low white pines.
The winds sighed lonesome in the creeper vines,
And night and day the winds kept calling back:
"Yours is the party of the long ago,
But years must pass before you really know
Yours is the party of the long ago."
I can remember how the winds called back
And how I heard the lapping far away
Of Sandy water moaning over stones,
And how I loved this lapping night and day,
The waters' lapping, lapping monotone.

126

Somehow the years recall—I do not hear
After I've freely spent many a year,
I could say "black" to crow and "brown" to bat,
But I could never grow to peace at that.
Now I can only view this place again
And keep these scenes in album of my brain,
And scenes may come and go—these shall remain
Because they have become a part of me—
Still part of me when I feed roots of tree—
Sleeping, sleeping, sleeping, mortally sound.
If there will be a picture on my brain
When I am sleeping, sleeping underground,
Only the wind and corn-field crows will know
I was one of the party of the long ago,
My scenes now dust while sleeping here below.

127

Stand in your ruins, you tumbling mountain shack,
Though years may call, your inmates won't come back.
You keep their secrets, House—you keep them well,
Now keep them from the wind—the wind will tell,
Now keep them, House, and keep them from the crows.
These crows will tell the secrets Mother knows.
Stand in your splendor, tumbling mountain shack,
Stand high and dry amid the autumn days
And do not call, for no one will come back
Except to stand beside your ruins and gaze.
To me you are a picture of the former days.
When I was young and lived between your walls
And did not know there was a world at all,
I was happy then—memory recalls.

128

Now do not leave me, love, for rugged lands;
Don't leave me, love, for beauty of the stars;
And do not leave me, love, for honest toil.
The food and strength of life come from the land.
The beauty of the flowers come from the land,
The land is all—the golden locust soil.
The stars are things a baby cries to love,
The white stars in a blue, blue sky above.
Be with me, love, that I may not forget
The silver wind, the leaves, the clouds, trees;
Be with me, love, that I may not forget,
And if I pray to Gods in winds, remember these—
For such as these, words are the frailest things,
Frail as a white moth on its air-thin wings.

129

The first Monday each month in Finnisburg,
The country ikes come in to buy and sell—
And they come in half-teaed to Finnisburg.
This only day the merchants wish them well.
And one may easily tell a country ike—
Mud on his shoes and patches on his pants.
And when "Blind" Frailey comes to play the fiddle,
These country ikes will come and start the dance—
And if they dance, come out some day and see
To Finnisburg—come to the courthouse square,
For all dancers and fiddlers gather there
Under the shade of any courtyard tree.
And if these country men can dance, my friends,
It's up to your decision—come and see!

130

When old "Blind" Frailey starts his magic fiddle
And a Plum Grove man is there by chance,
You ought to watch this man step out and dance.
Of course he has some patches on his pants
And by his side the old men jig a little
And laugh and listen to the talking fiddle.
"Blind" Frailey stops for resin on his bow
And when he starts to fiddle up he cries:
" 'Girl With the Blue Dress On!' Boys, let's go!"
And then coarse shoes like mauls thug on the ground
Until they nearly drown the fiddle sound,
And soon a jolly crowd is gathered there
With best of drink upon the courthouse square
And talk about dancing and the fiddling there!

131

The boys give freely to "Blind" Frailey here,—
Nickels, dimes and quarters that the boys can spare,
The boys pay freely for good drinks of booze,
And they pay dearly for new soles on shoes;
But it is dance and drink these countrymen choose.
And of all days first Mondays are the best
Of each month when the boys come in to rest,
Come in to town to rest and buy and sell—
This day of all the merchants wish them well.
But fiddler Frailey takes the boys by spell,
They dance and let all business go to hell,
Under the maples on the courtyard square,
And all you have to do is venture there
And listen to "Blind" Frailey play the fiddle
Where a crowd is parted under the maple tree
And dancing men step up and down the middle.

132

This is a fiddler when he gets to Heaven
As people say "Blind" Frailey's sure to do—
He'd go up to the golden gates of Heaven,
"Blind" Frailey would, and fiddle his way right thru.
He'd fiddle all round God's children with harps,
"Blind" Frailey doesn't know the flats and sharps,
But all God's children will throw down their harps
And listen to a blind man fiddling thru.
"Blind" Frailey will fiddle on the golden street
Till dancers will forget they are in Heaven,
And they'll be swept away on dancing feet
And dance all over golden streets of Heaven.
"Blind" Frailey will fiddle for the dancers there
Up where the Lord sits in his golden chair,
He will sit down to jolly fiddling there.

133

And if one Plum Grove man has gone to Heaven
And if he hears this fiddle by a chance,
He will call out the angels here in Heaven;
The sweet fair maids here all white-robed in Heaven,
And they'll renew again the old square dance—
The old Kentucky mountain "Waltz the Hall"—
The most Kentuckian of all dance calls—
The Lord will sit in his high golden chair
And watch "Blind" Frailey from Kentucky there,
The Lord will sit wistfully a-looking on
But the Lord will never say a word at all,
Not when he sees his angels "Waltz the Hall—"
And when he hears Frailey from Kentucky there
He will sit back and laugh from his golden chair.

134

And if "Blind" Frailey finds rest in Heaven
And if the Plum Grove folks knew it back here,
I'm sure these folks would try harder for Heaven
To follow the "Blind" Frailey fiddler there—
They love to dance to his magic fiddle—
They could dance all the night and all the day—
And if they would become light spirits in Heaven
And get all the thirst and the hunger away
Their light spirits then could dance till Doomsday—
There's danger that they would forget to pray—
But when "Blind" Frailey starts sawing his fiddle
Only he stops long enough to resin his bow—
When he does this, spry dancers will jig a little—
Jig on till Frailey says: "Boys, let 'er go!"

April 1, 1933

April is here—the peach trees are in bloom,
Their pink blossoms wave in the bright-blue air.
April is here—white moths break from the tomb
And go a-flitting, flitting everywhere.
And may I say: "White moths, this is your Spring.
Go, flitting moths! Go flit on crumbling wings!
Go hunt the pink peach blossoms in the wind!
Before they fade drink their sweets from within!
After your season, moths, you will remember,
The season of your lives was bright-blue Spring
When you were young to flit on air-light wings.
It's hard to gather sweets in your September,
For sweetest blossoms die before the autumn
And you must die ere cool winds kill the blossoms—
High hills of goldenrod—pinks at the bottom.

April is here without a doubt in mind.
April is here—look in the cool fresh wind!
See how the buds begin to burst again!
So fresh they burst after this April rain!
The dogwoods spread their white sails on the hill.
They are the sails of many thousand ships.
When winds are still the dogwood sails are still,
When the wind blows the white sails toss about.
These sails move up and down—move in and out!
Pine trees are sailors with green-bearded lips,
They stand beneath and help to shift about
These great white dogwood ships with flapping sails.
The high green hills are rough waves on the sea,
An ocean of green water beckoning me!

137

April is here—the wind is fresh and fine.
Green buds are bursting from each living tree.
Winds blown from bursting buds is good to breathe
As wine to drink—fine to breathe, deep and free.
What is there, tramp, from keeping you and me
To breathe this April wind down deep and free!
Breathe deep to lungs and let it touch our blood,
Remember it has kissed the bursting bud,
Remember it has kissed the blooming tree.
Friend tramp, this is the wind for you and me,
Friend tramp, this April wind is good to breathe.
Get plenty April wind before it leaves!
April is just a month of thirty days—
April, a light-green month with silver ways!

138

April brings back to man in fresh array
White sprays of blossoms on a silver day.
April is here—we welcome sunny Spring.
I laugh to winds—birds work and sing and sing!
And even I have laughed for swift strong wings
To bear me far into this April blue.
Oh, I would soar though I have work to do—
The cane is yet to plant, so is the corn.
The oats are up—dew-match stems in the morn—
Small weeds are growing now among the oats.
These should be cut—rings put in nose of shoats,
Stove wood's to cut and put in ricks to dry,
There're coming times for stove wood by-and-by.
My word, I love April in such a way
I want to put off work from day to day.

139

The empty fields are left and dead weeds there
Must be turned under for the crops again,
For April now has brought fresh days and fair
With precious little interludes of rain.
Spring leaves unto the wind white blooming flowers
Where lazy honey bees waste precious hours.
Can one blame them for living with the flowers?
When I go out to plow these fields again
I love to sit down on the beam of plow
And think: "When shall I plow this land again
And will it turn as fine as it does now!
Cool, soft, it turns and moist like after rain—
What will it matter if I plow again
Or sit here dreaming on my bull-tongue plow!"

140

The chickens cackle under leafing trees
And scratch old leaves and chase the honey bees,
They're out to get fresh worms from sweet Spring soil
And mate and lay white eggs on stained oak leaves.
This is blue April here among the hills
And chickens love to cackle in the sun—
Hens hear the roosters' "kir-kirks" and they run
To eat choice worms their roosters hold for them.
The shedding snake crawls on the white-oak limb
And falls to break hen eggs he has in him.
This is one way snakes celebrate the Spring—
They love to writhe around and steal the eggs
And then there is the crazy thousand-legs
That cannot eat but loves to crawl on eggs!

141

White in the moonlight the valley lies sleeping
And frost has whitened dead leaves on the ground;
Deep in the valley moon shadows are creeping
And March winds blow through pines with lonesome
    sound.
Through pine needles the white moon is a-gleaming
And on ground-frosted leaves the white moon gleams.
Under the bright March stars the valley's dreaming,
Spotted with moon-shadows the valley dreams.
My hound has come with me, I hear him bark,
His voice to me is clear and sweet and shrill.
He brings the red-fox through pine woods where dark
Shadows now lie—he runs with a good will.
And on a frosted hill where white stars glisten,
I stand chilled by the wind and listen, listen!

142

These yellow banks are very dear to me.
I know where each gray stone lies on the field;
I know about where stands each sweet-gum tree
And hollow trees where squirrels are concealed.
I keep these facts—why tell them to the others?
Why tell them where the crows have built their nests?
For man and squirrels and crows are not brothers—
But men are killers with God in their hearts.
These white corn stalks in March moonlight to me
Are receipts here to show I pay for bread.
One of my prayers has been for me to be
Strong as my oaks—if this is ever read,
Remember, I once prayed to write words pure
As gold to rhyme—and prayed they would endure.

143

Why pray for words—my words will soon be lost
Same as the leaves fall from the trees each year
In first wind-gust—after a little frost.
We first see beauty in them lying here,
Rich-colored autumn leaves now on the ground,
Under the autumn trees so slim and bare
We hear the winds blow with an angry sound,
And these words from the trees die with the year.
And there is not one man to pause and hear
The wind-words that go drifting, drifting down,
The wind-words that go drifting softly down,
Wind-words a-drifting yellow, scarlet, brown,
Wind-words to die forever—drifting down.

144

My words are wind-words lying on the land.
My words are worthless words the people hear
They are true words—the soil-men understand;
They will die in their season with the year.
But let them die for you and I must die;
Our words must die—and die forever too!
Our words must die we fling to wind and sky—
Like leaves must die and rot the long year through.
The words I spoke to many loves are dead—
Dead as these humble lines I write shall be;
Dead as one Love now sleeping in a bed,
Under the yucca and the cedar tree.
I love to say these words and I shall write,
Knowing that they and I perish tonight.

145

The years have passed and prayers still are needed.
I pray to winds and gods in the night winds.
They do not hear—my prayer is still unheeded.
Gold words I chose are cankering in my rhymes.
And when I walk the hills alone and pray
For powers it takes to spin words in a rhyme,
It seems to me that silence tries to say:
"Why pray, my youth, when you have plenty time.
You are strong as an oak behind your plow.
Go make your living with an honest toil.
Live clean at heart, for growth is in you now.
And as the oaks root deep into your soil,
Go with a courage just as deep and strong,
Go plow the soil and sing your corn-bird song.
Go face the world and pay your honest debts,
And live a life to die without regrets."

146

And as I tread the bosom of my clay,
High yellow hills where I have spent my days,
There's something in my bosom seems to say:
"Here is the place where you were born and raised.
This is the place your mother prayed to God.
This is the place she gave you children birth—
The place where your brothers lie under sod—
To you it is the greatest place on earth.
Here some fine books you've read and once grew fond
Of them and worked enough to go beyond
These austere hills that hold you to their slopes
And let you share your family's joys and hopes.
Now if you could rise up and sing their fame;
Wonder, of your poor hills you'd feel a shame!"

147

That time will never come to me, my soil,
When I am wreathed in little oak-leaf fame.
The time will never come when I unfold
My leaves and fly to mountain heights of song.
I grow too close the earth in sterile soil.
It would be hard for me to make a name.
It's hard for me and I am still to blame—
For over me the sun slants rays of gold,
And over me the stars are white and cold.
And I am rooted in the land I love—
I do not care for sun and stars above
And if I should drift singing to the skies,
I'll not forget the black oak land I love—
Land where starlight and shadow fill the eyes—
And rugged hills and trees—a paradise—
This is Kentucky I am speaking of.

148

In paradise I found life first a battle.
When I was six I worked at thinning corn,
I went to work before day in the morn.
I got up four at morn to feed the cattle
Before the chickens flew down off the trees.
And when I found the cow on autumn morn
I drove her up and stood on the warm leaves
Where she had lain, to get my cold feet warm.
Cold feet and cattle are dear memories.
This is the land still very dear to me—
The land of oak trees and the scrubby pine
And sawbriars under the persimmon tree—
These scenes I claim forever to be mine.
Can one forget home waters from his birth?
How can a man forget his native earth!

149

Spring in Kentucky hills will soon awaken;
The sap will run every vein of tree.
Green will come to the land bleak and forsaken;
Warm silver wind will catch the honey bee.
Blood-root will whiten on the barren hill;
Wind-flowers will grow beneath the oaks and nod
To silver April wind against their will.
Bitterns will break the silence of the hills
And meadow's grass sup dew under the moons,
Pastures will green and bring back whippoorwills
And butterflies that break from stout cocoons.
Spring in Kentucky hills and I shall be
A free soil-man to walk beneath the trees
And listen to the wind among the leaves—
And count the stars and do as I damn please.

150

Ah, April's here—the corn is young and green,
The meadow larks are soaring to the skies,
And I go down to walk with bonnie Jean,
Wherein the sun the pale-green meadow lies.
And we go there to hear the wild bird cries.
The meadow is clothed in light April green
And I am proud to walk thereon with Jean—
And it is here that swiftly the time flies—
I know I do prefer to walk with Jean,
I love to walk with her across the meadow.
She walks as nobly as an April Queen,
She steps as softly as a silver shadow.
I know I love to walk with bonnie Jean,
Upon the velvet carpet of the meadow.

151

As I came by I heard a running stream.
I heard the water falling over stones.
I stood and listened to the monotones.
And there between the dark hills was a gleam
Of silver water in the white moonlight.
I paused and blessed the gods for such a night—
The dark hills sharply etched against the sky—
A ribbon stream of water flowing white—
A ribbon stream of water in moonlight.
The night winds made the naked oak boughs quiver
Longside the wooded shores of this small river.
The night wind sang a song to soap-stone oaks.
The winter ferns bent down with finger strokes
And kissed the moonlight on this placid river.

152

The naked willows in the meadow wind
Is fine net-work of iron tracery,
Tonight my ears are tuned and listening in.
I hear these willows swish the winter wind,
And the night cry is like a violin.
I wonder if the gods are listening too!
I wonder if the silent stars and moon
Are listening to the wind and willow tune!
I wonder how the moon and stars refrain
From hearing this music of joy and pain,
Too fine to be conceived by mortal brain.
And yet these willows in the wind can make
A music that can make one's own heart break.
Sounds born of beauty, joy, sadness, and pain!

153

Now I do not belong to clique and clan
But I am free—free as the wind that blows.
And I have never known the fear of man
Nor failed to love the beauty of a rose.
Deep in my heart I love the sweet primrose
Just after summer rain, after the wind blows.
Why should I tie myself to any clan?
What is this difference when man is man?
Each has a heart that beats deep in his breast.
Each lives and loves and hates and then takes rest.
Who knows the worst of us—who knows the best?
We are children only, under the sun,
And we are children half afraid to run,
For clay temples will easily come undone!

154

Come on, comrades, let's click the cups together!
The wine is rich and let us drink together—
Let's drink tonight, tomorrow we may never—
The best comrades that ever tramped on leather.
Turn your face to the stars and drink tonight.
Red wine is good to drink beneath starlight.
Comrades, starlight may get into your eyes
When you are drinking to the starry skies.
Oh, drink tonight, for golden time now flies.
Tomorrow, comrades, we'll not drink together
Nor proudly walk on old and thin shoe-leather.
Now come and let us click our cups together,
And drink rich wine and face the starry skies.
Come on, comrades, for swiftly the time flies!

155

Life I have cried unto the gods in terror
When passion in this flesh remained superior—
Superior to this nervous mortal brain—
But the gods have been deaf to all my cries.
And what is there to do but still remain
A mortal man until this clay house dies?
I know the gods have never heard my prayers.
Prayers the gods immortal ought to hear
If man is patterned to a plan of theirs.
I pray: "Immortal gods, revise your plan
And for the future make a different man.
I have been told my faith is not secure,
My brain quite primitive, my thoughts unpure,
And I was one, gods' children can't endure."

156

The crows fly over empty fields of Spring
And carry mud and sticks to make a nest.
The meadow larks have early taken wing;
The wrens build in a place cats can't molest.
I plow the earth around my mountain shack;
Go out before the day has quite begun—
I'm proud the birds are here and Spring is back—
I work from dawn until the setting sun.
The cow-birds swarm along and trail my plow—
Never a one of them gets in a hurry—
Black birds are after dung of corn-fed cows,
Cat-birds are building in the blooming cherry.
I'm proud the empty Spring has come again
And trees are leafing after April rain.

157

The poplar leaves are silver in the wind.
The hay is getting duller in the ricks.
The white clouds float above in silver wind.
The naked hill-top timbers are black sticks.
But where the trees are growing by the water,
A sheen of thin leaves flutter in the wind.
Though river trees have leafed the leaves are thin
And plowmen sing about this merry April—
Green back among the hills—gold to the sun—
White, blow wind-flowers on the pasture hill—
Like new sap in the trees—new blood's begun
To reopen our body's winter veins.
Oh, Spring is here—power to live remains
Deep in our hearts—reprinted on our brains!

158

I love to turn the cold bare March sod over,
I love to turn the fresh earth down the hill,
I love to have my ground in shape to plant
About the coming of the whippoorwill.
Few days before the blooming of the clover
The plowing must be done when April's over.
The mules work better in cool days of Spring—
Better to work when larks first start to sing.
I hate to think I'll ever lose a Spring.
I love to watch the cool sod turning over,
I love to plant my corn in middle April
When crows are building on adjoining hill
And try to measure the bright April weather—
Oh, I do wish Spring would go on forever!

159

I plucked for you a goldenrod bouquet.
I plucked them from a bank of yellow clay
And put their broken stems in a blue vase.
Somehow you did not love the goldenrod.
Its substance came from the Kentucky sod.
I wish I could slip back and now erase
From memory flowers I plucked for you.
You are still young and have such ugly face—
Ugly in flesh—ugly in spirit, too.
I've no Kentucky goldenrods for you—
Not one to wear on your tremulous breast,
And certainly not one bloom to be pressed
Between the yellow pages of a book
Where you may fondly someday turn and look.

160

The years are creeping slow in Plum Grove hills.
The season has been short for daffodils.
Green leaves were late a-gettin to the hills.
The farmers planted little corn in April.
Summer was filled with lazy shifting shadows
Of clouds above green trees and light-green meadows—
Shadows of birds and bees and thin locust trees.
The fall was late—industrious honey bees
Gathered sweet fragrance from the shoe-make berries.
Winter came later and little blue-snow flurries
Pinned fresh beds of oak leaves down with the rotten.
Old winter snows passed off in a Spring rain
And left old fields so barren and forgotten.
The years go slow at Plum Grove—Spring, again!

161

I gather phlox for you, my sweet Elizabeth.
The bees love fragrance of the phlox's breath.
I gather these wild phlox to make a wreath,
A wreath of phlox for you, my Elizabeth.
A wreath of phlox above your shapely brow
While they are now in their majestic bloom—
A wreath of beauty for your snow-white brow.
The land where these phlox grew, I soon must plow.
Better to let a wreath fade on your brow
Than let majestic blossoms meet their doom,
For what is prettier than the wild phlox blooms.
Here is the wreath to crown your snow-white brow—
Phlox blossoms soon to wither and to fade—
These fresh phlox on your living brow now laid!

162

Why do you hold to me, my Jean Elizabeth?
I have not been all you expect of me,
You do not ask these things, my Jean Elizabeth
No more than do you ask if wind is free.
And wind is free, you know, sweet Jean Elizabeth.
Put your hand in the wind the way it blows.
The wind is free and very free one knows.
The wind is free and blows where no one goes.
It kisses more than one wild woodland rose.
And like the wind—I'm free and very free.
But when I kissed your petals, woodland rose,
I stayed with you—this carefree wind that blows—
With you soft-petaled rose, dancing and free!

163

I shall not go inside the church tonight.
She must not see me stagger down the aisle.
She must not be ashamed of me tonight;
Church will be over in a little while.
The music makes me want to venture in;
My Jean Elizabeth plays her violin.
I know she wonders why I am not there.
My Jean Elizabeth—she should not care
Nor ever say for me a silent prayer,
She should not care for one that does not care.
I hear the words they speak of God within.
The windows are all up and I look in
And hear the music of the violins
And men asking forgiveness of their sins.

164

I know the way she feels—my Jean Elizabeth,
She sees me by the window looking in—
I'm listening to the lonesome violin.
I don't care what the preacher says of sin.
But I do care for my sweet Jean Elizabeth.
I think I hear her utter prayer under breath.
I do not care for any lofty prayer
Prayed by one of the righteous strangers there.
I hear them preach of wild oats young men sow
And how these wild oat seed do sprout and grow
In whiskey, woman, cards and sweet rich wine—
I must be high tonight as a Kentucky pine.
My Elizabeth—I know she's not divine,
But she's a star above this night of mine.

165

I think birds roosting in the cupola
Have been aroused tonight by lofty prayers;
I think these sleeping sparrow birds would know
And see the bright grains in these lofty prayers—
I think they would peck at these words of theirs.
If I had wings tonight I'd reach the stars,
I'd peck them from the big blue bowl of sky.
Tomorrow I may be behind the bars—
A bird confined without wine-wings to fly,
A bird confined and sick enough to die.
Tonight, my Jean Elizabeth, don't spend your breath
In golden words with me—serious as death!
Outside the house I hear the lonesome prayers
Of night winds catching on the arms of firs.

166

I hear no more the lonesome violin,
At the church window I cannot look in,
The fault in me the preacher calls it sin.
My face is now upturned to the night skies,
I lie with starlight in my half-closed eyes,
My flesh is chilled with dampness on the ground,
My eyes are blurred to the sight of the skies,
My ears are deaf to wind and green leaf sound.
I am a lifeless lump of worthless clay,
When this wine dies, I shall be better clay;
I shall not lie and sleep the time away,
And I shall walk beside of Jean Elizabeth.
She will not mention where she found me last,
But Jean Elizabeth will keep this under breath.

167

The call to earth is pounding on my brain,
I want to walk with my bare feet on earth,
I want to go back to the earth again,
I want to breathe of clean air for my breath.
I want to get right down and dig in dirt
And get away from man and work and work—
There's consolation to be found in dirt,
And rest comes better after one must work.
I think life is too easy for us all:
We love the easy-sounding mammon call,
We hearken to this sounding mammon call,
The call to earth one seldom hears at all.
But when sap stirs in trees blood in my veins
Runs swift as flooded water in Spring streams.

168

I love to see corn bursting from the earth—
Three tender green blades growing to the sun.
I love to see the sown-cane bursting forth
And see bean sprouts with two half-beans on one.
I tell you then the call to earth comes back
And I cannot escape this deep-blood call—
Wheat in light waves—light-green—in thick **waves** black.
I watch wind waves of clover rise and fall
And walnut limbs wind-bent on shaded walk,
And here the whistling plowmen meet and talk—
They stand beside the wild raspberry stalks,
They speak of melons, sugar-corn and freezes,
Of sultry days and the cool summer breezes—
The voice of Spring will always call them back.

169

The green tobacco grows in crooked rows,
And here work Sarah, Jane, Mary and John.
One sees them in the sunlight raise their hoes
And cut the weeds and rake the dirt upon
Tobacco roots in little shapely mounds.
One sees them trail the field the live-long day
And peck their hoes deep in the golden clay.
And when they cut the weeds and loosen dirt
In the tobacco rows, they leave behind
Clean burley plants to wave afresh in wind—
And rows as clean as these are hard to find.
John speaks to Jane of the barn dance next Monday,
Jane asks Mary for her dress to wear Sunday.
They forget clean tobacco in the wind.

170

And here are long green rows of waving corn.
Unseen beneath tall corn are clicking hoes,
And morning glories blossom in the morn,
In heat of afternoon their blossoms close.
The loam is hot to filter between toes,
It's smothersome in tall corn to use hoes,
And cut pusley and careless from the rows—
The one in the lead row must be my mother.
She hoes in corn from dawn till set of sun.
She helps with corn until the season's done.
She loves to work out till the season's over.
She loves the smell of corn pusley and clover.
She loves to hear wind talking to the corn
And see dew-jeweled corn blades in the morn.

171

The wind that speaks of daffodils to me
Is wind blown from the hills of Kentucky.
The wind that speaks of black oak hills to me
Is wind that sweeps north-eastern Kentucky.
No hills on earth like these—honest there're not.
Come here and see the bronze men in the Spring.
They plow the land they say God has forgot,
They plow and listen to the cardinals sing.
They are such rugged tillers of the loam—
Hard drinking men—God-fearing, fighting men,
They are the men of earth that love a home.
Soil-men as free as blowing winds are free
And firm in words as hills in Kentucky.

172

The hills are calling me:
                      "Come back my son;
Don't waste pure blood on artificial places
Where men must toil with hungry haggard faces;
Come live with us until your race is run."
My lover's voice is calling louder still:
"Dear Lad: I've known the city all my days;
Flicker of light, her strange illuminous ways;
My dreams are not a cottage on your hill."
Dear hills: Your woods are dark—your rocks are cold;
I know your ragweeds grow around my shack;
I hear your voice and Lord I'm coming back.
Dear girl: The hills keep young. Woman grows old
Before her time and torturous to kiss.
I choose the hills mindless of what I miss."

173

It is not long until the winter's over;
Just February, March, and then green April.
Of all the months I choose April my lover—
Blood-root, wind-flower and the daffodil
Give new life to a scarred Kentucky hill.
April will make us want to start life over,
April will give us strength and fresher will
When we watch crows a-carrying green sticks over
Where skies touch pines on summit of a hill.
I shall be glad to see this winter over
And hear Spring swamps break out with thin-voiced
    frogs,
And see the kildees fly on whirring wing.
Oh, April is the month worth remembering
Green weeds and grass and blood-root by old logs.

174

Tear down these anthills made by men of Tobb,
For all these men have done is steal and rob—
They stole the pennies from the dead men's eyes;
Each sought to build a mammon-paradise,
These robbers took the country by surprise.
In stern reality one can discern,
They have taken fat farms they didn't earn—
These thieving men of Tobb—so penny-wise,
They take it easy in their paradise.
But men of bronze, I ask this thing of you,
Clean up their wretched house first thing you do.
Slap down the cocky thieves and take their bounty!
Gentlemen: they robbed you and your country!

175

White were the sprays of April apple blossoms
Waving in silver winds in light-green April,
When Lucy lay with roses on her bosom
Where fresh dirt was piled high upon the hill.
Lucy Riggs will not come back to bug the beans
And set her April cabbage in straight rows,
Lucy will not be back to pick the greens
Nor be here to use garden rakes and hoes.
A woman will come soon to work her garden
And have new dresses on the fence to dry,
She'll come before dirt has begun to harden
In April earth where Lucy's doomed to lie.
She'll come against the will of Lucy's children,
She'll come just when the garden work's laid by.

176

There's something fine about this May I love.
The call of earth is getting in my blood.
I walk the pasture, watch the skies above.
I watch the bursting of the black-oak buds.
The pasture winds are driving me to moods
The way they sing among the pasture briars
And waft the petals of the black-berry blooms
Down to the earth to meet their shriveled dooms.
The winds zoom on the rusty barb-fence wires.
A moth flies to a dew-drenched mountain daisy.
The cows eat too much grass, sleep by the daisies.
The lightning bugs flit through the sour-wood leaves.
The jar-flies sing among the dewy trees.
The cows lie under stars and chew with ease.

177

The road that leads me to my high-hill home
Leads over Greenup hills of yellow clay,
By looking from afar the sky's blue dome
Come down to shoulder one hill on my way,
And on the summit of this highest hill
The spare oak trees weave patterns on the sky.
One stream of water murmurs down the hill.
At evening trains of crows go cawing by.
And I must say it is a desolate land,
The contour lines of hill ledge-stones are black;
And in small corn-fields the white corn stalks stand
High there above the valley mountain shack.
The road that leads me home is not so far.
It takes me where my own hill people are.

178

Kentucky clay is golden clay to me,
And her black oaks that weave against the sky
(Against the white of a December sky)
Are harp string music in the winter wind.
Some winter leaves on oak boughs still remain,
And when the swift December winds go by;
Dead leaves on oak boughs tremble with a sigh—
Old leaves are marked with winter's jet-black stain.
Though I have reached the age of twenty-five
I wish to live this length of time again—
I wish to spend it on this golden clay.
I want to walk on earth a man alive,
A cricket now to dance and sing today.

179

When leaves of Spring adorn each barren beech
And shade the spring of sulphur water under,
Leaves will hide names cut high above man's reach,
The bearers' names Death has now torn asunder.
And they lie sleeping—sleeping on the hill
Beneath the wind flower and the whippoorwill.
New Loves will stand beneath the shades of beech
And drink the sulphur water from the spring,
And listen to the corn-birds flute and sing.
And they will cut initials out of reach
And laugh and speak of many silly things.
They do not listen to the corn-bird songs.
But they do love the silver wind of Spring
And they do love the water in the spring,
And here beneath the stars and April moon,
They laugh and sing the old, old songs and spoon.

180

And Bad-Eye Johnson Jiles and Kate lie sleeping;
Kate slender-built with eyes blue as the sky—
Above their graves pink love-vines are a-creeping;
A pair of copperheads are crawling by.
It is a shame Bad-Eye and Kate did die—
Two lovers kilt right in their prime of youth.
Steave Sloan loved Kate—he met and shot them both.
Bad-Eye and Kate are sleeping side by side—
Lovers in youth—at death, lie side by side,
And Kate was neither Steave's nor Bad-Eye's bride.
Where they lie sleeping on the lonesome hill
And vines are creeping there in daffodils,
At night one hears the songs of whippoorwills,
And Steave Sloan walks above a man of will
While they sleep silently upon the hill.

181

I've heard it said deep in the heart of Sloan,
He loved Kate Dills although her heart was clay,
And on a night when high winds made a moan
He pounded on the thick door of her clay
And asked for her on Resurrection Day.
And now the years go by in single file.
The hair on Steave Sloan's head is getting white,
Steave has been married only for a while.
He married Sue, a daughter of John Bright,
And Sue lies sleeping on the hill tonight.
Now Steave has gone to live with his old mother.
He says deep in his heart Kate is his lover;
Her dust he loves and not dust of another.

182

If truth were known Bad-Eye would never trust
The blue-eyed Kate now sleeping by his side,
Although her slender form has turned to dust
Bad-Eye could tell you that his sweet Kate lied.
She told Steave Sloan she loved him deep at heart,
She told Bad-Eye she hated old Steave Sloan,
And old Steave Sloan would not let her alone,
And Bad-Eye promised her he'd show Steave Sloan.
One evening under the white summer stars
When cows were coming to the milk-gap bars,
And deep green woods were dark and desolate—
There stood lip-pressed arm-locked Steave and his
    Kate.
Kate screamed and Bad-Eye ran there-in too soon,
Sloan pulled his gun too soon and shot Kate Dills.
Their mingled blood ran there under the moon
And sank to roots of grass among their hills.

183

Where is the fiddle that I used to hear?
Where is the party of the long ago?
Where is the old log shack that once stood here
And corn-field voices singing "Old Black Joe"?
Where is the girl I loved—sweet Laura Day?
And where are Charlie, Milton, Jack and John;
And Leathe and Murt, Jenny, and Lucy Mae?
Where are they now, I ask—are they all gone?
They are all gone—the wind sighs lonesome here;
Sighs through the briars where the house used to be
And hums over old chimney stones piled here
And through the branches of an apple tree.
Ah, lonesome like—these summer winds sigh low;
They are all gone—your party of the long ago.

184

Charlie and Murt live somewhere in the west,
Jenny and Jack are sleeping on the hill,
Leathe's Milton fell with five holes in his breast,
He sleeps by Jack and Jenny on the hill
And no one dares to speak of Lucy's John
Since he shot Milton five times in the breast.
And no one speaks of John since he has gone
With Lucy Mae to live out in the west.
And gone too is your sweet, sweet Laura Day—
Where were you when she called for you, Bill Glover?
Your Laura Day is sleeping under clay.
Where were you when she called for you, Bill Glover?
Ah, sleeping with some man's forgotten lover.
Your Laura Day is sleeping under clay,
She is not sleeping by another lover.

185

No one will hear and I can tell the wind.
I left our merry party of the long ago.
And I went to the west and tried to find
A party like the one I used to know.
I rambled through the west—at last I found
A girl not half as fair as Laura Day.
We settled down to live in a quiet way.
But all the time I dreamed of Laura Day.
I found Bess with a man and shot her down.
Then I went on to State of Washington—
I'm telling you, but please don't tell it, wind.
In Washington I lived with a wench woman
Until policemen were about to find
Where I was living since I kilt my wife.
If they had found me it would cost my life.

186

Don't tell it, wind—I want no one to know,
Those who have heads turned white as mine.
Don't tell it, wind, for they must never know
The merry party of the long ago.
Until this body has grown thin and pine,
I pray you, do not tell it to them, wind.
Here is one man, policemen never found—
I left my woman in State of Washington.
I slept California nights out on the ground.
I went gold-hunting on the river Yukon.
Oh, I have rambled till my hair is gray,
Ready to die, I come to Kentucky—
I've come back to my first love, Laura Day.
I've found her sleeping, sleeping under clay.

187

Now if policemen come from Oregon,
They can have me, for I have lived my life.
And if they want me for a crime I've done,
It is for killing one man and my wife.
I've had to dodge the Law all of my life.
The girl I wed and kilt was not my wife.
My wife is sleeping, sleeping on the hill,
For in my heart she's always been my bride.
And now if I die in the penitentiary,
Or on a scaffold or a limb of tree,
I want my clay to lie by Laura's side—
My disgraced clay to lie there by her side.
Don't tell it, wind—don't tell these things on me.
I have come back to rest by Laura's side.

188

Now blow you idle winds through summer grass
And gently sway green branches on the trees.
Speak to them kindly, whispering Grass,
And whisper to them kindly, talking leaves.
They are the party of the long ago,
And now they're doomed to lie against their will.
These corn-field voices singing "Old Black Joe"
So sweetly silenced on the black-oak hill—
When you were gone they thought of you, Bill Glover,
And Laura often wondered where you were,
Not knowing you had slept beside a lover
That you had kilt her and a man with her!
Yes, Laura Day has waited for you, Bill,
Now Laura's dust is waiting on the hill.

189

This summer green will turn to autumn brown,
And trains of crows will be a-flying over,
And flocks of leaves will be a-drifting down
To cover Laura Day and her Bill Glover.
When gusts of wind blow through the autumn trees,
Blow through the autumn trees with lonesome sound,
Brown in the wind are flying flocks of leaves
That silently will settle on the ground,
And they will settle here year after year,
Beneath these rich Kentucky floating skies.
People will never know when passing here,
That here beneath if one or many lie,
They will not know of Laura and her lover;
They will not know when dead leaves are strewn over.

190

I am the wind—I speak to you, Bill Glover.
You were a happy man when you were young.
And you danced with sweet Laura Day, your lover,
And you and she were happy there among
The merry party of the long ago.
"We drank the gin and put our lips together.
All night our feet tapped on the hardwood floor
Where fiddlers wore the resin from their bows
And kicked up dust by patting of their toes.
These were the good old nights of long ago,
With the merry party that we used to know.
But, wind, you see—my friends, they are all gone
And I have come back here to live alone.
I have come back where lonesome waters run,
Run sparkling, splashing, in light of the sun."

191

I am the wind and I shall speak no more.
But where's the resin, fiddle and the bow?
Where is the cabin with its puncheon floor?
Where is the merry party of the long ago?
Where is the past, Bill Glover, I ask you?
The past turns ashes like your dreams turn dust.
The past—it goes like wind a-blowing through
The briars where this old house is turned to dust.
The past goes somewhere—never coming back,
Part of the past is sleeping on the hill.
Part of your past died in this mountain shack—
Died in the apple blossoms on the hill.
And part has gone with sound of mountain water
And Laura Day—your youth is buried with her.

192

You stand where once there stood a mountain shack.
Your head is bare, your hair is white, Bill Glover.
Kentucky hills kept a-calling you back
And your sweet Laura Day—your only lover.
You stand and listen to me blowing over.
Ah, I do love to speak to you, Bill Glover,
Before you go to sleep upon the hill,
Before you sleep—before your clay lies still.
I'd love to speak about your Laura Day.
She was too faithful to you in a way.
And now sweet Laura is a heap of clay.
Why did she always love a wretch like you?
Why does she sleep not knowing any man?
Why does she sleep not even knowing you?

193

How very well does Bill Glover remember
Kentucky hills where he was born and raised;
The hills where stand the pine and poplar timber
Was where Bill plowed the corn in youthful days—
The hills where once grew country's finest timber
Are now in massive coat of briar and sprout.
These were the fertile hills that Bill remembers,
But they have been tilled long and near worn out,
They have been left fallow to grow in sprout.
And now men strange to Bill live here about,
The old rail fence has rotted to the ground.
The sprouts grow tall, for earth is fertile here,
The thick sprout leaves like rain drip to the ground,
Like autumn rain they drip with lonesome sound.

194

Dark trees are etched on the white floating skies
And furrows on the hills lie dark as shadows,
The empty fields are filled with wild bird cries,
Spots of green grass are sprinkled on the meadows,
The wind is blustery and cries aloof.
At night I lie in bed and hear the cries
When it is flapping clapboards on the roof,
In March the stars shine brighter in the skies.
I have no reason for believing this
Than I have for believing March is bliss;
The month of sun and shadow and cold rain-kiss,
The month of freedom and the month of furrow,
The month of silver wind and changing skies,
The month of coming birds and greening meadows.

195

Farewell to Sandy water flowing here,
Farewell white sycamores among dark trees,
I leave you, for the winter time is here.
I'll come again when you are clothed in leaves,
I'll come and sit beside you, Sandy River,
I'll come to you again when summer goes,
I'll come and listen to your green reeds quiver
And sit on grassy banks when sweet thyme blows.
I want to come when April days are here
And when the frogs are singing in the pond,
I want the April sun a-shining clear.
Rise white at morn—sing red at night beyond
The hills—Farewell, you waters, I esteem
You are the scene of many a wasted dream.

196

Roll on forever, Sandy waters roll!
Roll on forever, Sandy, to the sea,
Roll on beneath where April buds unfold,
Roll on beside my Lucille Aims and me.
For on your banks grow April thyme and phlox,
And down your rippling stream the marsh hen cries—
Her cries are loud as water-beating rocks—
She flies above foam white as April skies
And Lucille plucks a sprig of April thyme
And throws it to the water drifting by;
And I sit down to spin an April rhyme
And fling it to the breeze a-blowin by.
What is the use of rhyming useless words,
Amid the songs of water and of birds?

197

Darkness is settling in the woods around,
Less than one hour night will be falling here.
And now the shadows lengthen on the ground
And it is time we should be leaving here.
I know of one woman here with a bad tongue,
She keeps her words well trimmed and ringing clear.
She is suspicious of the night and young
Lovers who love the darkness and the night—
Dew-jeweled leaves are waving in starlight.
I think it's time that we should go, my dear.
I'd hate for this woman to find us here.
We can slip down beside this running water—
She cannot hear our voices for the laughter
On the rocks and on the surf of breaking water.

198

One night I have remembered Quadroon Mott—
The night when you and I were last together,
It was a night that I have not forgot;
The night when last we put our lips together—
And since that time you have had many lovers,
And since that day I have had many too.
But of that night one memory still hovers,
And you remember this last night with you.
The stars were brighter in the cold March sky
That night when you and I walked down together
And heard the marsh hens on the rivers cry
And dreamed if this life would go on forever.
There are fond nights one in his life remembers,
When fire of life has burned his youth to embers.

199

Swirl through my silver leaves of green and gold
And dance like fairies on an April lawn—
Dance while the sun is warm, for winter's cold!
Dance now, for your summer will soon be gone.
See how the fireflies flit upon the lea,
And don't you hear the plaintive whippoorwill
A-singin down beneath a green-wood tree?
And katydids sing on the cornfield hill.
This is your season, leaves—dance while you may
And fling your selves through silver with a will!
Ah, dance you leaves—you only dance one day
And then you lie in debris on the hill.
And you are dust before you have grown old,
And then, leaves, you will lose your green and gold!

200

Oh, don't you see the willow leaves this Spring
And bright green finger needles on the fir?
Birds choose to light among their boughs and sing;
It's where the summer jar-flies choose to churr.
And don't you love the silver maple leaves
Upturned by silver winds to skies deep blue.
And don't you love the leaves on white oak trees
And beech tree leaves when winds are blowing through?
And don't you love green whispering corn blades
And wild fern leaf where placid waters lie
Beneath a tranquil lazy summer sky.
And don't you love the smooth-fan poplar leaves
A-wavin in a silver summer breeze.
I ask these questions and I don't know why. ·

Blades
>from a field of
>>Corn

201

There's something that I always want to say
When I cross moon-lit meadows bright as day.
Last night I crossed the meadow going home
And watched by moonlight mating rabbits play.
The frosted grass was silver in moonlight,
Gray stones were dish-pans with their bottoms up,
The quarter moon was a brass drinking cup.
I watched the fairy White-Clouds come to drink,
I know I saw them drinking from the moon.
The stars looked at each other—gave a wink,
They thought the White-Clouds would be reeling soon.
The rabbits down below were drunk on love,
On moon-lit meadows I am speaking of.

202

Ten years ago Dad set these peach trees here
And they have borne good fruit for seven seasons.
They bore their fruit each season of the year
Except for winter freeze and other reasons.
The blight and frost—worms working on the roots,
The drouths and surface washings of the hill
Have caused the death of many bearing shoots,
And they are black stems standing on this hill.
The man who set these trees with his own hands
Has borne fruit good to eat for many seasons.
He stood storm-washing surface of rich lands,
He stood a little giant for no good reasons.
He is a good fruit tree that's gone to wrack.
The seasons call, but he will not come back.

203

Two men are grubbing from the golden soil
Tall locust trees, grape-vines and green-briar stools.
They are tall men—bronze men—strong sons of toil.
They are the type of men 'soft-hands' call fools.
I see them dig up roots of wild wood ferns
And tear long-rooted shoe-makes from the clay.
They work together—not by taking turns—
Ungloved they work—this gray December day.
They pile their brush in windrows down the hill.
The yellow roots are upturned to dark skies,
And dismal sun that's wading through the skies.
They work for this brief winter daylight flies.
Sons of the soil are clearing land together,
Shoulder to shoulder, despite December weather.

204

Tobacco will grow in this golden clay.
Land three year's farmed will be used for the corn.
Corn will be planted long the first of May
And burley set on some wet April morn.
The oats will be sown on the thinner lands
And orchard grass will be sown with the oats.
The oats and grass will be sown by rough hands
On a still day—a time when no seed floats
Upon the wind and drifts beyond the reach
Of furrowed land. I've heard the old men say
Best time to sow the oats was when the beech
Buds swell and plant corn round the tenth of May,
And time to set young burley was in showers
Of April when blood-root donned white flowers.

205

Oh, don't you hate to hear this monotone,
The incessant flow of water over stone?
Elizabeth and I, stars and woods hear this.
Maybe an owl, a lizard and a frog.
Elizabeth and I together hearing this,
Sitting alone here on a wet beach log.
She beats the falling water with a stick.
I throw black chunks into the foaming stream.
Such monotone—I cannot hear the lick
She strikes—we sit here silent in a dream.
"Life is the monotone of flowing water.
Life is a stream flowing toward some sea.
The stream goes on, but leaves life coming after
Incessantly flowing to some infinite sea."

206

I walk the hills tonight beneath a sky
That's filled with stars—I hear the rustle of
Thin dead leaves on oak boughs—I hear the cry—
A lonely cry—of wild geese lost above.
It's strange to hear the cry of geese at night,
They have been shot at when they started down,
And now black lines of them fly by starlight,
Over the dead-leaf earth long faded-brown.
I walk the hills tonight in solitude.
There is a rapture that I get from this.
Night plover going through a long dark wood,
And finding quiet night earth a perfect bliss.
A Voyager that has gone forth to find
The voice of some great god on the night wind.

207

The road's muddy and I've miles to go.
It is a long road and I have grown weary.
In these mud-weighted shoes I'm walking slow.
The road is long, but there's no need to hurry.
The moon and stars hang high above my path.
They give a lantern light to show me on.
The soft night winds sigh through the barren brush—
I must keep walking walking till the dawn.
High sky with stars hung in its night-blue dome
And sliced musk-melon moon that glides among
The stars and rides above my mountain home.
I'll soon be there and hear some old songs sung.
Though I have many muddy miles to fare,
My heart and lungs and legs and brain don't care.

208

I put away madness like an old shoe.
I said that I would never fight again.
Fist-fighting's not the nicest thing to do,
I said, I still shall fight, but with my brain.
Madness is an old shoe worn at the toe,
The shoe is thrown among the weeds to rot.
Strong men stand up and trade a blow for blow—
They kill—are buried—then, they are forgot.
I put away fist-madness, but the brain
Is mad—mad forever beyond control.
It even loves the sour oak-leaf stain
And on the winter boughs it finds some gold
In dead leaves clinging to the white-oak bough.
Oh, for fist-madness I have long been through!

209

I shall remember an old southern town
With her dirty bricks and her loose-strung wires;
I shall remember pigeons flying down
Between the sooty stacks and sharp-pointed spires.
I remember wandering penniless through her streets
With hunger in my guts and trying to find
Some work to do (washing windows, cleaning streets)
And believing hunger was a state of mind.
Days have gone to oblivion since that time
And I've plowed many furrows on the hills
And at the plow spun many useless rhymes—
(Verse from the soil is a good balm for ills)
But this December I've returned and feel
Good in new clothes with money to buy a meal.

210

I have remembered winey sunsets here
That left red radiance round the hack-berry trees;
These came so often in the fall time of the year
After the winds had stripped the trees of leaves.
I have remembered Spring's blue crystal days
When life was young and I was very young,
And I've remembered summer's milky haze
And patches of street-grass I sat among
Under musk-melon moons in city noises,
Then evening winds blew cool as cellar glass.
I've remembered how I saw the winter pass,
Reviving Spring, the summer and the fall.
Even the hills are native to my blood,
Though Nashville is no bad town after all.

211

There is a pie wagon down on Broad Street
That keeps good pies and coffee black as ink,
The place where intellectuals used to meet
Survey their scanty food and eat and think.
I was no intellectual, but I went
And listened to the silly things they said,
I got more for the money that I spent
Is why I went—I drank coffee instead
Of listening to Will Shakespeare's "Tragedies."
And now I think I shall go back and meet
The intellectuals there and discuss fleas,
Order my lunch with five baked pies and eat
And drink black coffee with white rings of cream,
Discuss Shakespeare and fleas and eat and dream.

212

I have grown hungry for the hills at home
And low black clouds that scud the winter sky.
I took a notion—left the dead-leaf loam,
I thought I only would return to die.
I'm long from Death—I know that I'll return,
I start today to hills and mountain loam,
And as I conquer miles this heart will burn,
These feet will walk contented on the loam.
And I'll walk out again beneath the stars
And put my arms around the black oak trees
And thank my gods there are no prison bars
And are no lovers like the black oak trees,
(No lovers faithful as the black oak trees)
Standing under a winter sky of stars.

213

I know a place where the wild pansies grow
Among dry chips of cow dung where sedge vines;
It is the ugliest hill on earth I know,
So poor it only sprouts sedge grass and pines
And multi-colored pansies sweet as light
When the eyes have been closed all of one's life
Then have the films removed and restored sight
And sees the things he touched in his blind world
Pine needles and petals of pansies curled
Up to the midday sun and browsing winds
And dry chips of cow dung they're growing in.
They are sweet colored to this earth they're in—
Growing where it was not their choice to grow,
But they give color to this drab I know.

214

Let this blue unvexed mountain water run
Forever on to some infinite sea,
Across green meadows sparkling in the sun
And under long blue shadows of the tree.
Do not pollute the cleanness of this stream
With human waste, but keep it free from filth.
But let it flow forever to that sea
Kissed by the drooping ferns and clean sand silt
Of earth and petals from the dog-wood tree.
This blue pathway of water is a life,
(Not mine, however, of unfiltered sands)
The dregs have long been in this stream of me,
But let her flow unfilthy to some sea!

215

I hear the lapping of the sandy water,
I hear it lapping—lapping night and day,
And I go down and sit beside this water
And throw in sticks and watch them float away.
Long years ago, barefooted, I walked here,
Unlocked the old john-boat and let it glide
Down the birch-shaded isle of lapping water—
I had a Spanish Lady by my side
And how we mingled happy words and laughter!
The rain-crow croaked for a downpour of rain.
The lizard roved the scaley bark for sun.
My Spanish Lady sat close by my side.
I do not know how water kissed the grain
And if that lizard found his patch of sun.
But I do know who said she'd be my bride.

216

And when I hear the lapping, lapping water,
I think of her whom I once loved so dearly.
It all comes back in music of the water,
The childhood Love I thought I'd marry surely.
Her skin was milk-weed dark, her eyes sky-blue,
Her teeth were blood-root white—her hair was black
As thick rain clouds—her lips were soft as new
Bark peeled from a slippery elm and her back
Was straight as a horse-weed upon the shore.
Her legs were brown as the buff-colored corn.
As I hear water lapping on the shore
And as I see the sun rise up this morn,
I think of her that I shall see no more,
The sweetest mountain girl I've ever known!

217

The night is fine—the wind and moon and stars
And trees and skies are loves of mine tonight,
And I cry to the skies and moon and stars
As I am guided by their mellow light—
I fear to trust the wind the way it sighs.
I leave the trees, for they are stand-pat lovers.
And every time I look I see the skies—
The moon and stars are left my only lovers.
Oh, yes, this January night is fine.
I just say life is great to live tonight,
And I look to the stars and drink good wine,
I walk a pathway white with mellow light,
In solitude I am in love with life,
I pray to Silence that I'll live forever!

218

The lark is flying in the morning clouds
And pouring forth the music from his breast.
And I have stopped my mules from harrowing clods—
(My mules are always glad to get a rest)
A song rings cross my pastures leafing early—
It sounds across the bottoms of green wheat.
These notes do not come from a small bird surely,
A small speck where the skies and hill-tops meet.
The mules—if they could have some sense to listen—
Would please me better, but they fight the flies
And everlastingly keep trace chains jingling—
I strain my ears to catch a sound that dies.
The speck gets fainter—weaker grows the sound,
The mules and I must go on harrowing ground.

219

Oh, I have done some crazy things at times,
One time when I was sick and took the tea
Made of wild cherry bark, spice-wood, bone-set,
I drank till it was near the death of me.
Sometimes I've hid in corn-fields making rhymes
And had Dad looking everywhere for me—
My Dad could see no good in silly things
Like scribbling down some crazy poetry,
Trying with words to mock a bird that sings,
Trying to speak of sunlight on a tree—
The best thing Dad could see for me to do,
Since I was strong, was wield the fastest hoe,
To hoe my row and help the others through
And never leave a weed in any row.

220

But when one wields a hoe in talking corn
And feels the summer sun sting through his shirt,
I'm telling you it's tough to have to work
And miss wild strawberry nooks in the cool morn,
And sweet wild honey-suckle blossoms in the woods
By Hylton's worm rail fence on green-briar flat.
Just think of wild-bed moss and solitudes
I miss—barefooted and without my hat
The way I went and let weeds take the corn—
The long bright isle of crystal channel water
Be broken by my body plunging down
And little swirl holes in the water after
I have gone down to touch the muddy bottom,
Thinking some day corn would grow from my bosom.

221

I cannot sing tunes that great men have sung.
I cannot follow roads great men have gone,
I am not here to sing the songs they've sung,
I think I'm here to make a road my own.
I shall go forth not knowing where I go.
I shall go forth and I shall go alone.
The road I'll travel on is mud, I know.
But it's a road that I can call my own.
The stars and moon and sun will give me light.
The winds will whisper songs I love to hear;
Oak leaves will make for me a bed at night,
And dawn will break to find me lying here.
The winey sunlight of another day
Will find me plodding on my muddy way.

222

I love the chiseled forms of red-oak trees
Standing on hill-tops at the setting sun.
I love to walk beneath and hear the leaves
A-rustling in the wind when day is done
And I am leading mules back from the plow.
I love to see the shining red-oak bark
Reflected in a sunset after-glow,
And crows fly over just before the dark
Has settled in the trees and left the sky
A starry world above a winter earth.
I love to hear these red-oak night-winds sigh,
Knowing that I shall soon be on my hearth
And warm my feet before a good wood fire,
Eat my supper—forget all worry—retire.

223

Muddy waters, how I have loved your crying
Night and day—forever past my open door,
Down through the reckless breaks along the shore
Where winter wind in ankle-sedge is sighing
And infant moon circles above the hill.
I have gone down at midnight—sat beside you
In woven reeds when winter winds whistled through
Your lonesome bank-side trees— Your pulsing will
Was surging your body down one lost way,
Like some deep singer in the void you fling
Futility to the wind and flow and sing—
New songs, perhaps, for new youth molding clay
While I return to where my candle flame
Burns low and the world will never know my name.

224

Batter me down, you who are strong, I plead.
I, who am weak, in the little ways I know
Will learn to battle young and soon take heed.
I know when cherry buds learn to obey
The gusty April rain-drops' stern command.
I know that night will usher into day
Sun-gems of dewdrops to bestrange the land.
I know the lark will rise in after-glow
Of storm—proud wings above the scarlet lea;
And a river young will wear a way to go
Until it cuts a channel to the sea.
Batter me down, life! Give me blow for blow!
I'll take the bleeding lips and liberty!

225

My loves will remain when I have passed
Beyond this certainty of time and light
And positive decay— But surely this night
I shall remember—these spiral massed
Pine silhouettes against the horizon.
Nocturnal things have been my loves: moon-downs,
Valleys of fog and sleepy mountain towns,
Dew on the grass and play of wind upon
The hill— Night sounds, I've loved: the cold
Nosing winds in November corn stubbles;
The zoom of wires and water that troubles
Creek mosses and ferns— Happier loves will not unfold
When I have passed—far beyond this night,
Beyond all loves and swimming time of light.

226

I shall sit down to watch the autumn pass
Where black-oak leaves go windward to the ground;
That cry like wounded quails with ghost-like sound
And settle like the dust on road-side grass.
The clean-mown meadow has no use for moles;
The willow leaves have left the willows bare;
In wheat-brown grasses limps the timid hare;
The corn-fed chipmunks house in wintry holes.
I shall sit down to watch the wild geese flying
Far out of sight into the autumn blue.
I bite my lips and try to keep from crying;
Gray restless birds, I want to fly with you.
You are the words from this brown autumn's mouth;
I see him come and you in streams go south.

227

Mother America, I am telling you
In words the flavor of old stagnant pools,
Out in your streets I've asked for work to do.
I've served Apprenticeship in your Hard Schools.
I ask what made you give this body birth
With tempered blood and flesh by no means brittle,
And send it out to battle with the earth?—
A hungry hound to lick some Master's spittle!
Ah, well—money—money—is all your cry—
Your rest-room fees—machine fee postal stamps—
Money! Money! Street haggard faces sigh
With signs above their doors: NO ENTRANCE,
   TRAMPS.
Mother, I'm sound in body and in mind,
I've walked your streets, but nothing can I find.

228

Be with me, courage, for I walk alone,
Although I have no fear of night and gloom.
The earth is wide and there is spacious room
For human creatures on her streets of stone.
Be with me, courage, in this trying hour
When stars are hard to barter for thin bread
(Be with us all in this dark hour of need)
The lonely poor with dreams, the rich with power.
The leafless tree in winter stands alone
Dreaming of leafy days and sunny Spring
When birds alighted in her boughs to sing.
Now somewhere out by changing winds I'm blown
A yellow leaf to drift with time away
The silver moments of my swift brief day.

229

Kentucky, I shall return to you someday
To live out in your wind and rain and sun
And watch your trees and fields together run
And orchards whiten with the blooms of May.
I shall go back and sit before the fires
At home and tell tales with a fellow rover;
Before I'm cold and the best of life is over;
We'll tell of drinking days and fighting sires.
I shall go back to tramp the crimson leaves
That spread like quilts upon the frosty ground.
I'll take my gun and faithful hunting hound
And be alone where wind in treetops grieves.
Kentucky, your dwindling autumn streams,
Flow out across old meadows of my dreams.

230

I saw Kentucky's windy oak trees weave
Thin patterns on a white December sky;
And I'd been sick of life and wished to die
Until I saw those eastern hills and banks
Of reddish shoe-make clay—I yielded thanks
For oak trees patterned on this windy sky—
I'd been a fool to ever wish to die.
Silly I was in younger days to leave
The winding willow lanes, the sky-blue streams,
And apple blossoms gleaming in the sun;
And night-time meadows' drowsy soothing words.
But now I have come back to where all seems
A higher world than where mere fancies run,
And words are tuneless by the fluting birds.

231

He would return to a hollow he once knew—
Follow the road to where the last house stands,
Six-draw bars and a gate he must go through
And cross three hills of worn-out sedge-grass lands,
The road is grooved with many a rain-washed rut.
Over this road the teamsters used to ride
And give their mules the long keen raw-hide cut,
And now both mules and ruts the rag-weeds hide.
He would go back this old, old trail at night,
And look for ghosts of horses he once drove;
He'd see a rag-weed road in the moonlight
A-winding through the honey-locust grove,
And he would see an ulcerated hill
Where slate-dumps in the moonlight lie blue and still.

232

Deserted now you stand with lichened walls
Moldering into dust. Your window panes
Are shattered by reckless winds and rains.
Your birds and bats will come when darkness falls.
Once we gathered in your eerie halls
To share life's meeker gifts of joys and pains.
But now my folks are gone— Still your remains
Abide with me when your haunting spirit calls,
Even your yard trees whisper from their height.
They see my eyes, heavy-lidded, wet with dreams,
They see my candle soul send forth its beams
And wonder if I shall share the coming night.
But oh, this place is lonesome, lonesome here,
And no one, oh, no one anymore goes near!

233

When I am gone the grass will grow again
Beside the streets and then the grass will die;
Springtimes will come and go and summers wane
And autumn leaves will blow across the sky
And fiddle through the brown stems of the grass.
Low winter suns will sink into red flames,
Old streets will bear the burdens of new feet,
And golden words will crown new heroes' names
When I have gone back where rich fields of corn
Are nourished by the full breasts of the earth.
When I go to the land where I was born,
When I go there to give this flesh rebirth,
There I shall dive into a deeper stream
And I shall drown or come up with a dream.

234

TO THREE LOW GRADES: Vanderbilt

My hands and brain created you dream stuff.
They fashioned you, but not to my desire;
For now I wish I'd thrown you in the fire
Or taken time to build you strong enough.
God knows my time was spare and timber rough—
Deceptive things that made of me a liar—
Trying to raise you dull pavilions higher.
Must I sit down victim to scorn and scoff?
Not I—though in steel corridors you lie
And boney fingers sour as drain-pipe rain
Will turn you over once, but not again,
And catalogue against me your old cry:
"Not good enough. We'll choose a higher grade!"
Better for me if you were never made!

235

The earth turns brilliant now—color of leaves
Is on the streets. The wind's bright lips of laughter
Smile half-reflected on the tarnished water.
The night clouds race above the tangled trees.
The earth turns yellow now—the narrow street
With signs of the footprints we left are lost.
All of our past is carved in autumn frost.
It lies beneath the dead leaves and the sleet.
"Soon frost shall pass," you say—and soon shall we.
Then let the earth turn brilliant with the flow
Of yellow leaves to hide the things we know—
For soon we'll sleep, you by the side of me,
Beneath blue moons suspended like blue-ghosts
Where signs of the footprints we left are lost.

TO B. G. 236

Do you remember April evenings when we
Tripped side by side on tender orchard grasses
Beneath the spreading cloud-white apple tree?
Do you remember night birds' fluttering passes
Into shower-drenched wind-quivering leaves?
And the cloud-patched sky, the wry-faced moon
And sleeping valley mists do you remember? It grieves
Me to forget—Our lives broke then—broke soon,
Too soon we drifted down corridors of time
With new lovers following after. And now
The grass is dead, the winter's rainy slime
Marks jet-black each leafless apple bough.
Can you remember a dread that banished?
A love that faded? A joy that vanished?

237

Murt is a queen of beauty lying here.
The earth to her is like a blinded moon.
And where she sleeps Lill Hoffman won't go near
To see her sister-to-the-dust this soon.
Lem Hoffman said she often cursed her birth.
Lem said her body and her lips were warm.
But now she lies a captive to the earth
And she can do Lill Hoffman's Lem no harm.
The warm caressing wind of Spring now blows
In rose-vines growing from a dust that's rare.
And at her head falls petals from the rose
Like once she wore to crumble in her hair.
Lem Hoffman comes and lifts his hat in vain
To planted flesh he will not mate again.

238

Long soughing winds zoom in the beech-tree tops
Unheard by dreamers in quiet beds below
Sleeping soundly beneath the fluffy snow.
The keen-eyed crow alights above and flops
Sharp wings against the frozen timber.
"Who sleeps beneath this frozen January cover,"
Cries he, "many a forgotten lover's lover?"
His voice is hoarse from the cold of last December.
"Elizabeth Hale sleeps with her athlete John.
Sly Marvin Smith sleeps by his faithless Joan,"
Answer snow-drifts in cold white silence blown.
Drifts hear and know they lie so close upon
The mounds, Joan's Marvin and his roommate Death
Quarrel over the lips of John's Elizabeth.

239

What facts are certain?—not even cities,
For yesterday they were built on a plain.
Today of all their splendors, dusts remain.
And for the laughter there, the wind hums ditties.
Facts are most uncertain, for even stone
Disintegrates into positive decay
And a breath of wind could blow the dust away.
There is futility in everything.
And the thing most beautiful soonest goes—
Beauty of flesh, white fragrance of the rose,
The colored feathers on a rooster's wing.
And when we turn to look upon the past
We find few chosen words are things that last.

240

How silent the countless billions who have died.
They cannot speak to tell us where they lie.
We, who tramp above them, how are we to know
Who lie beneath our feet where saw-briars grow?
We only know men born are men to die.
And they too will ride if the dead must ride
Out past all space and where all time is vain;
Where their rich dust will be a hidden urn
That will not hear nor see nor even know
If the beat upon their face is rain or snow.
Why does it matter, they cannot return
When they give up the body and the brain.
Yet deceiving is this epitaph I found:
"How soft and sweet is sleep beneath the ground."

241

I was not made to search cold streets of stone;
To walk these streets and search and never find.
But I was made to search the woods alone
And listen to the music in the wind.
And moss is carpet to feet bare as mine;
And moss and leaves are warmer than cold stone;
And music's sweeter in the beech and pine,
Than braying trumpet or a saxophone.
Oh, there is music under the white stars.
Each naked beech tree is a violin.
The wind is master and the notes and bars
Are stones and ferns for a beech-tree violin.
I stop and listen to the Master Wind
Play Titl's Serenade on his Violin.

242

And if I follow the cold streets of stone
And listen to the music in the street;
Cold notes that do not touch the heart of one;
And interrupted by the tramping feet—
Yes, music's cold upon a street of stone.
There is no music there—all is a grind.
There is no place for one to be alone.
There is no beech top for a violin.
Ah, once, I tried the city and its ways.
It would have been better if I had been dead.
I could not ghee-haw to the city's ways.
I tried and could not barter work for bread.
And I went mad—I soon became a knave.
Two years of such would put me in the grave.

243

And I came back where there is poetry
Among the streams and hills and skies I love;
And I came back a brother to the tree;
My home the roof of flying clouds above—
I came and threw myself upon the ground.
I put my hands upon green growing weeds.
And then I said: "At last, my life I've found.
For this is all my hungry body needs."
Who doomed my body for a steel machine
And patterned it for dollars and for cents?
This brain cannot forget when weeds are green.
This brain cannot forget the body will be spent.
But last the call of earth I have obeyed.
I found life in the heart of earth and stayed.

244

And what can force me from the land I love
Where life is tranquil as a mountain stream,
And where the white clouds spread their sails above?
Nothing can force me from the hills I dream
That will hold me and all my heritage—
Hold me forever and sweet Lydia Doore.
This is the land where my forefathers lie.
This is the land they loved—the world they knew—
This is the land where-on I choose to die
And lie deep-down and sleep the long years through.
Then who will know if I were saint or knave?
And who will know I have a resting place?
For there will be no markers at my grave.
The wild rose roots will grow into my face.

245

The high wind roars tonight through cove and glen
And bends the arms of pines and stems of oaks.
The gaunt red fox sneaks from his rocky den
And tilts his ears to winds and timber strokes.
His warm breath steams toward the cold blue sky,
And trotting by, he howls to stars and moon.
The dead leaves rustle and the pine cones sigh;
The dead sedge shrieks an old and lonesome tune.
The hound dogs take his cold-trail at the den,
And on and on they speed through cold moonlight,
Around the ridge and round the cove and glen;
And on and on throughout the starry night.
Next day on mountain trails the feet of hounds
Have left blood-tracks upon the crusted ground.

246

Here once horseshoes struck fire to ledge slate stone
And wagons creaked under the heavy loads.
But that was years ago and time has flown,
Horses have died and men have changed the roads.
No more men laugh with cracking horses hoofs
That broke the silence of the countryside;
No more do they bend for the bramble roofs
Of locust limbs and grapevines as they ride.
This dirty-ribbon road's forsaken now,
Bedded with fallen trees and brush and grass.
Rabbits and quails hide where its grasses grow.
Let drivers come and go and horses pass,
These old dirt roads have more appeal to me
Than horseless carts and roads of finery.

247

You went somewhere and left our rugged lands.
I don't know when you went—I asked not why.
But I remember us a-shaking hands
And you a-telling me a long good-by.
Though years and years have gone we have not met
To view our initials on the school-yard tree;
Though stubborn years stalk by, we shall not meet
By trees where lies the youth of you and me.
But Mabel, I keep you forever young;
I keep you in the rough lines of a sonnet—
Though you are gone, I still keep you among
The green corn with your apron and your bonnet.
And I shall keep you, dear, forever young
With braided hair and wide blue ribbons on it.

E. H.   248

This small white world of crystals carved in frost
Has grotesque shapes of trees upon the hill;
(All of yesterday's brownness has been lost)
That stand as guarding sentinels and still
As stone— The blue-chilled morning water flows
Down avenues where frost-thin sheets are spread.
High in the heavens move the trains of crows
Above a world that's neat and clean and dead.
Yesterday our love was brownness of the world
And mortal eyes could see the brown-wet stain.
Today that has been buried with the frost.
Tomorrow our new buds shall be unfurled
And we shall blosom in the woods again;
That will be Spring, our winter shall be lost.

249

"The Law will send me from my highland home
And I will travel in the south and west.
I do not have the fever, but I have to roam
To some strange land where I can do the best.
I made some licker, apple-jack and rum.
I sold these drinks to make my daily bread.
Somehow, the Law found out—a farmer comes
To buy a drink and ease his aching head.
I sold to him—he turned to walk away,
Lifted his coat, showed me his badge, 'The Law.'
Says he, 'Old boy, we'll meet again someday.
I'll keep your half-pint here to show the Law.'
We'll meet in hell—I shot him through the breast.
I mean to get a-going for the west."

250

"My children may go hungry for their bread.
I kilt that stool-pigeon in farmer's clothes.
I hate to kilt, but glad I left him dead.
Now Kate will have a time—God only knows!
Must keep eight children in their bread and clothes.
Would God keep me from making daily bread
For my eight children and their shoes and clothes,
Or see them bare of clothes and underfed?
I think that God would do as I have done,
Shoot through the heart a man that tells him lies—
Betrayed me to the Law and thought he'd won.
And that's the only reason why he lies
Under a sheet, shot through and through the breast—
The only reason why I must start for the west."

251

Green maples in the woods after a rain.
They stand among the oaks serene and tall.
Some men would say that they are beautiful.
Their leaves upturning—so dew-cool and white;
Upturned to winds and moths and starry light—
Maples among dark oaks after the rain!
I think I shall not see their like again.
The moonlit brook holds images of them.
And in this mountain water blue and still,
I can pick out each maple on the hill.
With wind-blown leaves now drinking to the moon,
Drinking a health, I think, to moths and me
And to white blossoms of some young percoon.

252

Today, my brain, you are a young green tree.
You are one in a wood with other trees.
Some people pass and say: "What a fine tree
This is—the bark is smooth—has pretty leaves."
And others pass: "This is a rugged tree,"
They say, "we ought to burn it roots and stems.
Leave it, perhaps, it will foul other gems."
The things both say are all the same to me.
Go on, my brain, and speak now while you may,
Speak while you're young—these are the words I say.
Go to it, brain—tomorrow you may be
A dead-ringed corn-field tree upon this hill;
Your leaves and bark and limbs blown off by winds.
You there—a shattered hulk forever still.

253

"Land is poor as a snake where pine trees grow.
Cut them today, you Tom, and Bill and Joe,
And burn the burrs so they can never sprout.
Pine trees sap all the life from land I know.
I aim to put that land in corn this year.
Because of them damn pines it will not sprout
Them black-eyed peas—I aim to try it out
And every year it will keep getting better
By letting cattle feed on it in fall,
For fodder stalks and cattle dung is better
Than all this fancy fertilizer you buy—
Remember the price is not half so high—
Remember, boys, there's something 'bout them pines
Like ghosts a-talking when the night wind whines."

254

I've loved the deep damp places where the sun
In summer seldom ever penetrates—
Where weeds grow slender for the lack of sun—
(A place where writhing black-snakes wait
For toad frogs and young rabbits playing there).
I love to sit down in these cool recesses
And watch the green flies and the honey bees—
(Green flies suck watery plants when they are hungry)—
The bees work on the blooming black-gum trees.
I love to break the tall weeds with my feet.
And tramp pokeberry stalks and cresses under
And see the fresh-dug holes craw-dads have made;
To see where he's been pinching off corn blades;
Pinching them off for, I suppose, to eat.

255

I shall be going soon where no one knows:
I shall go to my pine pole mountain shack.
Before the autumn comes and summer goes
Before the leaves fall—I must be going back.
I was not made to walk on streets of stone
And breathe into my lungs the City smoke;
I must go to the highland world I own
Where I can breathe the air of pine and oak.
I shall go back to where the jar flies sing,
Back to brown hills that shoulder to the sky.
I want to see shikepokes on whirring wings,
I want to hear the bittern's lonely cry,
I want to hear the beetles sing at night,
I want to see the owl fly in the gray starlight.

256

I never saw a prettier flower in the wind
Than a white blood-root when March woods are brown.
I love to see their white heads tossing in
A wild March wind, that bends their thin stems down.
I know a pea-vine hollow where they grow,
And I shall certainly go there this Spring
To see brown woods with flakes of blood-root snow
Before ground sparrows have returned to sing.
It does one good to rove his native haunts
Of blood-root, ferns, larkspur and daffodils;
It does one good to take long daily jaunts
Into recesses of his own Kentucky hills—
Among his ferns, blood-roots and daffodils
And listen to Spring songs of whippoorwills.

257

I know a place where violets should be,
Under a sheet of leaves this time of year;
Days are too cold for one to rise and see
If winds still freeze or mellow Spring is here.
It does not matter violets will know
If over them are April suns and showers,
Or over them are leaves and January snow.
They are much earlier than the other flowers—
The wind-flower, sweet-williams and blood-roots—
And they live safely under dead-leaf cover,
Protecting stems and blades and blossom shoots—
They hug close to the bosom of their mother—
When early stock's turned out to browse,
They nose for violets—it's true of cows.

258

I never felt so tough in all my life.
I think it is the fever I am taking.
The pains above my eyes cut like a knife,
My flesh is sore and all my bones are aching.
I keep on going, but I feel like hell.
I'll lie in bed when I am forced to lie.
I'll make myself keep thinking I am well—
(Some people think that they are going to die
And they do die—could be the other way, I guess).
Tonight I drink a pint of bone-set tea
And spike it with best whiskey Dad could find.
And it's begun to break the sweat on me;
I think I'll tear this feeling all to hell
And get up in the morning feeling well.

259

I've heard the old men say at peddler well
They'd seen a headless man walk there at night;
They'd seen him rise from this uncovered well
And walk the W-Hollow road in the moonlight.
The old men say that peddler Nick was kilt
By three young men and thrown down in this well.
Of course, there is no exact way to tell
Who these men were and when old Nick was kilt.
The old men's fathers told these tales to them—
Our grand sires told our sires and they told us.
They say the robbers broke the buggy up
And threw it with the harness down on Nick—
They took the peddler's money and his pack;
Buried the blood and started the horse back.

260

And now that well is plain for men to see.
Tall trees are growing round this peddler well;
By its dark brink a thick-bark black-gum tree
Stands up to shade this hole—it shades it well,
Its entwined roots keep dirt from falling in;
These roots and old fence rails that's laid across—
And these keep black-gum leaves from falling in.
The top rocks of the wall are green with moss,
The briars are growing tall around this well
And they are holding leaves just where they fell.
After they've gathered leaves year after year
The rotting mass will make a carpet here—
A carpet of dead leaves around the tomb,
But in the Spring are thick-bark black gum blooms.

261

And peddler Nick can walk on dead-leaf carpet
Without his head in meadows of moonlight,
He can step lightly so no one can hear it
When he goes out to show himself at night.
He puts the passers-by to panic fright,
This lone headless peddler going out at night.
Sol Spraddling saw him headless in his buggy.
Sol said that he was driving in a hurry.
The sight that T. L. Shelton saw was worse—
Met headless Nick a-leading home his horse—
And children claim they've seen Nick cross the road
And on his back was strapped a heavy load.
The old men who have lived close said they heard
The cracks of heavy whips and drivers' words,
And when they looked they saw an empty road.

262

Old headless peddler Nick may come at night
And drive his sorrel over gravel roads,
And he may take long strolls in the moonlight
And he may show men how to pack a load.
For all I know is what the old men say—
I know that some have said they'd seen him walk;
I know that some have said they'd seen him ride.
They say old Nick was buried in the well—
The well was cleaned and man's bones were found there.
Some of the old men still are left to tell
They found wrapped in well leaves some curly hair.
And if we could be by that well, they say,
We would see Nick arise on Resurrection Day.

263

Last Wednesday night of this December
I got my feet wet when I crossed the creek;
And I came home and stirred the dying embers
And lit the lamp and set it on the dresser,
Undid my shoes and left my socks to dry
On a chair-back before the ember heat.
I heard somebody in the chicken roost,
I grabbed the gun and ran out in bare feet—
That is the reason why I'm sick to die—
I found a nice big owl upon a limb.
This chicken owl sat by a nice white hen
And tried to nudge her off the white-oak limb—
And I'm not saying what I did to him!
White chickens are a flower pot at night.

264

I know he made cross-ties to earn his bread.
I know his crops burned in last summer's drouths,
And this is all he finds to buy the food
That goes to fill ten hungry children's mouths.
He gets eight cents to make a standard tie
Of hardwood tree— I think a man can make
Fifteen of these—a dollar twenty-cents per day—
Keeps his children from starving in a way.
Better to work on just a little pay.
It's all because the summer fields stayed dry,
Crops failed, and there was nothing left to do
But make cross-ties for men that pay so little;
Go home and eat corn-bread and play the fiddle.
They say the rich are having hard-luck too.

265

I guess I look too much into the past.
I know damn well the past is worth my gaze.
For I look back upon the meadow haze
And backward glance upon my youthful days.
By mother's days I know life's going fast—
(It's got to go—no single life can last).
There are the peach trees where she smoked her burley
And rested on the Sunday afternoons—
Sat under April peach trees wafting blooms
And free as she was ever free from worry—
"Mitch, you will plant that hill in white corn surely.
That ground is better for the white bread corn.
I want to plant fall beans in each corn row,
That land is rich enough for beans to grow."

266

And I look back upon the little creeks
Of water rippling down between the hills,
I think of peppermint—cool peppermint
In a clean stream of water—how it fills
The nostrils and how good it is to taste.
I do keep looking back, for something speaks
And tells me the old things have gone in haste.
(They have gone long ago to wrack and waste)
I hear a voice—to me it seems to say:
"The past is past, but keep on looking back,
Though you will not see buggies in the lanes.
You will not see a rubber-tired family hack
Beside the garden hollyhocks again—
Your age is not—but we're established facts."

267

I always felt uncertain when I went
A-past the house where Rudy Starke lived.
I can remember when my mother sent
Me to a neighbor's house to borrow meal,
And how I would slip out across the meadows
And wade the branch beneath the drooping willows,
To dodge the house where Rudy Starke lived—
I was afraid of birch trees' shifting shadows
(Wind sagging trees threw on the moonlit meadows)
And when I heard the banging of the door
I hugged the earth, for I knew Rudy Starke
Was in the bed with Monnie—his stepdaughter,
I feared a volley of his shot-gun thunder—
It was not safe to pass there after dark.

268

Rudy grew old and Monnie craved a youth
After she'd lived four years with her step-father.
And when he bought her silks to court her favor
She laughed at them and told him not to bother.
Now she had younger men to buy her clothes
And take her to the Greenup picture shows.
The youth she craved met her and took her out;
Along the dark roads they would ride about—
Then they would park out in some lonesome place.
Rudy would go at night and hunt for her;
Make threats to kill, and cuss and tear his hair.
But when old Rudy saw her angel face
He would become meek as a little lamb;
He'd draw her close and kiss his little lamb.

269

One night his lamb did not return to him
And Rudy searched all night and tore his hair.
The morning did not bring her back to him.
He told his neighbors that he did not care,
For Monnie's mother had appeared to him
And said: "Rudy, you are not right with God.
The Devil ought to swing you to a limb—
In bed with Monnie and me in the sod.
My daughter by Sol Greene—the man I love;
And Sol and I lie down together here
And know just everything you do above."
"I know I heard my last wife speak these words
When I was mowing briars the other day;
And Pet has been nigh four years in the clay."

270

Monnie is living with some younger man.
Rudy is tottering on his sourwood cane
(Too old to work, he does the best he can)
Lamenting youth that will not come again—
He hunts for Monnie but she's far away.
He cannot hope to lie with her again,
For she has gone forever and shall stay.
Why would she come to Rudy Starke again?
Rudy got on his knees and prayed to God,
And in this prayer I know Old Rudy said:
"Young Rips will put the old men in the sod,
The reason, God, why I shall soon be dead;
The reason why I've doubted if you, God,
Will pardon me before you plant this seed."

271

I do not know what Rudy does today
But I do know that he is under clay.
And I do know the ground's begun to harden
On the long mound of earth that Rudy owns.
I do not know if God gave him a pardon,
A written scroll and laid it on his bones—
I do not know who Rudy Starke's God is.
I do not know who Rudy's Devil is.
The heaven he prayed for was perfect bliss.
His lasting rest I think would come to this.
Heaven for Rudy Starke I think would be:
Blue water flowing over a white stone;
Plenty to eat, a fiddle and shade tree,
And fifty Monnies he could call his own.

272

White stars are lanterns in deep velvet space.
Black winter trees are etched against the sky.
Dead leaves hug down to earth, rocks hide their face.
A stream of water is a-murmuring by.
Adelia and I walk by this mountain stream,
We watch white lanterns in the velvet sky,
And high bluffs with a rugged pine-tree seam
Reflected in the water flowing by.
We hear the highwinds blowing in the timber;
We talk of winter, crops, and youth, and love;
And life is sweet to us this gray December,
The night around us and the stars above.
Tonight our lips meet and we love and trust;
We love tonight, tomorrow we'll be dust.

273

I hear the rusty court bells ringing now.
They strangely sound across the autumn land.
The farmers leave their rakes and hoes and plows
And go because the farmers understand.
The bells are calling men to justice there—
Handfuls of justice for the yellow gold.
They hear bell vibrants in the crisp blue air;
Harsh music to their ear-drums—harsh and cold.
They say: "We've done no harm that we can see.
We make our living from these sprouty hills.
Our money goes to pay a lawyer's fee
Because we operate our moonshine stills.
We drink our licker as we rake and plow.
We make our living by sweat from our brow."

274

This place is one of earth's most wretched places;
Tobacco breath and brown tobacco spittle;
Dirt-sodden clothes, limp forms and broken faces;
Old men that come to talk and chew and whittle
And hear smart mammon-lawyers speal their pleads
And prosecute men for 'intent to kill';
And men and women lying in the weeds;
And finding on one's farm a moonshine still.
Lawyers arise and make their speal and splash.
Poor wretches bow their heads and cuss the pen
(For laws are hard when men don't have the cash);
And if you die the damn law beats *you* then.
Think of this house—the hell-house for poor devils!
They are brought here to answer for their evils.

275

Beware you yellow jackets of The Law.
(The Law, I warn you, wears a badge of brass)
Beware of our America's Great Law,
Beware of drinking cider when you pass.
You're drinking cider when you suck the juice
From wine-saps rotting here upon the trees.
Bugs of the field, Our Law, won't turn you loose.
They carry pistols, black-jacks, locks and keys.
You yellow jackets have your stingers primed
And sting hell out of dirty constables,
And sing for stool-pigeons a drunken rhyme
And give the county sheriffs a bellyful
Of poison stings to make them groan and fret.
Sting them and sting until they can't forget.

276

Throw on me—I can stand you howling pack!
You thugs—you thieves—you politician bores.
Come on you vulgar pack, I'll fight you back,
Give you the whip, my sympathy to whores.
You God-damned crooked sticks, my slate is clean,
And then you offer bribe! And do I sell?
Hell no—as long as there is breath between
These ribs and I have breath and tongue to tell,
I hate you crooks and I am not afraid
To meet you face to face and tell you this:
I know the rotten politics you've played,
Afraid of pennies that your purse would miss.
Green parasitic flies, you cling to dung,
With green-saprophytic flies among.

277

When I am tired and weary, O sweet woods,
I find a solace in your deepest gloom;
Silence is soothing in your solitudes;
Silence is soothing in your spacious room.
I put my hands against your leaves and feel
The tender ribs that hold heart-shapes to leaves—
I kick the last-year dead-leaves with my feet;
I put my hands to cold green bark on trees.
I hear the willows swishing in the wind;
I see the white clouds floating in the brook;
I see September's leaves now drifting in
The briars—I turn the pages of a book;
It is a book that I can never read,
For every page I turn I see it bleed.

278

I see the long black train of hungry crows
Fly hard against the cool September wind.
They must be looking for the old shock rows;
They have been hauled and grain is hard to find.
I see the white clouds floating high and slow,
And oak leaves drifting in the windy sky.
The earth is looking big and brown below;
The sky is looking big and bright and high.
The dwindling streams are murmuring in sleep;
They tell their secrets to the willow limbs.
Something this is that makes one want to creep
Out of the world away from funeral hymns
Sung by the lonesome winds and dying leaves
And plucked on harp strings in the leafless trees.

279

The earth is desolate and his rock-ribs
Show out like scaley monster's broken teeth.
There are rock monsters back of our corn cribs
And many young are sleeping there beneath
The bellies of old monsters—and thin dirt
Over the rocks that's woven into quilts
Of sheeted snow aside to see the sun—
This yellow sun of winter on the barn
And on the mules after their work is done,
And on the long-haired cattle getting warm—
Forgetting all about the summer skies,
Forgetting all about the biting flies.

280

I see the moon rise in the mair-tail sky
Behind the ridge road—through the inky firs.
From the dark hill I hear a night hawk's cry;
I hear the beetles' songs and jar-flies' churrs.
An old Kentucky night is slipping through
Dark holes in dewy laps of pasture lands,
And arms of trees and mair-tails in the blue.
Beyond tree-fingers on the earth's brown hands;
Dark hills and trees and crisp winds blowing through
The lonely valley where I used to live
This night is etching sharp against the blue—
Profiles of dark hills where I used to live
Sweet benediction in the golden days.
I hate new life since books have changed my ways.

281

How strange the dog will come back to his vomit;
How strange the dog follows the bitch—his mother;
How strange it is a man will write a sonnet;
How strange it is a man will kill his brother.
This earth and everything there-on is strange.
It is all strange—the trees, the dirt, the grass.
Nothing is lost—it only makes some change
Though centuries will roll and men will pass
And life move swiftly on—it moves too fast.
Life is too strange, first birth, then death to one,
And then one's life is buried in the past.
Beautifully strange: sunrise and setting sun.
Beautifully strange: dark fingers of the pines.
Beautifully strange: this flesh of yours and mine.

282

Your God is rich—your God has much to spare.
My God is sandal-footed with the poor.
You say your rich God hears your prayer.
My God hears frail bones knocking at the door.
My God is giving treatment to a whore.
My God is strong and his broad shoulders bear
The load of man—he does not hear your prayer.
My God's with poor men down among the poor.
My God tells me to go and meet the night
Where his tree fingers point to lonely skies.
The earth's his altar—the moon and stars his light.
The universe his heart—the wind his cries.
My God has sense—he is no infidel
Nor little man to preach you to his hell.

283

Last night the rain thumped on the clapboard roof
Like feet of house rats running over tin.
I laid awake beneath this sheltering roof
And listened to a cold wind blowing in
The trees outside and blowing through a crack
Into my room—stirring the covers on my bed.
I slept upstairs in a Kentucky shack.
Last night some verse kept running through my head
And I got up and lit the smoked-globe lamp.
I took a sheet of paper from the stack.
I wrote about a mouse and brown oat stack—
The room was mighty cold and dark and damp.
I threw the poem out into the rain.
Its destiny was darkness and the rain.

284

I had grown chilled by staying in this room
Without a fire on such a rainy night.
The yellow lamp did offset some the gloom
In the little circle of its yellow light.
There were some books stacked on the old wall-plate.
I opened one to marked passages and read
About a farmhouse old and desolate.
And then I thought I'd better go to bed.
But first I stuffed a quilt into the crack
To keep the cold-damp draft from coming through.
Now everything was done and I went back,
Pulled down the heavy quilts and jumped into
The bed and thought: verse writing is a mess.
And yet some fools call it sweet loveliness.

285

The wind kept playing with the loose-hinged door.
I laid awake and listened to the wind
Flap smoke-house boards, and mice run cross the floor.
This was a fine predicament to be in.
I must be up at four and milk the drowsy cows
And feed before the chickens left the roost.
Long as wind kept a-whistling round the house
And rain kept pounding on the leaky roof,
I could not sleep—there was no use to try.
For when one tries to sleep, one thinks of sleep;
The brain keeps active and one has to lie
Awake and think of darkness and the deep
And let things keep a-running through his head
About old books and poems he has read.

286

The rain kept drumming on the leaky roof.
The wind kept playing with the loose-hinged door.
The chickens still dozed on the black-oak roost.
The mice still ran across the cold room floor.
The rain thumped washtubs on the smoke-house door.
It tom-tomed on the old chip-yard wash kettle.
The wind played reels on a coarse oak-limb fiddle
And yard trees drunk on rain zigzagged a little.
And I got up—put on my overalls
And went downstairs to build a fire of wood.
The wood—was wet—I did the best I could.
I built the fire and heard the grunting calls
Of hungry fattening hogs in their wet pen.
I went to feed bare-headed through the rain.

287

When hollyhocks bloom in July and August
The hens sit under their broad leaves and wallow,
Shuffle their wings and beaks in the loose dust,
Under white blossoms, purple, cream and yellow.
They dream of white eggs in round pretty nests
And gold-plumed cocks a-calling them to bugs—
June-bugs, and jar-flies, are good food for chickens.
Under sky-roofs and by green grassy rugs,
The geese waddle up the bright-blue August stream.
And they swim out and mate on running water.
They sun on the rug and cross their necks and dream,
Positively of a little son or daughter.
They dream of straw-stained eggs in stolen nests
And gardens they could rogue in the easiest.

288

The woods are fresher now, and good to smell:
Water has made them fresh and washed them clean.
Water has washed the bark and washed it well;
Water has lifted dirty haze between
The hills, and from the corn and stacks of grain;
Water has wet the parching rain-crow's throat.
We heard the rain-crow singing in the rain:
He sang a new rain song—he tried to quote
The song of fresh-rain water giving blood
To thirsting roots of corn and pasture grass;
And giving Earth's intestines a cool mud
Where water snakes can writhe when feeders pass.
The song is fine to water moccasins
And to the cool, mud-burying terrapins.

289

I shall feel wet oak leaves close to my skin
And I shall smell these dead leaves after rains.
The winter of this life is setting in—
I do love oak-leaves' coffee-colored stains.
My body will be stained from head to toes
And I shall have the oak roots through my skull,
And fern roots through my lips and eyes and nose.
Each summer I shall wear loose green in full.
I think I shall be able to discern
You and the rain through hard eyes of the trees,
And I shall hold with fingers of the fern
The nourishment there is in my dead leaves.
And I shall taste the oak leaves and the rain.
I shall not feel the oak roots groove my brain.

290

The greenbriars, shoe-makes and the goldenrod;
The pine trees, chestnuts and the sycamore;
The dry disturbing winds, the floating cloud;
All this is autumn—and the leaf-strewn floor.
And long dry ridges sheltered by the sun—
All this is autumn and the brown corn shocks
Men cut before the day has new begun.
They cut the corn, leave bare the stumps and rocks.
The mold-board moon rides high above the fields,
A white disc plowing through the blue-sky dirt,
And leaves no trace behind of mellow fields—
But brown plow men leave traces of their work.
All this is autumn—such a bone-dry world;
Tree-leaves, corn-blades, flower-petals frost-curled.

291

I shall go back to life sly as a fox,
And follow mountain paths through huckleberries,
Shoe-makes, grapevines, and deep red rocks,
Where blacksnakes sun and the gray lizard scurries.
I shall go to the life that's home to me
And bare my flesh to wind and sun and rain.
I shall go back to life—I shall go free
With earth to live the old wild life again.
I want to worship gods: White Flying Cloud,
Red Evening Cloud, Sun, Wind, and Moon and Stars.
I do not want to live a life too loud—
No louder than the blowing of a wind,
No swifter than the passing of a cloud,
But higher than oak limbs against the stars.

292

I shall go back to earth and lonely skies
That float above the earth—I shall go back
To earth where I can hear the wild bird cries.
I shall go back and make a small bark shack.
I want to feel dead leaves beneath my feet;
I want to throw my arms around the trees.
These feet were never made for cold stone streets,
But they were made for soft-loam and the leaves.
These eyes can see no visions in white blocks
Of city stone—and dry electric fires.
These eyes were fashioned for to find the fox
And worming green snakes on green berry briars.
These ears were made to hear the music in
Night falling water and the pine tree wind.

293

There is shrill music in high winds at night
That break dead limbs and shake the pine-tree cones.
And it is life to walk in gray starlight
And hear winds snap the dead brush like dead bones;
To slip through brush and let one's footsteps fall;
Lighter than autumn rain falls on dead leaves,
Slyer than snakes that writhe close to the earth,
Quieter than dead leaves falling from the trees.
Shrill music that sinks to the heart and bone
And buries in the blood and brain and flesh.
Such night as this was made for man alone;
The stars and wind and pine tree cones and brush;
Alone for him to worship gods and trees,
And hear the music of the wind and trees.

294

The black birds and the geese are going south.
The grass has died before its time to die.
The grass has browned and purpled from the drouth
And copper clouds are ledged upon the sky.
The earth has hardened for the corn-field moles.
Jay-birds are scolding from the acorn trees.
The ground-hogs bury in their winter holes.
Squirrels are nesting in the hollow trees.
The blind blacksnake hunts for a winter-hole
Under the roots and rocks and rotting leaves.
He wants a place before his blood turns cold
And he sleeps like a stick through winter freeze.
For this cold-blooded snake lies down with earth
And sleeps till Spring gives his cold blood rebirth.

295

I came the Womack Road from Sandy Bridge
When red shoe-makes were nodding with the dew.
The sun rose even with the Seaton Ridge;
Under the leaves a golden ray came through.
A man with horse and buggy passed me by,
A jar-fly sang upon the weedy hill;
A mallard duck flew over with a cry,
A crow flew by with something in its bill.
I went the Womack Road from Sandy Bridge
When red shoe-makes were drinking back the dew.
The moon rose even with the Seaton Ridge;
Under the leaves a silver ray came through.
I could pick blackberries along the way,
For moonlight on the fields was bright as day.

296

No fife can wake young soldiers sleeping here
Under the ferns, blackberry briars and grass;
No fife can ever break their slumber here
With marching songs from out the braying brass;
Though years will roll and dynasties will pass.
The grass and leaves will try to talk to them.
The grass and leaves get nourishment from them.
These men knew not what they were fighting for,
They never knew just why they had to die
For men now calculate about the war
And wonder what young men were fighting for.
And young men forced to die! Will you and I
Be forced to face young men and take a shot,
Leave them, or be left, in such lonely spot?

297

He took you out and roped you to a tree
Because you were a bitch—he took a gun
And shot your brains into eternity
And you roped there without a chance to run.
Before he shot, you barked and wagged your tail
And whined to him—surely he understood
You meant you did not want to take the trail
Of Death— But then he shot and your warm blood
Ran in a stream on dead leaves down the hill.
When you were kilt your body was in heat
And hound-dogs came that night and ate their fill
Of you because you were in heat—next day
The crows flew down and picked your carcass clean.
The ants licked where blood-stains of you had been.

298

You used to eat crow carrion on the hill
And scare the crows and whip the dogs away;
You treed the possum when night winds were still
But none of this is true with you today.
Your bones are dirty sticks upon the hill;
Your friends came here and feasted on your meat
And let your cold blood drip like dead leaves fall.
Now possums play in the persimmon trees
And eat persimmons in the white moonlight.
The rabbits doze in the fresh fallen leaves.
The thieving fox prowls round the house at night.
You do not come for bread when Jammie calls.
Because Brigg, you are dead, they have no fear.
If you were living they would not come near.

299

The winter birds are roosting in the fodder,
I hear them twitter when I pass at night;
I hear September winds in low-lipped laughter
Combing the gray cornstalks in white moonlight.
I see old stubble fields and fresh green weeds
Beneath old ferns and leaves and blades of fodder.
I see the timid rabbit coming out to feed
And then I see his playful mate come after.
I hear the long notes of the hunter's horn
Sound over silent hills in gray moonlight—
It is not music like the wind in corn,
The notes are coarser than the warring fife.
And I have picked a solitary star
Above the pine-cone fire where hunters are.

300

From in this frozen corn-field where I stand
I hear the lonesome Greenup church bells sound.
Far out across the gray December land
They carry high above the frozen ground
Like winds that shake dead oak leaves on the bough
And stir through bleak December's white corn-blades.
The sound of old church bells is ringing now
Over the silent fields with a strange sound
And through the treetops and the dead grass curled:
My heart is stirred, though all the world is cold.
O bells, with your chimes, shake the sleeping World!
He is asleep—his fiery heart's grown cold!
O rusty church bells, wake the dreaming World!
Then warm him, Sun, with your white arms of gold!

301

This night is dark, but let the night be dark.
Let darkness be upon the face of the deep.
This night is dark and let there be no spark
Of light save lightning, sun, and moon and stars.
Oh, let us have the earth back clean again!
Nature improved upon has been destroyed.
Let us go naked, wild, like beasts again!
Let us go nameless strangers to the void.
Let us go wild—I lift my hands and pray
Up to the gods: the Moon and Sun and Wind;
White Flying Cloud, Red Evening Cloud and Stars;
And listen to sweet music on the wind,
And leave the record of our days behind.

302

This night is dismal, gray and desolate.
There are no moon and stars to penetrate
The dead-weed piles of low-hanging rain-cloud.
This night has valleys filled with wisps of fog
And winds that smell of ferns and pine and rotted log.
The earth is dead—this night's the funeral shroud.
Black fingers of the naked trees up-loom
To murky skies and unseen stars and moon,
Offering benediction to the earth.
The thunder's loud enough to shake the earth.
It may wake terrapins in slimy mud;
Cold-blooded snakes and frogs that sleep beneath
The leaves with blood temperature same as mud.

303

This night is dark—the drooping stems of weeds
Will wet the prowling possum, fox and coon;
And cover under earth the rag-weed seeds—
This night is dark, only a dismal moon
Can be seen wading through a thin rain sheet.
And all is silent save the limbs of oaks
That loom where hill-tops and the rain-clouds meet,
And water dripping dripping from the oaks—
This dismal night was made for man alone.
This darkness, mud, thunder and jet-black slime,
And songs of water running over stone
And winds in naked brush that hum a rhyme,
Not giving place to it nor any time—
Surely, this night was made for man alone.

304

The rain falls from the slack-pile heavens to
An earth that's covered with dead grass and leaves.
The rain falls down among the barren trees.
The lightnings scar the heavens—flashes through
Dark pages of the earth—the grass blades quiver,
And strong trees bend to reckless elements.
Ah, I would love to say: Storm rage forever!
I love to see your lightning cut the sky!
I'd love to see your naked woods washed clean!
I love to hear your wind and waters cry!
I love that cool incessant monotone;
This would make me go wild and live alone!
The passionate surging of the elements!
Surgings like passions of primitive men!

305

This is the land where sweet blue violets grow;
It is the land where there is thyme and phlox—
This is the land where pretty blood-roots blow
In early Spring beside gray hill-side rocks.
This is the land where oak and ash and beech
Leaf early to the sky-blue winds of April;
This is the land of pretty vale and hill
Where poplar trees grow to the low sky's reach.
Look now and see a violet in the wind;
Look now and see a modest growing jonquil
And you will say, fair is Kentucky's hill.
It is my land and I am part of it—
I think I'm clay from in the heart of it—
My land—a green quilt hides its rocky scars
When it sleeps under Kentucky sun and stars.

306

Life now is awakening in the chicken's combs.
See they are red as blood when first it runs.
Life is reviving like swift sparkling streams
As they flow under late-march mellow suns.
Life is reviving in the flesh of us
And showing as it shows in rooster combs
As we go working round our log-shack homes.
There are a thousand blossoms in plum trees
And they are filled with a thousand noisy bees.
There is the burdock by the rotting sill.
It is so green and pretty as a slipper heel.
There are the hollyhocks in chimney corners,
And by the palings grow the lady's-fingers—
Reviving Springtime and the earth's awake.
The blood has warmed in the veins of the snake.

307

I hear the crickets singing on the hearth.
When night has come I lie awake in bed
And hear their songs of sadness and of mirth.
I wish I knew the words these crickets said.
I only know what men have said they say:
"Be of good cheer, be of good cheer—good cheer.
Be of good cheer, be of good cheer—and smile—
Wish for a merry prosperous new year—
Be of good cheer, be of good cheer and smile."
I'll tell you what I think these crickets say:
"So many nights we've watched the dying embers,
And danced together in their golden light—
These are the merry parties we remember,
When we danced together in their golden light."

308

I hope when I have settled down at last
It will be by my Jean Elizabeth;
I know I must, for youth is going fast,
And someday she and I must sleep beneath
A quilt that will not be so easily moved.
The things that we have done are ours to keep;
Days when we were young and eager how we loved;
Days when we little dreamed of a long sleep—
We plucked the blooms of phlox and goldenrod
And laughed together under windy skies;
For we were young and fresh above the sod—
We laughed and listened to the wild bird cries.
I hope when I have settled down at last,
It's in the earth where Jean Elizabeth lies.

309

I know the wine in Lydia Doore's strong blood
Will weaken and the rose fade from her cheek;
I know the petals of the wild red rose
Will fade and die—and she shall cease to speak.
Her lips will turn cold as two frozen stones;
Her fingers wither to brown stems of grass;
Her bones be as the gray sticks on the hill—
Only her dust will lie beneath the grass.
I shall love Lydia Doore, my highland flower,
Until the frosts of winter strike her down
And leave her there in winter's darkest hour,
A stem of grass, wind-bent and autumn brown;
To lie forever on the darkest hill;
A rose to lie forever on the hill.

310

I shall love you, my Mountain Lydia Doore,
When other loves have drifted with the leaf;
I shall love you Sweet Mountain Lydia Doore;
The season for our love is summer brief.
Oh, we shall walk beneath the sycamore
And watch the moon rise high above the river.
And I shall love you then my Lydia Doore
When we walk where the ankle sedge-grass quivers.
And we shall listen to the night winds sighing
Through sandy-bottom corn-fields wet with dew;
And we shall listen to the shike-pokes flying;
Flapping their wings against wet winds of night—
When we walk through corn-fields on Sandy Shore;
I shall love you, my Mountain Lydia Doore.

311

When we lie down forever, Lydia Doore,
A rhine of dirt will be between our beds;
A quilt of dirt will hide the sycamore
And slabs of oak will pillow then our heads;
Our ears shall be deaf to the night winds sighing;
Our ears shall be deaf to the talking corn;
Our eyes shall be blurred to the shike-pokes flying;
Our eyes shall be blurred to the rising moon;
We shall lie down together—side by side—
And maybe dream our slumber shall break soon;
For what is it to any groom and bride
When heart and eyes are blinded to the moon?
If I could push—I'd push our wall apart;
But what are dead lips and a cold clay heart?

312

Yes, I shall come tonight, the moon is full;
A block of white-ash wood caught in the leaves—
We'll listen to the beetles' drowsy lull
And jar-flies singing corn songs in the trees.
I shall be there and we must dance together;
And we shall dance until the early morn—
Oh, we shall dance and put our lips together
When we go home through dewy fields of corn.
And Lydia, if we see a shooting star
You make your wish before it fades away—
Then we can hold our hands in running water
And make one wish of all the things there are—
Choose that one wish that's been a cherished dream;
Old women say it will come true hereafter.

LUCAS LITTLEJOHN *313*

It would be pleasure to you sons-of-bitches
If I should go for never to return;
Why don't you kill this scum from country ditches
And stretch me on a high-hill slope of fern?
Kill me for crows to eat my flesh and eyes
And bare my carcass to the wind and sun,
And leave it shining under the white skies;
Just leave it there and say: "His work is done."
For I would rather die than lose the fight
That you have waged on me, you bastard pack;
And if that time be day or darkest night
I stand here back to wall and fighting back.
I shall not leave if Death looks at my face.
I'll meet Death here; I'll meet Death anyplace.

314

Oh, man, you are a bubble on the water
That drifts into current, bursts to foam.
And man, you want to dream of the hereafter
And say a space in ether is your home.
Ah, man, you want to dream your fragile dream.
You are a coward and afraid of life.
You want to drift a bubble on the stream.
You want to miss the current and the strife.
Ah, man, insipid bug, you want to rest!
You want to float a bubble on still water.
You want some class distinction for your blest,
When you are old and dream of the hereafter.
You are a coward and you know you are.
Bubble shall never get beyond a star!

315

I am a man and I have tasted life;
The taste and then I mastered all I could;
Lived dangerously without a gun or knife
And plunged into the darkest solitude.
I've gathered life—I've caught it on the run.
I try not let one spark of life depart;
Let it be in a bottle, book, or gun;
Let it be vows congested in the heart.
I've gathered life—I've thrown the idle hours
Back into time—and danced on feet of clay.
I've been no working bee a-sucking flowers—
I did not gather roses when I could—
I am a bubble on a reckless stream;
A moment here to laugh and drift and dream.

316

I've gone cold-hungry in this moneyed town
(I do not have desires for this again)
When winter moon and silver stars shone down
And language there was profit—loss—and gain.
I could not speak with thread-bare words like these
When there was little left for one to say.
Could I describe a white moon in the trees?
Could I describe a derby hat and cane?
I have seen far more wretched things than these
But not words vile as "profit, loss, and gain."
And such a town where wretches save and save
And want to take it with them to the grave.
It is hard to go hungry in a town
When the winter moon and silver stars slant down.

317

Civilization has a bed-rock stand.
His ears are heavy with the mammon-gongs;
His eyes blood-shot to beauty of the land:
His brains are stunned to any wind-grass songs.
And what is he but trials to bones of men?
What is he but a weariness to human flesh?
Better for us to go quail-wild again;
Better go wild and naked in the brush
And live on roots and wild fruits from the trees,
And let our flesh get lean as a running fox—
Better for us to sleep on dry oak leaves
And find a winter shelter under rocks.
Better to hear a pine-top violin
And music from a wind-grass tambourine.

318

The money that I owe I know I'll pay.
It comes too slow and hard and easily goes
To pay for shelter, paper, books and clothes.
I further paying debts from day to day.
My friends, it's hard to squeeze a corn-field stone
And earn above the nourishment I get
For a mammon-chaser on his soft tabret.
He gets my gold, the little that I earn.
And he can have my copper, silver, gold—
He is the man to take it to the grave;
Poor fool, he is the kind to skimp and save.
My words above his coins when we are cold;
My words above his coins, don't you forget;
Above this lazy ass on his tabret.

319

"I am a poet—tell me what to write.
I've read 'Poetic Principles' by Poe—
I am inspired on pretty starry nights
When I see hills and rivers here below."
I would advise you get a coffee pot;
I would advise you then to write and riddle:
(A coffee pot is coffee pot is not)
Rats lived therein, but mouth and drink a little.
Then bottle up and send it to the Payneys
And pay them for to solve your inspiration;
Lucille and Sid, they have a use for pennies—
Ten lessons will put you before the Nation.
Come on, true poets, let us laugh together;
A jackass poet and two cockade feathers.

320

This flesh is eternal Kentuckian
Walking among her hills, breathing her air;
Plowing her soil, feeling her wind and sun
That stream as gold and silver in the fair
Blue days of Spring and summer corn-field haze.
Surely, I am eternal Kentuckian—
My people have lived here all of their days,
Plowed the same soil, felt the same wind and sun
They have been sons and daughters of the soil
And made their living by an honest toil.
This flesh will not go down eternal dust;
At least, I proffer to the gods and trust
It won't—but I do think that this flesh must
Be one eternal Kentuckian's dust.

321

Oh, singing world, you are too beautiful
Tonight—upon the misty moonlit hill
I hear the plaintive singing whippoorwill,
And down in white-top fields the beetles lull
A drowsy song—and jar-flies sing to rest
The sweaty mules that lie on pine-tree needles.
Oh, world of whippoorwills, jar-flies and beetles!
And now a corn-bird fluting from the nest!
The katydids are singing everywhere—
And down among the trees the night-hawk screams.
The pasture branch is fretting sod-grass seams.
The lazy cows lie under dew-drenched willows
And dream of calving time and better meadows.

322

The grass is getting dull—the days are colder.
The yellow leaves fly in the crispy wind.
White thunder clouds roll over ravelled, thinned—
The willow leaves drift on the Ohio River.
And I shall swim today, for soon the water
Will be chilled by the autumn rain and wind
And water from the small streams running in.
And soon the best of swimming days are over.
Today I split the water with my shoulder;
Swim on my back and watch the changing skies—
Swim on my back with water in my eyes.
I do not care if water has got colder—
I'll swim so I can see the clouds beneath
When I pick willow leaves up with my teeth.

323

You came too late to see us, my Elizabeth,
Wild roses by the rocks have lost their bloom;
And their soft petals now have curled beneath
The barren stems to meet a dead-leaf doom.
You came too late to see the blood-root in
White blooms along the worm rail fence corners;
Too late to see wild yuccas in the wind—
You came too late to see wild lady's-fingers.
But you are here to see the wild larkspur;
Blue beggar lice, and wild wind-loved jonquils.
You have come to my Kentucky where
The goldenrod are turning on the hills.
Susans are yellow as a brush-pile flame;
You have come late, but I am glad you came.

324

We walk together under the night trees.
I carry you across the swollen streams.
I wonder how you like the smell of leaves.
I wonder how you like the night-hawk screams.
But you are with me and we go alone—
We go alone together in the night.
We step from shadow woods to white moonlight
And here we sit upon a pasture stone
Where moonlight floods the pasture hills like water.
We hear the water leaping over stone—
We love to hear its drowsy monotone—
We hear the low-lipped creek along sod-lines.
We breathe the wind from dewy green-briar leaves,
From pasture daisies and from scrubby pines.

325

And if I kiss you, why should I confess;
Tonight the things we do are our business.
These pasture fields are wide, the sky is high.
Only young rabbits are a-passing by—
Sometimes a night-hawk passes with a cry.
We are alone beneath the tall green trees.
I know a place where Mother seldom goes,
It's on a knoll where a soft night wind blows—
We should go there and see the ramble rose,
Smothered by brush, sawbriars and wind-leant pines;
By honey-suckle and blackberry vines—
It was there where my mother first kept house;
Come let us stand beside this smothered rose
And ask the wind for secrets Mother knows.

326

Do you remember now, my Elizabeth,
The night we sat down on a rotted log;
We smelled the young corn and the pine trees' breath;
We listened to a night-hawk and a frog.
The wind blew your fine hair down on your face
And played the harp and viol in the young corn.
Have you forgotten then our long embrace
And how we left when stars had set for morn?
Do you remember how you were afraid
When blighted hickory nuts fell through the trees,
And when you heard the popping night corn-blades
And foxes tramping through old last year's leaves?
We heard the sobbing in the dark night-time
Like some old tune or half-forgotten rhyme.

327

And when you went away, I went around
Under the pine trees on our pasture hill;
And there among pine cones and grass I found
The slender footprints of your slipper heel.
I went the same path, Elizabeth, we took;
Down in old W-Hollow filled with mists;
I walked along the singing pasture branch
By wild rose stems where we had stopped and kissed.
I saw the gray owl on a starry limb
So wisely talking to the bright full moon;
The jar-flies and fox-hounds were mocking him—
The trees and wind were sobbing some old tune.
My Elizabeth, I could have told the wind
That you could beat him on your violin.

328

Elizabeth Hale, I know you are composed
Of finer clay than you find in this man;
Something is in you that is in a rose;
Something is in me that is in a stone.
The wind loves you, all things that smell the breath
Of wind love you—I know they love a rose;
Thin-petaled, waving in the wind, Elizabeth—
Wind passes over me and never knows
I am a gray stone lying in the grass,
And over me night wind and grass make moan;
And over me the writhing blacksnakes pass—
But wild rose roots are under this gray stone,
And winds can't shake it from its pasture earth.
This stone will hold it here and show its worth.

329

I've loved no one as I've loved you, Elizabeth,
Where moments swifter than the wind go by;
Never did pine trees give a sweeter breath
Than you, Elizabeth, under this starry sky.
Your eyes are colors in the green Spring timber;
And you are slender as the wild phlox stems;
Your hair is blond grain straws in damp November;
Your fingers are the shapely percoon stems.
I know, my Elizabeth, you'll be my bride;
I know, my Elizabeth, I'll be your groom.
And in our lives we shall lie side by side;
At death lie down together in the tomb.
Remember, I shall keep the best of you
And let the cold earth have the rest of you.

330

I wonder if the stars and sun and moon
Will be the same to us when we are married.
I wonder if white flying clouds and moon,
And purple hills (where youth is partly buried)
Will be the same to us—and willow trees
Drenched in night mists and moonlight by blue streams—
And if the youth that you have spent with me
Will pass on silently into old dreams.
I wonder if crab apples in the Spring
Will blossom white on thorny limbs for you;
I wonder if brown-breasted thrushes will sing
As sweetly as they used to sing for you—
And if you'll care to hear the whippoorwill,
Like we loved in our youth on pasture hills.

331

Elizabeth Hale, we've lived our youth together,
But we have gone with many other lovers;
The times did come when those loves had to sever,
And in the end we are again together.
Elizabeth Hale, I could love you forever.
Your lips are sweeter than the annis shoot.
Your hair is fragrant as a dewy rose,
Your teeth are white as inner poke-berry root,
Your voice is musical as wind that blows.
These lives of ours are most too brief for love,
If we kept young we could love on forever,
But love's uncertain as a cloud above.
We do not know the time that we must sever,
And lie with Death forever and forever.

332

When I take you, my Elizabeth, to wed
I know where we shall make our marriage bed.
We shall move by the Sandy River bottoms
In a log shack where pinks and larkspurs blossom;
Where we can hear the river's monotone
And see white water flashing over stone.
We shall live in this shack where we can see
The moon rise high above the white-birch tree
And July corn green-blanketing the bottoms—
A broad brown blanket made of tassel blossoms.
I think we can make our food from the soil,
For I am strong enough to stand the toil;
The food made from the soil will not come easily,
But it will be an honest living surely.

333

Oh, fighting kin, you have marched into war
And you marched madly into death and strife;
You did not know what you were marching for;
You loved the drum and the shrill blowing fife—
And when I go to clean your graves each May,
To rake off sprouts and briars, I shed warm tears—
I think of glory and I think of clay
That has lain deep and cold for all these years.
Now what to hell was marching to a fife,
And what to hell was marching to a drum,
Marching out to give a life or take a life—
Just stepping proudly to a fife and drum!
You rest: Commercial war gods did their best.
You rest: Deep holes are torn in your clay breast.

334

If I could hear the old shrill blowing fife,
If I could hear the old old beat of drum,
I would be with you old—I'd meet my life,
I would step proudly to a fife and drum!
And all the rugged lines I could have penned
Would die in this brown arm and brain and breast—
Just one more man in the dead world of men,
Under the briars and sprouts to take his rest.
I would have been a man to kill and fight,
But now I am a farmer tilling loam.
I plow my fields and sow my grain and write,
I hunt and have my drink and live at home,
I do not have desires to kill a man
Nor clean the sunken graves of fighting kin.

335

How could I stand to lie deep in such night
When young warm eager lovers come from church
Down corn-field paths in floods of gray moonlight
And stop and kiss under a water birch.
How could I stand the cloven hoofs of cows
To tramp above me and their teeth to eat
The grass above me—and, maybe, plows
Above this temper in a different heat.
How could it be fair for this warm young flesh
Be slashed by swords and riddled by coarse shots.
Remember there is power in young flesh
And think to butcher it for lonely spots
For brush and briars and for this desolate earth;
Better, if never cost the pain of birth!

336

And when I walked with one young far-off friend
Where honey-suckle was so freshly wreathed,
And Spanish bayonet waved in the wind
And yuccas in the heat just barely breathed—
Said he: "Do you suppose if Robert Stuart
Could have come to this Plum Grove hill in life
Before a bullet rent his stubborn heart—
Before he marched to beat of drum and fife—
That he would care to know he must lie here
Under yucca, honey-suckle, grass and stone?"
It's all the same—let him be sleeping here.
It's all eternity of dirt and stone—
And he must lie somewhere under the grass
While generations come and generations pass.

337

When I am gone, have some respect for me.
Have some respect for me when I am dirt.
Don't read my rugged poetry at your tea.
Don't make those sweet comments upon my work.
If there are any comments to be made
Above the stories pretty folks will tell,
Just say I lived and felt both sun and shade,
I saw some heaven and I saw some hell.
My hands were calloused by an honest toil;
My shoulders broad and brown my legs were stout;
By birth I was a bondsman to the soil,
And not a straw the wind could blow about.
Dear readers, please have some respect for me.
The best is: Please forget me at your tea.

338

If there is malice in this stubborn heart,
Remove it, blackness of this mountain night.
This man's an oak tree that will play a part.
Oh, night, don't let him stand to kill and fight.
Don't let his ears be deaf to music in
The wind and oak trees sobbing in your night.
Don't let his eyes be blurred to moon-clouds in
The starry heaves and the gray moonlight.
Oh, wind, blown fodder blades caught in the briars,
Don't let this heart grow heavy as a stone.
Earth needs this man, preserve his heart's hot fires,
But kill the malice in his heart and bones.
Just call him Night, Wild Night, you are his prayer.
Out in your gloom, he finds some solace there.

339

Your god is dead—your little god is gone.
The spoils you shared with him are gone today;
But you're enough to work and stagger on
And bring the money back—he could not stay.
Your spider god has spun his daylight lines
And you are blind to blue-air lines at day.
You followed him, now look, you shriveled flies
Caught in his web—alas, you had your way.
You Mammon Chaser fed you from the piles;
You grabbed like dogs, the gold was good for greed.
And now your Mammon god is gone—he smiles
And thinks of you—he thinks back of your needs.
Winds laugh at new thoughts running in your head.
Your god is gone—what more can now be said?

340

Jammie has gone to cut the corn tonight.
Jammie has gone to earn a little wage.
But I sit here alone and write and write;
My work the candle and the written page.
I snatch some busy time and write my song
And get no further on that first beginners—
And to the wind, I sing my weedy song;
I sing for plowboys and the seedy sinners.
I pay my debts and do not bow to man.
I live on the fruits of my sweaty labors—
I hate the law—God damn the politician—
I divide without a fuss among my neighbors.
I live among the earth a dirt-colored man.
I'm just an ordinary citizen.

341

I've not forgotten yet, Dear Wilma O'Shean
The purple mountains in your Tennessee
And blue Clinch River winding there between
And fair Spring days you walked its banks with me.
We loved each other then—and you and I,
We cherished April nights of loveliness;
Wind in the leaves, the white stars in the sky
And silent hours when lips to lips did press.
Have you forgotten now, Dear Wilma O'Shean
The night you said: "This will not last forever.
This night, someday, will be a vanished scene.
This night, and other nights we've had together
Someday will be our youth carved on the beeches,
Initial carved along the cool recesses."

342

We carved our initials on a roadside beech
And talked and laughed—you said a silly speech,
About our youth would lie forever here—
Our youth would lie forever in dark mountains—
Beyond dark hills would lie for many a year—
And we would not be there to see blue fountains
A-flashing in the sun and sweet clean air—
And rhododendron hanging from the cliffs.
Lovers would come, but we would not be there.
Our lost youth would remain beyond the hills—
"Beech bark is smooth where our initials were;
Deep scars are there, but they have long grown over—
Maybe, someday, our ghosts will come back here,
When you and I are buried by new lovers."

343

We could not love forever—that meant lost.
We could not live forever—that meant death.
We knew for all our love we paid the cost
And we were free with love as with our breath.
The rose was golden that you gave to me,
And there was sweet harp music in the wind.
The leaves were silver on the maple tree.
The grass played dance reels on his violin.
Do you remember any tunes they played?
For one lone tune here are the words I made:
"Oh, you must love forever and forever,
From Spring till leaves turn golden on the tree;
For don't you know that you will die forever,
A dead leaf falling from the golden tree."

344

Sweet Wilma O'Shean, please say, why did you marry?
You were not old—why were you in a hurry?
Your youth lies buried now beyond the hills.
We could not love forever and forever—
Silly for me to dream of roads and daffodils
And starry nights we walked the hills together.
And when our bodies parted, our love went.
Love in the flesh is greater than the mind.
Our bodies parted and the life we spent
Together parted—our youth was left behind
The hills—each went a separate way
With memories of one long youthful scene—
Blue starlight on the hills and purple day—
I've not forgotten you, Dear Wilma O'Shean.

345

Wilma, I have not seen the man you married,
But he is like the average man, I guess.
I cannot understand why you have married
When richer lips to yours would gladly press.
Your dancing days are over, Wilma O'Shean,
And you've begun the days of "looking back."
You live among hills, blue water flows between.
You live there in a tumbling mountain shack.
This life is yours and it keeps calling back.
Your husband is a tiller of the loam
And you now lie with him and make a home.
I wonder if the leaves on that same tree
Are golden to you now, Sweet Wilma O'Shean!
And I would love to know your thoughts of me
When you ride with him over certain scenes.

346

I speak again to you, Dear Wilma O'Shean,
You know I've lived free as the wind that blows.
And since we parted, listen, Wilma O'Shean,
I have met only one wild woodland rose;
But I have met some lesser since that day
And done some foolish things that no one knows.
My Elizabeth has eyes as blue as you.
Wilma, My Elizabeth is fair as you.
She is fairer than any woodland rose.
She is as fresh as any wind that blows.
The fragrance of the phlox is in her breath.
And now I fight for her—I fight with Death.
Sweet Wilma O'Shean, you cannot pair with her.
For Wilma O'Shean, you are not rare as her.

347

Water is all we want, water to drink—
To moisten lips and dust between the teeth,
Water is all—water is good to drink—
And men and plants are thirsting near to death.
The roots of corn and goldenrod are dry.
The juice is drying in the stalks of cane.
The wind and grass and silking corn stalks sigh
For water and the rain crows cry for rain.
"Oh, heavens, send rain to our dusty teeth,"
They cry, "and send cool water for grass roots—
Send water soon—we're thirsting near to death—
Send water soon—water is good for guts—
Our guts need water and our roots are dry—
Oh, wash our dusty teeth before we die!"

348

This lazy day—the sun is scorching hot.
The snake feeders fly up and down the creek
And dry winds blow through graveyards long forgot
And soothe the church-house half-afraid to speak.
This lazy day—the cows stand by a pool
And chew and chew and swish their tails at flies.
They're half content to find a place so cool
Where they can dream under the scorching skies.
The dry winds blow—the yellow leaves drop after
The shoe-make and the black-gum berries fall—
And drift on shaded pools of stagnant water.
They drift where shike-pokes drift and mud-hens call—
They drift beside the church-house and the graves,
And by the cider mill that's gone to staves.

349

O storm, rise up!—and lightning, cut the sky
And pour your water—wash the earth to ruts!
Oh, give earth water, for the earth is dry,
The earth is dry—her lips and teeth and guts.
O lightning, rip the seams of dirty clouds
And tear the hearts out of the strongest oaks!
Oh, cover the dark womb of earth with shrouds
Of falling water, wind and fog and smoke!
O storm, rise up and hide the huts of men
And show your teeth of fire on muddy dark—
Show us just what the old earth might have been!
Oh, rise up, storm, and let your thunder bark
And wake cold-blooded snakes and dusts of men!
Wake them—eternity is long and dark!

350

The muddy rain-clouds rose in the northwest
And muddy rain-clouds rose in the southeast;
Winds sang the thirsting corn and grass to rest
But they woke drinking in a water feast.
The earth had cried for rain and the rain fell:
Potato wagons rolled across the sky,
The lightning cracked like popcorn over hell,
And Earth cried out: "O Rain, My guts are dry
My long intestines are dry as dog bones
And dirty-colored, as a dead man's veins.
My long intestines are cramped with dry stones
And I need gastric juice of heavy rains.
Water is new life for my wrinkled skin;
Water is sweet red wine: I soak it in."

351

Dead leaves and damp—her bare feet touch the leaves.
The high winds blow—black pine trees wave and sigh.
The oak limbs crackle and a tree-top weaves
Black fingers patterned on the silver sky.
She waits—her lover comes—her brown-skin comes—
She knows he will come by a moon-lit stream—
Her steps are lighter than a far-off drum
Of rain against the leaves—she waits—she dreams—
"Tata-tatum—tata-tatum—tum—tum—
Tata-tatum—tata-tatum—tum—tum—"
Her lover comes—her brown-skin lover comes—
He proudly marches to the old war drum.
"Tata tatum—tata-tatum—tum—tum—"
Her lover comes—her proud young lover comes.

352

Her lover comes and they lie down together.
They lie down on the starlight and dead leaves.
And who will tell? No one but Wind and Weather
Will tell of two they found a-lying there.
The Wind is jealous and the Weather grieves.
Her lover comes with starlight in his eyes,
His flesh is brown—his hair is black and straight.
Her lover comes and limb to limb they lie
Where stars shine down and winds in tree-tops sigh—
This starry night is beautiful to them.
And they could lie and love forever here;
He with a warrior's clothes to cover him;
And she with jewels in black-waving hair—
After they've tarried where the leaves dropped down;
People can't wonder why his skin is brown.

353

This is the place my mother's mother lies
Under these poplar trees and honey-suckle;
Under these lazy Carter County skies
And roads near-by where wagons wheeze and chuckle.
It will be forty years sometime next March
Since two black horses pulled a light express
Upon this hill—their manes and tails were arched.
They brought my mother's mother here to rest.
Fresh yellow clay was piled there underneath
The trees where children stood and shed warm tears—
To think their mother would be housed with death
To lie there for the coming years and years.
They heard them pray for her a lofty prayer
And then left with the small crowd gathered there.

354

The two black horses pulled the children back
To their deserted pine-log mountain shack.
They left here there to sleep among the dead;
Tall Sextons, Penningtons and Leadinghams;
Shoveled her under after the prayer was said,
Among grave-stones with Bibles and White-lambs.
One crumbled dirt and put into her box:
"Ashes to ashes and dust to dust," he said.
And at her head and feet one put field rocks.
Violet Hylton was sister to the dead.
And forty years have passed—her grave is flat.
And no one now would know a grave is there.
No one would know here-by five children sat
And looked last on their mother's straight black hair.

355

Violet, I've cried in terror to the gods
Who whisper in rose-scented winds at night;
Violet, I've proffered prayer up to these gods,
But their ears have been deaf to prayers at night.
I've cried to them: "O gods, why can't you hear
Why don't you hear, these futile words I say?
Why don't we taste of life while we are here?
Why don't we gather flowers while we may?"
Violet, the gods won't hear this futile cry.
I wonder if they heard the cries you cried
When you were young and youth was going by
And if they heard, if your cries were denied!
Violet, what is this great eternal strife
Crying to gods, playing with passions—life?

356

Violet, your younger daughter is my mother,
And same as you she loves the wind and sun and rain;
Not fair as you, but brown-skinned is my mother
And she hoes in tobacco, corn and cane.
She loves music and taste of sweet rich wines;
She loves the good earth and the fields and brooks;
She loves the starlight hanging through the pines;
She does not care for cold stone streets and books.
She loves to work—get out in fields and work;
She knows all wild plants growing in the woods;
She loves to dig her hands into the dirt—
She loves red evening clouds and solitudes—
She takes her time and lives close to the soil;
She finds sweetness in wild labor and toil.

357

The sourwood leaves hang clustered red as blood,
The dogwood leaves are falling to the ground,
The poplar leaves drift in a windy flood,
From their tall tops drift slowly to the ground.
The autumn winds creep mournfully through the woods.
They kiss with piercing chill the solitudes.
These autumn winds blow loud with angry sounds.
And listen, friends: this autumn I am proud
That back when warm Spring sun burst into flame
I planted seed regardless chill and floating cloud,
And it grew well— When days of summer came
I toiled through hazy heat behind the plow.
I hoed my corn, tobacco and my cane—
I'm glad I worked before the autumn came
For I am proud to reap this harvest now.

358

The leaves are drifting from the autumn trees.
They drift like birds beneath the windy skies.
Look in the heavens now—the flying leaves
Have turned away the sunlight from our eyes.
When Spring first tapped the valleys and the hills
I tried to be the first and beat the crow—
And welcome back new life with the new year—
Be first to shout: "You know the Spring is here!"
But I was beaten by the cornfield crow.
And then I saw green fields of waving clouds
And crows swarmed down among them with a caw.
Now see these same leaves are an autumn shroud;
Leaf-birth, leaf-death—these are the things I saw.

359

Oh, I shall put my cutter plow away,
And rakes and hoes and spades back in the shed;
I know the season's over and today
I'll haul away the little spoils I've made.
It is not much for any man to see;
Too many briars are raked in with the grain
And dead leaves fallen from the white oak tree;
It is rough cropping, but it is my cane
And corn and words and I shall rake them here
And leave them here, for I shall soon go on
To clear strange fields and use the cutter plow
If I can use a plow when I am gone—
And men can come and plow and sow and reap
The land I leave when I am taking sleep.

360

Autumn is coming now; plowing is over.
Pastures are sprouted clean and gardens tended;
The cane is thinned and all the fences mended;
It's cool for bees to gather from late clover.
And we must gather now the rakes and plows,
And mattocks, spades, pitchforks, and garden hoes,
Stack them away just as the summer goes;
And we must watch the water for the cows
And keep the holes cleaned out, for land is dry
And pasture grass is short this time of year.
The martins gather and the autumn's near—
And August clouds go floating slow and high.
When it's too cool for bees to work in clover,
It's time to gather tools, for summer's over.

361

The wind blows high tonight—the wind blows strong,
The yellow leaves fall on the Sandy water,
The leaves are grains of meal that sift among
The naked boughs and the buff-colored fodder,
The moon rides high—a grain of yellow dent,
The oak trees rock—the yellow dent goes by,
He smiles at silent fields in half-contempt—
The wind and trees sing him a lullaby:
"Tra-la—tra-la—tra-la—the moon is high,
Tra-la—tra-la—tra-le—the moon is corn,
O corn-moon, do you hear the hunter's horn?
O corn-moon, do you hear the dead leaves sigh?
Tra-la—tra-la—tra-le—tra-le—tra-li—
Tra-le—tra-li—the moon is yellow corn."

362

Oh, I remember my Elizabeth Hale
Down by the clear mountain waters so still;
Green corn was waving, my Elizabeth Hale,
When we sat by the water at the foot of the hill.
It was there by that stream, my Elizabeth,
We dipped our hands in water, made our vow
That we should meet again, my Elizabeth.
And then I went back singing to my plow—
I've plowed much green sod over since that day,
And I've kissed many a dancing mountain girl.
My dreams are all my Elizabeth Hale someday;
My Elizabeth before the frost has curled
The goldenrod, the phlox and daffodil
Down by the stream at the foot of the hill.

363

"Stuart, when you came cross the hill today
Did growing corn and tall trees talk with you?
Last year when I was well it was that way—
I heard them talking when the wind blew through
The leaves and blades— And do the crickets and
The jar-flies sing out on the pasture hill?
Stuart, I do wish you could understand
How hard it is to lie against the will.
For fourteen months I've lain here on my back
And listened to the Spring and winter rain
Beat on the board roof of this mountain shack,
Knowing that I shall not be well again—
To walk upon the grass about the place,
To see the trees and feel wind on my face."

364

"As I came cross the high green hills today
I never saw the skies so high and blue;
Tall trees were talking to the growing corn;
A wind that smelled of hay was blowing through;
Jar-flies and crickets sang upon the hill
And bees were working on the shoe-make tops;
A dove flew by with pine-straws in its bill;
A rabbit crossed my path and took long hops
For the tall weeds and briars—I hate to see
You Kyon Murray lying there in bed;
I'd love to see you well again and free.
I think it is a notion in your head
That you will not get well enough again
To feel the touch of sun and wind and rain."

365

"You, Jesse Stuart, don't know, for you are strong.
Your skin is brown as any autumn leaf—
Strong as the oak, you work and sing your song
(The life of any oak tree is not brief)
I know why I lie here and have to die.
When you and I went down the creek together
And through the rain and snow and sleet to school,
I did not have good clothes for winter weather;
You went without a coat and stood it well.
You, Jesse Stuart, will be a man alive
When I am dead and black boards cover me;
And long before the bees are in the hive
I shall sleep with the worms eternally—
Before the oak leaves fall I shall be dead
And two gray stones will mark my feet and head."

366

And long before the bees are in the hive
And long before the honey's in the comb;
I walk upon the earth a man alive,
Kyon Murray, has left her mountain home.
The wild flower has wilted down at last,
And pale, pale is the wild rose on her cheek,
The naked stem is waving in the blast.
Too silent are her cold, cold lips to speak.
And if there is a gray stone for her feet,
And if there is a gray stone for her head,
I have not been upon the hill to see—
But I do know that this wild flower is dead.
I know someday, black boards will cover me,
And I'll sleep with the worms eternally.

367

These parent birds the hunters have concealed
In hunting coats—once followed at my plow.
They were insect destroyers in my fields—
And think, their blood is staining brown coats now.
Last winter when the wind blew loud and shrill
Through frozen timber with a creaking sound
And stirred the ragweed stems upon the hill
And left their frozen seeds upon the ground,
These parent birds walked on this frozen ground
And ate of the black worthless ragweed seed—
They ate the worthless grain where corn was pulled.
These gave the food and warmth bird bodies need.
Here in these woods, secure from roaring blast,
These bobwhites lived until the winter passed.

368

It does hurt one to see the warm blood run
From timid birds that walked behind the plow;
Bloodthirsty man, why did you take a gun
And kill these birds that chased behind my plow?
They walked beside me in the furrowed field;
I heard them making love down in the oats,
Down where they had a nest of eggs concealed—
And now their blood drips from the hunting coats.
Now listen, hunters, let your shotguns rest
If you must walk here where my father owns;
You cannot take the blood of bird and beast,
That live among the hills my father owns.
When you shoot down a timid quail for sport,
I think something's the matter with your heart.

369

Farewell to winter frost and sleet and snow
And winds that snap branches of frozen timber;
Farewell to hollows where slush-waters flow
On gray days in this desolate December;
Farewell to log corn-cribs and yellow corn,
With white corn sorted for to make corn-bread;
Farewell feed baskets on a frosty morn;
Farewell white cattle breaths and warm stall bed
And chestnuts roasting in the log-wood fire,
And white corn parching on the old cook-stove;
Farewell potatoes roasting in the embers—
They are all gone, these winter things I love,
For to the frozen earth I have retired—
The wind and rain and black-clouds scud above.

370

Farewell to birds a-roosting in the fodder;
Farewell to naked hills with white-rock seams,
To black leaves drifting on the slushy water;
Farewell to all my native hills and streams—
The dark hills there against the threatening skies;
And cold white leghorn chickens in dark trees;
The trains of crows and their soft searching cries.
Farewell to all and cold snakes under leaves;
Farewell to ragweed fields where rabbits hide
And high rock cliffs where foxes make their dens;
Farewell to straw-pens where the quails abide;
Farewell to smoke from huts of hunting men;
Farewell to winter winds that make their moan;
Farewell to families by their warm hearthstone.

371

The August sassafras leaves are turning red;
The black-oak leaves are getting tough and thick;
The corn is dying and the beans are dead;
The pasture grass is short, and cattle pick
The leaves from sprouts and reach between the wires,
They crane their necks to gather tall grass there.
The yellow leaves are dropping from green briars
Like drops of water fall on the field stones.
The summer blood is dripping from the trees;
The trees are in a windy autumn mood
To give their blood in drops of flying leaves.
It must hurt trees to lose their summer blood.
The trees are drunk till Spring gives them new birth;
Their blood is whiskey for the thirsty earth.

372

This is the night for song; the windows shake.
I guess it is the wind that shakes the windows.
This is the night for everything—I take
My clothes and hang them up and get in bed.
There in the fireplace lie the dying cinders.
Dying cinders—and dreams are in my head.
The cat lies by the fire and sleeps a spell
The wind sighs by the door its sweet farewell.
Only the cat and I are in the room—
The wind is out beneath the golden moon.
This is the night for song: this windy night.
And I get up from bed before the cinders.
I find there are more songs the cat remembers
When I get up and take my pen to write.

373

Farewell to winter's frozen water-weeds.
Farewell dark hills and clouds that foul the sky;
Farewell to snowbirds eating ragweed seeds
And winds that blow dead leaves against the sky
And shake old sparrow nests among the eaves;
Farewell to daisies under pasture stumps;
Farewell warm rabbit blood upon dead leaves
And greenbriar thickets where the rabbits live.
Farewell weed fields so gray and desolate;
In hunting season where men searched to kill.
But now the scattered birds call to their mates
And coveys reunite upon the hill—
Late winter and the hunting season's over;
Wild crippled rabbits sleep without a cover.

374

Someday I shall return to dirt and stone,
And grass and briars and trees and growing things;
And over me night winds shall make their moan,
And over me white dogwoods bloom in Spring—
And rats will leave their footprints over me;
An epitaph for only rats to read
When I am rotting in eternity,
When I am sleeping soundly with the dead.
Only the rats and wind and briars will know
I was a poet—and the place I sleep;
Only the roots of grass and briars will know
About the ringed worms that writhe and creep
And feast upon the matter of my brain;
They will go down and know—they shall remain.

375

Oh, Brother, come! Now let us put our hand
Upon each other's shoulder and march to cut
The briars and locusts growing in our road;
Oh, let us march and cut and smooth the rut—
For Brother, don't you know that we together
Can march and cut and lift a heavier load!
I hear men crying like the winter weather
Down in the darkness on that thorny road.
Oh, Brother, come! My face and feet are bleeding;
The locust thorns have all but pierced my eyes!
Come, Brother, we can whip the night and darkness;
Oh, we can fight beneath the threatening skies!
We'll take a broad-ax, hew out slabs of night—
Let's go and meet the darkness and the light!

376

Kentucky dust and lone, lone evening sounds:
A pair of doves wing-fanning dusky air,
The far-off drowsy sheep bells' jingling sounds,
A brisk horse-snicker answered by a mare,
The winds hum and dead churchyard grasses wave;
These winds hum tunes men sang in former days;
They sing for old men sleeping in the grave—
They sing: "We loved old men and golden days."
Kentucky evening slipping fast away—
A barking dog—some pounding at a shack;
Kentucky dusk with hills brown as the clay.
The moon arose—went down—the night is black—
Dark hills—night autumn hills and lonely sound,
Lonely as water running under ground—

377

I hate to see the lazy summer pass
And blackberry blooms curl off the thorny briars;
I hate to see cows taken off the grass;
I hate to see the death of cornfield flowers—
The phlox must shed its petals to the ground
To wither with the phlox leaves bedded there;
The shoe-make leaves will fall without a sound,
For now they flaunt their banners to the air.
I'll say I hate to see this summer pass
And see white blossoms dying with the year;
I'll hate to hear the wind blow through the grass
When it is dead and autumn days are here.
Autumn is sure to come and summer pass,
And many of our dreams die with the grass.

378

O Death, you can frighten the king and the slave
And leave them by the flower and the tree;
Death you can teach us mortals to behave
By leaving us silent under the tree.
But come, you comely Death, and frighten me,
For I'm neither king nor cowardly slave—
I'm tiller of the loam and I am free;
I'm not afraid of the hell of your grave
And silence under roots of flower and tree—
Silence under the tufted grass and stone;
Silence and sound will be the same to me,
Down in a small eternity my own.
If there is new life in the womb of night,
I'm ready for to meet you, Death, and fight.

379

On with the dance—tonight may be the last.
On with the dance and let footsteps fall lightly.
On with the dance, for yesterday is past—
On with the dance and swing the girls ghost-lightly.
The "dew" was good tonight—now did you drink?
Some "dew" is here—go back in the dark room,
Where rays of summer moonlight now drift through.
The "dew" is good and don't you love to drink?
"Kentucky dew" will put new life in you.
On with the dance—the midnight stars are white.
Oh don't you love that peppy violin?
It says: "The bird flew out—the crow hopped in."
The way the boys are dancing is a sin.
Oh, life is great—on with the dance tonight!

380

Tomorrow may be bitter, who can tell.
Oh, listen to that call: "Move Children, Move!"
Tomorrow may be bitter, who can tell,
So spend this night a-dancing with your Love.
Oh, can't you hear that lonesome violin,
And can't you hear the strumming of guitars?
Better than listening to a lonesome violin
Out by oneself beneath the winter stars.
Now listen to that call: "Move Children, Move!"
First couple out—waltz up and down the hall,
"Move Children, Move!" Step lightly with your Love.
"Move Children, Move!" Oh, don't you hear that call!
"Move Children, Move!" That lonesome violin!
You see the bird flies out—the crow hops in.
"Move Children, Move!" Too slow that step you're in.

381

The dance is over—I take Jenny home.
The barren trees are black—fields are frost-white.
The path is rough that leads to Jenny's home.
The hills are covered in floods of moonlight.
We talk about the skies and fields and trees
And the warm days to come when winter's over.
We talk about the little mountain meadows
And warm days when bees will work on the clover.
And Jenny speaks of hollyhocks in bloom
And of a flower that blossoms in the morn,
And I speak of the hay and new barn room
And morning glories vining round the corn.
Below our path we see a mountain stream—
A ribbon in the moonlight is this stream.

382

Jenny and I walk through the night alone.
We walk beneath the winter stars together;
And Jenny is the strongest mountain girl
I think that ever put her foot on leather.
For Jenny does not care for mud and mire,
She does not care how far we have to walk.
I think her body was not made to tire,
And Jenny's always happy as a lark—
She works out in the fields and hoes the corn.
She laughs at life and says: "One time to live.
One time to dance; one time to hoe the corn—
Always to love—only, one youth to give.
Only one youth to give, but let it go.
One life to give, but I hate leaving so."

383

I've stood and listened to the night wind crying
And looked on beauty of the winter skies;
I've stood and listened to the dead leaves sighing;
I've listened to night water's lonely cries;
I have been reverent to the lonely night—
I've loved night with the little power of love—
And old brown stubble fields in gray moonlight;
The frosted trees—the moon and stars above.
I've loved the night—to Night, I am a friend—
Night is so filled with lonely monotones,
And I know Night will take me in the end—
Never a doubt, I'll sleep with night at last;
Forever Great Night shall enclose my bones.

384

There's something to the night that stirs my blood—
The beauty of the stars and winter skies,
Wind in the pine-tops in dejectful mood,
The low sad laughter in the river's cries,
There's something in the beauty of the flood
Of moonlight on bare field and winter tree.
There's something to these things that stir a mood
And makes cold blood run warm through veins in me.
And many nights I've sat beside the river
And listened to the water's monotone—
I've listened to its winter sedge-grass quiver
And thought night was not made for man alone.
And there beside the singing Sandy River
I cried: "Life, why can't you go on forever!"

385

Why should I have one fear of man and night?
Man is an enemy—man is a friend,
Man is one journeying into the night;
Why should I have one fear, night is the end.
Night is the end, my friend—never a doubt;
And while we're here, we should partake of life;
Be gay until our candle is blown out
By changing winds that will soon end our light.
And if there is a life beyond this life—
A life beyond all that we think is night—
I shall be one undaunted, unafraid;
Ready to go to conquer and to fight—
Let night be what it is—I do not worry.
And let this night come slow—I'm in no hurry.

386

I do not have one fear of enemies,
Though one could hide at midnight on some hill
And shoot me down from a bulwark of trees—
I know this is a treacherous way to kill—
This is the way of cowardly enemies.
But I have traveled near and far at night,
I went alone without a knife or gun.
I went alone where I had enemies,
I went alone with no intent to run,
I do not have one fear of enemies.
When I walk under hanging cliffs and trees,
My only lantern is the pale moonlight.
I do not have desires to cut and kill;
But I am not afraid to face and fight.

387

These men, I think, saw pleasure in the night.
Laid here: feet to the east, heads to the west.
To fighting men, I know this is a rest.
They must lie still and that will be the best.
They only tried to live a little while
Before feud rifles barked: "They die forever!"
And face to face they met death with a smile,
And rifles rang the shots that kilt forever.
In furrowed fields, fairest under the sun,
Yard weeds will grow—the house be desolate.
Little their deaths matter to anyone.
And long for them, the bull-tongue plows will wait;
Their widows will go on and lie with men;
Brothers to husbands, maybe—next of kin.

388

If I am ever forced to leave this land,
Luck be with you, my honest Greenup friends;
Long as the rivers flow and high hills stand,
Luck be with you—I pray no ill attends,
For we are of one flesh, my faithful friends;
We've helped each other at the bin and stack
And man for man we have done death-like errands.
Many of us have sought the world's far ends.
The hills kept calling and we all came back
To white frame houses and the rough log shack.
My friends, remember, I shall stand for you
Solid as stone, long as the waters cry for you—
A troth of truth, I give this hand to you
That I shall stand by you and die for you.

389

My friends, I wish not one of you an ill,
I think you do not wish an ill for me—
When the time comes this body must lie still,
It is a wish, my friends, that you will see
I am brought back to lie on Plum Grove Hill.
Dear friends, I choose to lie with jolly fellows,
Although you jolly fellows must lie still.
And when the heat of this strong body goes
Into a house of fungus and of mold—
Down where there must be neither heat nor cold,
Too deep for finger roots of the primrose,
But not too deep for worms and rain and moles—
If you are where you can, I hope you give
Your hands to bear me to a Plum Grove grave.

390

Tonight, my Love, you are the fairest girl
That ever lived among these hills near home.
You are the fairest in our little world
That ever set bare feet on sun-scorched loam.
And we keep drifting on and on and ever—
And let us drift—forever drift apart—
Remember we shall not live here forever;
Since we must sever, let one make the start.
Sometime this body would be cold to you,
If you and I were sleeping two by two.
There is a night I'd sleep beside of you
And you would not know whom you slept beside;
And we would sleep together the night through,
This bridegroom never turning to his bride.

391

My mother said Liz Reeder's baby died.
It lived ten minutes after it was born.
The Doctor could not come, or else he lied.
My mother came at four o'clock this morn.
Liz carried too much water, too much wood,
Knowing she was heavy with Bill's child.
Liz Reeder did all of the work she could.
She worked until the night she bore the child.
"Liz looks awful bad," my mother said,
"She's lying there flat on her back in bed."
My Dad had gotten up to build a fire.
Said she: "And Mitch, Liz Reeder's baby's dead."
Said he: "Must be Liz can't deliver well—
No Doctor and I'll bet it was some hell."

392

I was lying awake upstairs in bed.
I listened to every word they said.
I knew before the July sun was up
And dew dried on the corn and buttercup,
Bill Reeder would take his own child to bury—
In sheets perhaps he'd wrap its mangled form,
And then he'd put it in an oak box surely
And plant it somewhere on his hill-side farm.
It was a seed, but it would never sprout,
And it had cost its mother pain of birth.
After he'd planted it, who'd know about
A body sleeping under pasture earth?
Bill would remember mating time again.
Liz would forget about the childbirth pain.

393

At eight I saw Bill going up the hill.
Under his arm he had a bundled sheet.
And in one hand he carried a sprouting hoe.
A lean white hound dog followed at his feet.
He walked half-mile and put the bundle down.
He took his hoe and threw up yellow dirt.
He took loose clods and chased away the hound.
He stood a bronze man in a slit-back shirt,
Coarse leather shoes and root-stained overalls.
He took the bundle—hid it in the clay.
He stood in silence then—I think he prayed.
The crows swarmed over with their caw-caw calls.
And Bill picked up the mattock—went his way.
The lean hound slipped back to the grave and stayed.

394

Men say these are the children of the night,
These mountain men who cannot read and write.
They may not know the ways to shape a word.
They may not know the words when they are traced.
But they remember well the things they've heard
And soon forget the danger they have faced.
Some of these men are children of the sun—
Unnoticed things of earth one could show you,
And how to run your furrows straight and true.
They could teach many how to use a gun—
They are bronze men who have no fear of toil.
Their education is a book of soil—
They are men taught to work and pray and fight.
Let them be children of the darker night.

COUNTY SCHOOL SUPERINTENDENT'S OFFICE

I cleaned the desk of papers, laughed, and said:
"Who in this world would give their life to this?
Cooped in a room, better if one were dead—
Unless afraid of pennies one might miss."
And then I thought there'll be such thing as "cash,"
When I am gone, and there will be this room
Where another youth shall waste his mortal flesh,
Where he must age and slander be his doom.
And all the time I write these futile lines
I think of pasture lands, wild fern and phlox,
White evening clouds behind the swaying pines,
A chimney corner filled with hollyhocks—
I dream of things forever close the soil;
I don't want office work, but I want toil.

I should not curse this room, it feeds me bread.
But I'll go hungry if I must stay here
And do this routine work year after year—
And if I stay here long I shall be dead.
My feet are never patient on this floor.
This mind goes blank at questions all day long.
These ears hate hearing knocks against the door.
These ears would rather hear a wind-grass song.
But I must stay until my debts are paid,
And I must serve the PUBLIC while I'm here,
Go forward, clean, unwelcomed, unafraid—
I'll serve this PUBLIC only for one year.
Some buzzards crave this carrion meat I have.
Let them have it and vomit to their grave.

397

I get so damned tired of pretty politeness
From sissy men in small-town soda fountains;
Maybe they equally despise the ruggedness
And sturdiness of the men from the mountains.
I know one thing surely—I know it well,
I'll never stand at a fountain jerking drinks
And taking tips—this life would be a hell;
Taking of tips is softer than making drinks—
I have no love for soft men in these places.
They stand all day, make drinks and take their tips—
These little doll-men with white girlish faces,
Soft-voiced with thin moustaches on their lips—
To hell with men who bow and scrape for tips;
With powdered chins, with rouged and moustached lips.

398

We laid him here to rest a warrior done
Upon a hill that shoulders to the sky.
We knew if he could only speak he'd ask to lie
Where he could hear the thunder of my gun.
To us no man had been a better friend
On earth than Nig; and when we laid him here,
Above his grave we paused to shed a tear,
Knowing he'd gone unto his journey's end.
We hear his midnight howling at the gate
No more when strangers pass; the rabbits play
Around the house and foxes have their way;
In tall damp back-yard weeds snakes writhe in wait.
Nig took the wrong trail when he took the track
Of Death— We called, but he could not turn back.

399

The possums now are free to roam the hill;
Blacksnakes are free to writhe out in the weeds;
The fox is free to roam and prowl and kill;
Rabbits are free to clean the lettuce beds—
Old Nig is dead and he can never rise.
Around his bones the dirt's begun to harden.
Old Nig is dead and dirt is in his eyes.
He sleeps upon the hill above the garden.
He was a slave to us for eighteen years.
He was a fighting dog unto the end.
And when he died we shed some useless tears
Over this warrior and this faithful friend.
Since Old Nig's gone we have a fear and dread
Of dangerous fire-fighting copperhead.

400

Two months and I go back where Old Nig lies.
The dogs have come, exposed this warrior's bones.
And over them are swarms of bright green flies.
I cover well this debris with pasture stones.
The pilfering dogs can come since he is dead,
Disturbing Old Nig's peace upon the hill.
Over his bones the rabbits make a bed,
And he cannot get free from Death to kill.
This warrior has found peace upon this hill.
He did not wake—I covered him with stones.
He will not wake—his long life chase is run.
He will not wake, though flies swarm on his bones.
He will not wake to heat of July sun.
I wonder if his master, Death, has found
For him great game and happier hunting ground.

401

Wood-moss is pretty on the hickory butts;
The dew is silver on green leaves of walnuts.
Ragweeds are decorative to wind-breaks;
Cool mud is soothing to bellies of snakes.
The wild-rose blooms are golden to their stems;
Grapevines are ornaments for black-oak limbs.
The autumn shoe-make berries are gay plumes
Among the autumn flowers alive with blooms.
And fox-fire in the rainy velvet nights
Is prettier than a thousand white starlights.
The smell of rotten logs and percoon blooms
Is sweeter to the nostrils than perfumes.
This cool recess is one fine place to dream,
Where sunlight filters on a mountain stream.

402

One night I dreamed of thorny wild rose banks
Far back among the Greenup County hills;
I dreamed of wild rose blossoms rank on ranks,
I dreamed of these and the sweet daffodils,
I dreamed of swallows in the thin blue air
And martins sitting on the martin-box,
I dreamed of rye and green corn waving fair,
I dreamed of certain nooks and pasture rocks,
I thought I'd seen my Vivien Aims on Sunday
And we had walked among the primrose blossoms;
I thought I'd followed our "Jim" mule on Monday
Where corn and pusley springs from earth's rich bosom.
This was my dream hitch-hiking from the South
When I woke in a Georgia cotton field
One July night in nineteen-thirty drouth.

403

I love blue evening skies and sounds of water
Seething in moonlit streams across the meadows.
I love to hear leaves talk in the wind stir
And katydids sing from the dew-drenched willows.
I love blue summer evenings in the hills;
I love to smell the green corn and the rye;
Walk out with Mother, hear the whippoorwills—
I love to hear the foxes slipping by.
I know these hills lie in the heart of me,
This corn is in the flesh and blood of me,
I know these people are a part of me,
And I a part of them, and choose to be—
And I, a part of them—this rugged tree;
A part of them throughout eternity.

404

I know how we must starve by writing verse
And as I read a new anthology
I think of hungry poets there must be.
But I know of the hungers that are worse
Than food hungers of poets writing verse.
The millionaire still craves a fatter purse.
The hungry hound-dog craves his master's dung.
I know an old maid craving to be young.
The shoplifter now craves a better store.
The whoremonger now craves a better whore.
Poets crave shelter to tarry in
And music from the pipes and violin.
Poets want paper for wind-words they've said;
Not bread alone, but poets need some bread.

405

I hate to see a dead rat in the rain.
I know where one now lies between corn-rows.
The hair has started slipping from the skin.
This rat is getting blue around the nose.
It picked up a straw in its clutched fore-toes
When it was bleeding, dying, in our garden.
This rat kept climbing cornstalks in the garden;
I watched one day and filled it full of holes.
I never picked it up from where it fell.
I left it there to rot upon the ground—
A hog-pen rat is dirtier than hell.
At night they have a painful squeaking sound.
I know this rat will not eat corn again.
I hate to see it rotting in the rain.

406

I love the smell of dead leaves in the rain.
I love the clean-sweet smell of rain-washed woods.
I love black sticks a-lying in the rain.
I love rain-dripping ferns in solitudes.
I think the blacksnakes love the April showers,
They wake from freezing sleep and shed their skins,
I think they love Spring rains and thunder showers.
Spring is the time for them new life begins.
I think the terrapin would love Spring rain.
It's buried now beneath the hardened ground.
Rain melts the earth and it will rise again.
The terrapins awaken to the sound
Of April thunder and downpours of rain.
The terrapins, blacksnakes and men love rain.

407

I've loved white drops of rain in January
Falling on last year harvest fields and leaves;
I've loved white streams of rain in January
Nosing down jet-black limbs of black-oak trees;
Rain dripping, dripping to the leaf-strewn ground—
Oh, how I love the lonesome thugging sound!
I could lie here beneath in a cold bed
And sleep—I think I could sleep here forever
And listen to the rain above my head.
I could sleep nestled like the rabbits sleep.
Surely, I could sleep silent as the dead
And dream my dreams—while the realities
Of wind and rain would double sapling trees.
I know I could sleep under rain forever.

408

I stood out in the January rain;
My face was lifted to the foul-rain-skies—
And silver needles of the January rain
Came pricking down into my face and eyes.
I love to taste this January rain.
I love to feel its coolness on my eyes.
It is a pleasure to this flesh and brain.
I stand under the foul January skies
And on a path near-by I hear men talk:
"This blasted day is hell on brutes and men."
"This mud so thick it's worse'n hell to walk."
"When I get home I'll change these clothes and then
I'll eat my supper, warm, and go to bed."
I must be crazy after all they've said.

409

The sky's washed-in with ribbon-clouds and stars.
And far away the dark hills reach the skies.
Among these hills beneath the winter stars,
In long earth-evened graves my proud kin lies.
In many moods I've cried to lie beside them—
When Life was done—lie there for many years—
These strong men conquerors of the fields that hide them—
These fighting men—these sturdy mountaineers.
But what is here, I stop to ask myself?
Yes what is here? Black hills and windy skies.
The viney blackberry hills, the black-stone cliff
And richer earth of my proud kin that lies—
Forever brothers to weed, root, and stone;
Tall brothers to the earth that strangers own.

410

If there are other virgin lands to conquer,
I feel like moving on to conquer them—
I feel like going on and living where
The unspoiled wooded hills are free to roam—
Going to cleaner air and brighter sunlight,
And going on to make a bark-shack home.
I am a brother to the hillside trees.
I am a brother to the mountain loam.
I think, sometimes, I speak too much of these;
But I hear them a-calling, "Brother, come."
And if there is a land with cleaner air
And brighter sunlight on green-wooded hills,
And rugged cliffs where clean white water spills—
I know someday I'll pack and journey there.

411

I love the sound of muddy waters here.
I hear their monotone both night and day.
I love these muddy waters flowing here.
I ponder on the things I think they say:
"I am a stream of living liquid here.
And I keep rolling over brush and stone.
Yes, I keep rolling, rolling year after year—
And night and day you hear my monotone.
You hear my shrieks of melancholy laughter
When I am rolling over channel stones.
You know at midnight I'm the singing river
And night and day you hear my monotones.
You know I'll flow forever and forever—
She-wish, she-wish, lop-lop, lop-lop, she-wish.
She-wish, she-wish, lop-lop, lop-lop, she-wish."

412

Wild tiger lilies bloom by Sandy River.
I walk there-by and pluck a lily blossom.
The wind blows and I see the green reeds quiver.
I see rank corn sprung from a Sandy bottom.
Sweet Lydia Doore and I walk here together.
We speak of vows we made—vows that can't last.
For once we thought our love would last forever,
But now we know our better days are past.
We hear today the Sandy River laughter.
We throw wild tiger lilies in the water.
We watch the little water rings come after.
This singing river laughs with a strange laughter.
And as we sit here-by so quiet of breath,
Lydia makes for her subject, "Jean Elizabeth."

413

And my Elizabeth Hale's in Tennessee
And Lydia Doore's by this Kentucky stream.
We sit together under this birch tree
And Lydia Doore is silent in a dream.
The caw-caw crow flies through the sycamore.
He flaps his wings and hurries to his mate.
And I sit silent by Sweet Lydia Doore.
The sun is down, the hour is growing late.
The moon comes up and rides above the leaves.
The dew falls on leaves of the sycamore.
The water moans—the night wind slightly grieves.
I say farewell to my Sweet Lydia Doore.
We walk together under dewy leaves.
The water whines along the pebble shore.
I say farewell to my Sweet Lydia Doore.

414

Now Lydia, go your way and I'll go mine.
You know you are unto a stream of water,
That sparkles where the sun creeps through the vine.
You sparkle once and then you're gone forever.
Remember, there's new water flowing after.
It sparkles where the sun creeps through the vine.
And Lydia Doore, you are this running water.
But Lydia, go your way and I'll go mine.
The sun that shines on Greenup County hills
Has shown down on much fairer girls than you:
Girls of the fields in Greenup County hills—
Girls rare in form with work of men to do—
Girls pretty as young sycamores—
Girls young and pretty as the Lydia Doores.

415

Farewell to you, my Mountain Lydia Doore.
Farewell to you and hills you live among.
I say farewell to you—I close the door
That shuts you and your life apart from me.
I can't forget the day we spent together;
The nights your heels cracked on the hard-wood floor;
And how we danced the whole night through together—
I can't forget you Mountain Lydia Doore.
And I remember on the early morn
When white stars slanted on the loose green trees,
How we went through the dewy fields of corn
And listened to the wind among corn blades.
Remember, Lydia Doore, these lines I write
Will not express our living for one night.

416

Those spacious realms of leafy green-crowned hills
And you will be forever dear to me—
Those spacious hills where moonlight water spills
And where the wind plays with the willow tree—
And there among those hills will be your shack—
A rutty wagon road will lead one there.
In memory this shack will call me back
When sprays of apple blossom scent the air.
The moonlight on the fields will call me back
And silver chords of wind among the leaves.
Some other stream will kiss its pebbled shore.
And white starlight will fall on other trees.
But I leave you, Sweet Mountain Lydia Doore.
And when I go I shall return no more.

417

Jenny, hear the wind talking to the corn
And the corn-bird a-tuning up his flute;
Watch him a-sitting there just acting cute
Bending the tassel of that stalk of corn.
A corn-bird just a-fluting to the corn!
I'd rather hear him play his violin,
It's more melodious for the loving wind.
Out in this pretty July morning weather
When wind and corn are speaking love together,
It would be better for the talking corn.
Jenny, morning is filled with purple haze
And it is not too late for better days—
The corn-bird will be fluting summer long
And all his little world be filled with song.

418

I've met you many times before, Defeat.
Not everytime we fought you blacked my eyes,
For many times I've staggered to my feet
And hit you hard enough to break your ribs.
You know, Defeat, I whipped you at the plow.
I fought you at hot furnaces of steel.
You whipped me at the circus, made a show of me—
Of me for men to see—and now I feel
That when we meet again, one man must kill.
I'll meet you face to face and fight you fair
Though it be midnight on the darkest hill—
I shall come unafraid to fight you there.
I want to drive my fist straight through your head
And leave you there, Defeat—beautifully dead.

419

Autumn will come upon us like a thief
And autumn winds will blow and dead leaves fall;
Autumn will come upon us—birds will call,
And drift upon the wind with the dead leaf.
The trees will flaunt their yellow, crimson, gold;
The mellow earth in stubbles fields will freeze;
The sheep will gather closer in the fold
And pasture cattle sleep beneath the trees.
Autumn will come and whistling winds will sweep
Across the broken fields with lonesome sound;
The rabbit in a bed of leaves will sleep
Until its blood is spilt upon the ground.
Autumn will be here soon, there is no doubt;
Winter will blow the lamp of autumn out.

420

Pity her now, don't tramp her in the mud
And leave one full of life as Jenny there;
Remember she is young and she is fair
And there is weakness in the human blood.
Glass Gossipers, you're first to cast the stones.
One sees your dagger missiles fly about—
You thrust at Jenny while she's down and out.
Glass Gossipers, better to rest your tongues.
Jenny is now a winter apple tree.
Wait till you see her blossom in the Spring.
Wait for the kind of fruit this tree will bear.
Remember when you pass this winter tree
And see it changed to Spring-time blossoming
You'll think of nakedness it used to wear.

421

My friends, a constable is too low down
For mountain men to touch when he is dead.
I knew a mountain man who shot one down;
He put a silver bullet through his head.
The constable came snooping to the still;
The shiner heard his hands a-breaking limbs
To make his path through bushes up the hill—
He got his rifle took a crack at him—
He went on working at his moonshine still.
And there were night winds snapping the dead brush
And midnight singing of the whippoorwill
And gases gurgling in the barrels of mash—
But only this, for all the night was still.
The constable lay dead near-by the still.

422

The men next day saw old Bill stiff and cold.
They said his mouth would make a trap for flies.
One laughed and laughed and said: "God-damn his soul—
He's snooping for the Devil—telling lies—"
We want the hungry hounds to bury him.
We want piss-ants to come and eat their share.
The wind and briars can sing the funeral hymn;
The skipper bugs can come and offer prayer.
For what to hell's a low-down constable?
Shoot him like you'd shoot rabbits to the ground;
Leave him for hounds to get their bellies full;
He did not earn a place beneath the ground.
Six feet of earth is far too much for him;
We'll let hound dogs and piss-ants bury him.

423

The acorns hit the ground like heavy drops
Of autumn water filtering through the leaves;
They fall when lazy winds shake the oak tops;
They come a-bouncing through the leafy trees.
The jay birds sit up in the oaks and quarrel
Among themselves—over the hollow limbs—
And they sit quarreling with the squirrels—
Squirrels are hiding acorn food from them.
The time for summer pasturing is brief.
Our cow is eating acorns from the tree;
Her udders shrivel like the autumn leaf.
Squirrels and birds, your harvesting suits me.
And harvesters glean from the lower limbs;
Our cow will go stone-dry if she gets them.

424

The earth cried out for rain—the rain crow prayed.
And Brother Oakes prayed for the rain to fall
Before the blistering ears of corn were made;
But wind too hot to breath and sun were all
Earth got— Her grass was brown and creeks were dry.
The horse manure was dry for tumble bugs;
There was no sign of rain upon the sky
To fall and green the browning pasture rugs.
The doodle-bug worked in a new-ground hole
While tumble bugs worked in the old field pasture.
They worked before the days turned wet and cold,
For then manure and tumble bugs were nastier.
And Brother Oakes and rain crows prayed for rain
To bring new life to thirsting roots again.

425

I see the blood of autumn in the wind,
The wine-red blood of apple tree and peach;
The yellow blood of poplar tree and beech;
I see the blood of autumn drifting in
The fence rows and the stools of green briar thickets;
I see trees still a-bleeding down red drops;
Black-oak, birch, elm, black gum; from their tall tops
The blood drips like fresh water from old spickets.
O blood of autumn, you are in my blood—
Red shoe-make blood is in my dead-leaf veins;
O mood of autumn, you are in my mood;
Only, your red of shoe-make blood remains
And mine does not—I am a naked tree—
The winds have blown—my autumn is on me.
(O mood of autumn, you are in my mood!)

426

The season killing starts today—guns speak
With tongues of fire and smoke in every hollow—
The wounded rabbit runs for a water seap—
The hunters and the yelping hound-dogs follow.
Hot guns speak under the red autumn sun;
The hot guns speak—the red-oak leaves are flying!
The shots ripped out the wounded rabbit's guts.
The rabbit falls on dead leaves—bleeding, dying.
The rabbit dies under the autumn sun.
The hunter slings its guts upon the ground.
He sacks his game—the rabbit chase is done.
The hounds eat guts and lick blood from the ground.
Mad guns speak on under the autumn sun.
More guts are ripped before the day is done.

427

This furred creature played in gray moonlight
Among the fodder stalks upon the hill;
He played on autumn leaf-strewn hills at night,
For night is not the time that hunters kill.
He ate the green grass growing under leaves;
He ate the red tea-berries from the stalks;
He trimmed the bark waist-high from hickory trees
And gathered waste-leaves from old cabbage baulks.
And all the nourishment he could get
He squeezed from earth—earth barren as a stone—
The leaves and bark and grass and tea berries,
And often he went hungry to the bone.
He loved to hop upon and sleep in leaves.
His fur was soft and pretty as the leaves.

428

The slaughtering guns now roar on every side
Out on the rain-damped fields in gray November;
The frightened covey breaks its family pride,
Each seeks a shelter in the barren timber.
There is no shelter in the barren timber;
There is no shelter in the sunless sky;
The LAW has set the appointed time November
For coveys of these timid birds to die.
They die from number threes that rent their bodies
The wounded seek refuge in the tall weeds
Where they would rather bleed and die alone
Than be hit with the barrel of the gun.
And now these timid birds must bleed and die
In a red wreckage on the gray December sky.

429

"Son," said my father, "take you a strong wife;
Take you a mountain girl strong as a tree—
It takes a tree to meet the winds of life.
Your Ma, she was the kind that suited me.
Get you a wife with eyes bright as a star
And teeth white as a thunder-cloud's white head;
Get one with cheeks red as the wild plums are
And ankles thin as runners on a sled.
And get yourself about six right pert sons
So they will carry on blood of their fathers;
And let them nurse from their strong mother's breasts;
Your six strong sons—maybe three strong daughters—
Raise them to be men in a world of men.
Let them take wives and multiply again."

430

"And son, get you a wife while you are young.
And don't you spend your good seed on a whore.
You get yourself a tall clean mountain woman,
Make you an oak log house with puncheon floor;
Sleep on a bed of leaves and live alone.
Go clear the fields and break the ground for corn,
At first you may find life hard as a stone;
Crop failure and your first child to be born.
But then move on, reach out and grab for life.
Go face this life together, hand in hand—
You be a man and have a decent wife.
You live together—multiply the land.
You two strong trees can stand the storm and strife.
You two strong trees will stand and understand."

431

"I took your Ma when she was twenty-one.
Your Ma was a straight tree and she was strong.
She was a fine young girl of right much fun.
I knowed your Ma and me could get along.
I cleared the land and used a bull-tongue stalk.
And with my bull-tongue plow I broke the land.
Your Ma she worked till corn was in the shock—
I've never seen a better corn-field hand.
She bore me four pert sons and three fine daughters.
The fever put two of your brothers in the clay.
She bore you well—we hardly had a Doctor.
Them boys of mine that's dead will rise someday.
Your Ma's been strong—she had a right good will.
Your Ma and me are going down the hill."

432

"And Jess, your Ma and me are getting old;
Your Ma and me went up the hill together.
We've started down the hill since we are old;
Your Ma and me are going down together.
But I remember when the sun did rise
Your Ma was young and straighter than pine timber.
Her hair was black—starlight was in her eyes.
Her lips were fine to kiss I remember—
But listen, Jess—the sun is setting now.
We must go down the hill the best we can.
The lines are getting deeper in her brow.
The shovel and the pick have killed this man.
Your Ma and me have clumb the hill together;
And we'll go down a-helping one another."

433

You are the greatest of my enemies.
I've never had an enemy like you.
You've picked the gnat-size flaws that no one sees.
Your one-track mind has power to construe.
This is your one-track mind's great specialty.
One can't expect much wiser thing from you;
Deliberately choose to be an enemy—
If you keep up your talk I think I'll teach
Lessons to you that you should have long learned.
One lesson is to slap you out of reach
Of things where you're not intimately concerned.
I know you'll fight me to the bitter end.
I'll not salve you to have you be my friend.

434

Here is a message to your crafty pack.
Let law pursue the course—to hell with you.
Remember, we shall stand to fight you back
And I shall give your men a curse or two.
Your peanut-minded men with right good sense;
They are deserving of such gifts as these—
I see them hanging straddle of the fence;
Awaiting hush-money with patience, ease—
They are such valiant types of citizenry;
The men for fight that I have long preferred—
Now gentlemen accept these gifts from me;
I am delighted to present these damns.
Two damns for Groan and Scout and one for Steave
And ten for Toodle Wormlake's empty sleeve.

435

You are a belly-acher with a rope
Tied round your neck where you can eat the grass;
A belly-acher with a mental scope
Of black-ants and your back is streaked with brass.
Your heart is brass; your tongue is cankered brass.
And round the radius of your pasture rope
Your tongue lolls out—you eat and laze and mope.
Do people fail to watch you when they pass?
Lakewood: You are their politician boar.
The stems of grass are dollars that you flank
Down your intestinal channel with a roar;
Manure for hypocrite and whore and crank.
When grass gets short they set and stake your chain;
Gives you the chance to eat high grass again.

436

If my inheritance is drink and gun,
I'm sorry; for it is an evil chance—
To kill a man there is no victory won.
Drunk men are children in a circumstance.
Oh, I have used a gun—I shot it well.
I shoot with steady nerve—my eye is true.
I see no points in always raising hell;
Trying to do the best my gun will do—
Trying to take the lives I connect with—
To take a human life it would be hell.
One sire took lives and notched them on his guns.
And people say that blood is sure to tell.
I am victim of circumstances if one's
Inheritance is true—Life, what the hell!

437

I want a shack among Kentucky hills
With earth enough to raise my food to eat.
And I wish to attend my neighbors' ills.
I want to tramp the soft earth with my feet,
And squeeze old last year's leaves between my hands.
I want red-autumn in a leaf-blood scene.
I want grim winter with his desolate lands.
I want fair Spring with her loose green-snake green.
I want the summer with green fields of grain—
Just slightly moving under summer haze.
When I go off I seek the land again—
I cry for the good earth and rustic ways.
And I shall own a shack among the hills;
A shack among the music of the hills.

438

I have grown sick enough for food to perish
When I tramped roads that led me far away;
And I remembered then the land I cherish,
The land whose bosom loam I turn today.
I loved the road and high white floating skies.
I loved to rove with wind and be as free—
I loved the roads that seemed to meet the skies—
I loved the roads—the roads were home to me.
Like crows so many times I searched for food.
I sought rich gardens with ripe red tomatoes,
Green corn to roast, and turnips for to peel—
When one is hungry it is fair to steal—
And I have graveled out young sweet potatoes.
I love the road—but I prefer the loam;
A place for one to sleep and make a home.

439

These are the hills that's native to my blood.
These are the hills I choose to live among
And die among and let them drink my blood.
I drank of water here when I was young—
Of lonesome water, and I shall come back
To drink of lonesome water many times,
For lonesome waters keep calling me back—
I shall return to plow and spin my rhymes.
These waters will forever call me back—
The ox-eyed daisies are inviting me;
Sweet-williams, beggar-lice, pea-vine and phlox
And brown-thrush singing in a cherry tree
And scraggy pines that grow among high rocks;
You can see why the hills are calling me
With security as great as mountain rocks.

440

And I have never felt security
Sleeping in haystacks under different stars.
I've learned the highlands are the place for me
Where I can drive the milk cows to the bars—
Sit there and listen to the whippoorwills
And smell the white sprays of the apple blossoms.
There's something to one's life in lonely hills,
When one smells April winds from clover blossoms.
There's something to the wind among the trees,
Rustling the leaves under the white starlight,
And upturning the silver maple leaves.
There's something to the waters in moonlight.
I know the land where-on I choose to be—
High black-oak hills in eastern Kentucky.

441

When Spring in me has ceased to be no more
And rain has ceased to rouse my roots to growth,
I shall remember in my deep heart's core,
Dear Quadroon Mott, the girl I loved in youth.
My Quadroon Mott lived by the Sandy River.
Her father's lands were fair and broad to see.
Quadroon and I walked by the winding river;
Brown thrushes sang their songs for her and me.
The bittern sounded in the April green.
Kildees rose calling cross the light-green meadows.
A water snake slid down past our love scene.
Snake feeders played under the drooping willows.
Birch leaves in silver wind were tremulous
Brown moving Sandy water spoke to us.

442

We went together to dark woods at night,
Beneath the barren winter black-oak boughs.
We saw their chiseled outlines in starlight.
We stood beneath these oaks and made our vows.
We pledged good faith beneath white winter skies.
Our vows were witnessed by the sentinel trees.
We were alone out where the night wind cries.
I hear night winds and pause and think of these.
I know that vows are petals to be broken.
I know that Quadroon Motts are hard to find—
I know these words are better left unspoken
Than fling them free to blowing winter wind.
The black-oak stain is on that mortal vow.
Had I but known, it would not be so now.

443

And there are meadows I have not forgot
And blossoms bloomed thereon but bloomed to fade,
And I walked there beside dear Quadroon Mott—
And on that scene some of these lines were made.
And far away we heard a pheasant drum
And saw late larks ascending to the stars,
We heard one call and saw the cattle come
Trailing up by the river to the bars.
The apple trees were blooming in the yard
With blossoms whiter than the April skies—
Tall tender grass—the wind bent down a sward,
The wind passed on and then the grass did rise.
Your clean white-blossom soul, dear Quadroon Mott,
Blooms on a meadow I have not forgot.

444

The heavens were so far and blue above.
The maple leaves upturned by wind were silver.
The plowboy sang so sweetly in the cove.
He sang a song about his country Love.
He sang of moon and stars and skies above.
His plow was turning the dew-jeweled clover.
He stopped his mules to watch the crows fly over,
To black pines silhouetted on the skies.
He turned his ear to lonely bittern cries.
The bittern cries meant the cold days were over.
Lucy and I roved on the Sandy bottoms.
We were young lovers, eager, lithe and free—
Lovers of fireflies on the clover leas—
Of winds and starlight in the loose green trees;
Kentucky Spring-times, summers and her autumns.

445

Let us march on, the power to live is ours.
The power to grow in rich and sterile soil—
We shall be numbered hickories, thorns, flowers.
We shall feel sunshine, wind, rain and know toil.
We are blossoms to flourish and decay.
Our rugged beauty only lasts awhile.
We grow in season, perish in decay
When autumn bleak-winds blow our blooms away.
Our mating season was a little while.
The warm Spring rains were sweet to roots of us.
The summer suns were good to leaves of us—
And when winds blew our leaves were tremulous,
And there was music in the leaves of us
And there was fragrance in wind-words of us.

446

The yellow sun will shine upon our stems
When they are dead and drooping to the ground.
The winter sun will bless us in our dreams
When we are too dead to remember dreams
Our petals will drift on with a strange sound—
Their crumbled forms may fall upon a street
Of winter earth and there meet sure decay
There let winds blow our shriveled forms away.
On fallow fields let us dance on ghost feet,
For lives to me are very small, it seems—
We are as timeless, futile, thin-soil flowers—
One difference is our skull of crafty dreams:
We have less beauty and we have more power—
And yellow suns of winter shine on dreams
When they shine on our dead, dead winter stems.

447

Jean Torris, you and I have gone together.
We walked together when the moon was full;
When winds were sobbing in the mountain heather.
Jean Torris, you were straight and beautiful,
And I was proud to walk beside of you.
You were as pretty as a willow tree
When its sharp leaves turn silver in the wind.
We have gone out and danced the night together—
Swinging to rhythms of the violin—.
You neatly patterned as a willow tree.
Your auburn-hair so naturally was curled
With softness of a blossom first unfurled,
Your eyes were dew-drops in the early morn,
The sun left hanging to the blades of corn.

448

There will not come another time like this.
April is in the wind and we are free.
And you and I have found this April's bliss—
The white star-light is hanging through the tree.
We walk a broken street—you close by me—
And not too close the house we part and kiss.
I fear the barking dog will rouse your mother
And she'll peek wistfully from a dark window.
She has forgotten how she kissed your father
Under the April-night tree's lengthy shadow.
Wonder if we'll forget when we have married
And my tall son and your small daughter meet
Out in the moonlight in such April bliss
And put their lips together with an April kiss.

449

The night wind sings above us, Dear Jean Torris,
The night wind sings to us a lullaby.
The white stars swarm above us, Dear Jean Torris,
They gleam through fingers of the dark pine tree.
The katydid is singing in the corn.
The whippoorwill is singing from a log—
And these we hear and love tonight, Jean Torris—
These and shrill piping of a lean swamp frog.
We walk this night together, Dear Jean Torris.
We love these songs and the wind's lullaby.
I think these are words of the lullaby:
"Go out tonight, you young, and love tonight,
For lovers fine as you are under clay—
Go out tonight and drink of the starlight
For soon all hearts are silent under clay."

450

Be in me, mood, like sap is in the tree.
Run through me like the blood flows in my veins.
Life is all fiction, Death is eternity!
Then Life, good-by, when only dust remains.
Be in me, moods—dark as eternal night;
Incessant as blue water leaping stones!
Be in me, moods, when I walk in starlight,
When I walk with gods of the wind alone.
Be in me, moods, when the pink peach tree blooms
Set barren hills in early March aflame.
Be in me, moods, when the white apple blossoms
Go shriveling to the dust from whence they came.
Be in me, moods, eternal; for my dust
Will nourish growth to weeds from my rich bosom!

The
Enriched
Resignations

451

In summer when the pasture fields are green
And trees are leaved with idle swaying leaves,
The Plum Grove hills are pretty to be seen
By mortal eyes that love the grass and leaves.
Farmhouses stand upon the yellow banks
Where children and the chickens wear out grass
And leave their toys and feathers on the ground.
And here one seldom sees a person pass—
And here, a painted house is scarcely found.
The Plum Grove water runs in tiny streams.
From Plum Grove hills three streamlets flow away,
And minnows play in clear blue Plum Grove streams,
And water snakes and turtles have their way.
The turtles catch the minnows, so they say.
The water snake lies in the sun and dreams.

452

There is one hill among the Plum Grove hills
That gleams in sunlight from the hills afar.
It is the place where men have lost their ills;
It is the place where dead of Plum Grove are.
And one can see the headstones clustered thick
When one looks from the Dysard hills afar—
And one can see the myrtle-mantled niche
Down in one corner where the old graves are.
And one can see the winding rutty road
That leads to where the clustered headstones gleam;
In summer one can see grain by this road,
And one can see a silver meadow stream—
A sunlit stream and white as any star,
Flowing away from where dead people are.

453

There sets upon the hill the Plum Grove Church,
And from its cupola a white spire gleams—
The shining headstones face the Plum Grove Church;
And from each side one sees a meadow stream.
They flow westward and farther on they meet—
And farther still, they reach the Sandy River.
But here men have met glory or defeat.
They are lain side by side to sleep forever.
And all around grass-fields are fair to see.
The birds build over where these people dream.
And woodchucks bore for worms in a dead tree.
The streams flow on to meet a greater stream.
And men go down to meet eternity—
One planted for each white headstone that gleams;
Many have markers such as dead weed stems.

454

A thousand seeds were planted on this hill;
A thousand seeds and never one will sprout.
Never a-one has sprouted from this hill,
And never a-one will rise without a doubt.
All that was left to do was plant them here
And bed them down so they would be forgot—
Let rotten seed lie here for many a-year;
Lie hidden from the living eyes to rot.
Many were planted on this Plum Grove hill.
The mean and bad and good, the old and young,
The wicked, saved, rich, poor, the strong, the ill,
And toothless women with their wagging tongues—
They all are planted on this Plum Grove hill
And cannot wish their neighbors good and ill.

455

The bright stars hang above the windy hill.
The tall oaks tower to the wind-blown skies.
Beneath these oaks the Plum Grove men lie still.
They lie forever still with blinded eyes.
The quarter-moon comes up—the wind blows hard.
The light of stars and moon fall on the grass.
The night winds sing through each tall tangled sward,
And Plum Grove dead lie deaf beneath the grass.
White stars can swarm above their graves at night;
Their light can filter through green tops of trees.
But Plum Grove men will not know of star light
And summer dew that jewels black oak leaves.
The dead of Plum Grove sleep beneath the hill.
Beneath oak roots these men are sleeping still.

456

Strong muscled men that followed at the plow
And tilled the clearings round their mountain homes
Come to Plum Grove at last—they're sleeping now—
Strong sturdy women—makers of these homes
Lie close beside their muscled men that plowed
The rugged slopes and made the daily bread.
They sleep beneath a quilt of dirt and cloud
And wind and star, but in a lasting bed.
They sleep beneath where flower petals curl—
They do not dream of wind and grass and flowers.
They sleep beside each other in a world
Of silence and a world that kills their powers.
They sleep by those in life they feared to trust;
And those they fought and kilt, since all are dust.

457

Here is the hill where many youth are laid;
Hauled here by wagon, hearse, ox cart and sled.
This is the hill where roses bloom and fade
And throw their petals down among the dead.
This is the hill where life goes back at last
To dust—the hill that holds a thousand lives.
Some have grave markers giving their brief past;
Telling their titles such as husbands, wives,
Sisters, uncles, aunts and brothers, mothers,
Soldiers and infant sons and infant daughters.
No sinners, but all saints and saintly lovers—
Their pasts as calm and peaceful as still waters—
All Plum Grove headstone indications show,
A heaven is above—a hell, below.

458

These stars that shine above the slabs tonight
Are beautiful for mortal eyes to see.
May roses nod in wind and white starlight,
Thick leaves talk in the tops on each oak tree,
White yuccas point up to the golden moon,
The green-briars quiver to night floating skies.
Winds whisper to the yuccas, stars and moon;
These night winds whisper to the dead that lie
Down in a narrow room blind to the moon.
Like milk-white worms spun in stout cocoons.
Maybe the dead dream that they will rise soon
Like a worm turns butterfly in his cocoon;
A butterfly to greet the fresh May roses
And flit above dead dust that still reposes.

459

I shall be numbered with the Plum Grove dead
When time has come for me to lie in clay.
For me songs will be sung and prayers be said
To help one on not saintly in his day.
Old women in black shawls will kneel and pray.
The Shepherd some consoling words may say
When crumbling looser dust upon my clay.
I'd love to be alive and standing there
And listen to their songs and words of prayer.
I'd love to watch the old men shovel clay
And throw it in on me and hear them say:
"This is Mitch Stuart's boy we're puttin here.
And men, the clay will hold him here at last.
He's not the man that his old kinsmen were—
Not like old Mitch, and did not live as fast."

460

If I could speak to them I think I'd say:
"Old mothers of the hills, I love your prayers.
Good Shepherd of the hills, the words you say,
I'll keep them in the bosom of this clay.
You are the greatest people on this earth.
I know you are—I've known you since my birth.
And in the end you give to me your prayers,
Wishing me well in darkness that's to come."
They're disappointed in this son of theirs.
I found life was not big enough for me.
I did not think of immortality.
"One life to live," was my philosophy.
The good Earth was and is a friend to me,
And good as Earth are Plum Grove friends I have;
The last to bear me to a Plum Grove grave.

461

Myrtle Weir lies on this Plum Grove hill.
She was hauled here to sleep in nineteen-three.
She and her first-born Trevis were left here
To sleep under the grass and cedar tree.
She paid the price of love at twenty-six;
She died of measles and a cold child-birth
And lies beneath green grass and last year's sticks.
She little dreams of love down in the earth.
The wind blows through the fence around her lot.
The rusty iron fence can't hold the wind.
The wind will whisper Myrtle is forgot.
The bull-grass knows—it listens to the wind.
The cedars listen and the golden-rod.
The house is dead where Myrtle prayed to God.

462

It was not Willie's fault that Myrtle died;
She bore his child, but he was not to blame.
Willie Weir took Myrtle McElhaney his bride
And they lay down together when desires came.
Sweet as peach blossom were her lips and breath;
Sweet as peach blossoms blowing in the Spring.
They dreamed of love, they did not think of death,
For they were free to love and dance and sing—
They did not dream of Plum Grove hill, their doom
When they plowed and cut tall weeds from the corn—
She worked with Willie's baby in her womb—
They talked in secret when it would be born.
It was not seven months till Myrtle heard
The baby flutter in her like a bird.

463

And when the measles and the cold child-birth
Put Myrtle and her Trevis under the loam;
Willie could not bear his cabin hearth,
It was too lonely there to make his home.
And on dark nights when rain fell to the ground
And lightning streaked the valleys and the hills,
Men could hear in the grave-yard a strange sound;
A wailing plaintive as the whippoorwill's.
And Willie never took another bride;
And Willie lived till he was thirty-six.
And then they laid him down beside his bride
Beneath the green grass and the last year's sticks;
And no one now has heard the wailing sound
Since Willie Weir is sleeping underground.

464

"Why do you whisper, Grass? Why tell the Trees?
Whispering Grass, the Trees don't need to know,
For don't you know the Trees will tell the Breeze
Of Lovers who carved their names here long ago?
Why do you tell your secrets to the Trees?"
"Young Poet who remembers but the Grass,
Lovers in buggies coming to these trees.
Your Mother and your Father once came here
And cut their names upon that gnarled beech.
They were young lovers and the tree was young.
They cut the names as high as they could reach.
I remember a tune your Father hummed—
And I shall whisper for I am the Grass;
And I shall tell the old, old things that pass."

465

Beadie Blevins sleeps here beside Mont Reeves.
They were once lovers driving to this grove.
Why do you whisper, Grass? Why tell the Trees?
Why tell the Trees the secrets of their Love?
For Beadie Blevins and her Mont lie under
The sterile earth where they were born and raised.
Why tell the Trees and make the tall Trees wonder
Why they would live unmarried all their days.
What does it matter now you Whispering Grass?
Why tell the Trees and be a Tattle Tongue?
Years roll and generations of men pass—
Beadie and Mont had one time to be young.
And listen, Grass, they paid the price of love.
They sleep with their ten children in the grove.

466

John Forshee and his wife Birdie are
Buried under the beech trees side by side.
Their mother's quilts are dirt and wind and star;
And John is still the groom—Birdie, the bride.
The moon rides high above their beds tonight;
The moon rides high above the beech tree grove;
Their lichen stones are gray in the moonlight
Where John and Birdie little dream of love.
How can they dream of love since they became
Blood for the beech-tree roots, food for the grass.
Why do you whisper, Grass— the season came
In their young lives for love—why whisper, Grass?
They knew they could not love and love forever,
But they would sleep and sleep forever.

467

Ye moaning winds, what are you to the dead?
What are you and the dead leaves to them now?
All that was said for them has long been said,
And they dream not of forest, field, and plow.
Ye moaning winds, why tell them all you know?
There is no need in talking to the dead—
The dead are sleeping soundly here below,
And roots of fern and grass sink to their beds.
Ye moaning winds, why meddle with the dead
That long have slept upon the Plum Grove hill—
They lie forever in their narrow beds,
Down in the nether world where all is still;
Where no man moves, but ringed worms still writhe.
Don't whisper Winds, they are not men alive.

468

There is a mountain warrior sleeping here
Beneath the briars, poke-berry stalks and grass;
And no one dreams a warrior's sleeping here
Where the dead lie and living seldom pass.
But tall red men scooped out a shallow grave;
With tomahawks they scooped the rooty ground.
They left a Roaming Wolf—a bravest Brave—
They left him sleeping in a little mound.
Old Roaming Wolf sleeps in a world his own.
And he will sleep though men will come and pass
Over his bones that long have turned to stone.
His flesh and blood have been food for the grass.
His gods: the Sun and Moon and stars look down
Upon his mound of Happy Hunting Ground.

469

And now who ever hears of Sadie Blaine?
Who sees dirt on her back, straw in her hair?
For many years, Sadie in earth has lain;
Her grave is flat and not a marker there.
I think some old men know of Sadie Blaine.
They loved wild Sadie Blaine in her own fashion.
Some say they have not seen her like again;
A woman with her beauty, pride, and passion—
Now Sadie sleeps—her passion and her pride
Are gone—her beauty has returned to dust.
She sleeps: Not knowing whom she sleeps beside.
It does not matter for they are all dust.
Until in earth wild Sadie Blaine was laid,
Married women were jealous and afraid.

470

One doubts if virgin maids will get as much
From their clean lives as Sadie Blaine has gotten!
One doubts if married women get as much
As Sadie Blaine whose morals were so rotten!
The red rose blooms as sweetly on her grave;
The grass as green and yuccas bloom as white
As they do on the decent, saint, and knave.
The Moon and Sun and stars shine over her
Since she is bedded down to sleep the night;
The winds blow through the green grass over her
And whispers to her in the long dark night.
Like decent women dead, she's ceased to hear
Her name spoken among the living here.

471

She thought that beauty of the flesh was all—
The beauty of the flesh in Sadie Blaine;
And Sadie harkened to each lusty call,
Knowing each passion would not come again.
Wild Sadie Blaine: Flower for men to use;
Her passion-fragrance entering many lives.
Wild Sadie Blaine: Flower for men's abuse;
Her beauty was despised by lovers' wives.
But Sadie Blaine was here for eyes to see.
She met life with a smile and unafraid—
She met life with a smile and she was free,
Despite the accusations good wives made.
Heaven and hell she doubted—the grave she despised.
The curtain fell: what rolled before her eyes?

472

For her red wine is standing in the glass
And long, long silenced are the violins—
And silenced are the winds above and grass,
For Sadie's ears are deaf to whispering winds.
Wild Sadie Blaine is doomed to hear no more
The secrets lovers whispered to her ears.
Wild Sadie Blaine is doomed to dance no more;
Of lovers' wives she'll have but little fears.
Now she lies out of mind under the weeds,
And only winds have prayed for Sadie Blaine.
Her should-be children are abortion seeds
And they are planted not to sprout again.
The dirt and dark and rain are just to her,
Though people say there was not much to her.

473

Here lies William Charlie, he took his life.
When he was plowing in the field one day
He went back to the house and found his wife
Lying in bed with Honorable Will Day.
He took his pistol—shot Will through the heart
And then he unlaced Minnie Charlie's side.
The two lay dead—just barely pulled apart;
Honorable Will, and Minnie, William's bride.
Then William took Will's widow for his wife,
But William Charlie grieved for his young bride.
His mind dwelt on a pistol and blood-knife,
And the young bride he had lain down beside.
One Saturday he painted the town red,
Went home and put a bullet through his head.

474

Honorable Will Day's widow asked that Will
And William's Minnie be buried side by side.
And they now lie in peace upon the hill
And Minnie's William lies there-by his bride.
And people pass and wonder where lies Will
And where lies William and where lies the bride.
They have no markers sleeping on this hill.
Three lovers lie a-sleeping side by side.
Minnie may love to hold the hand of Will
But give her body to the young bridegroom;
But walls between the houses on this hill
Keep them apart and each sealed in his room.
They sleep: William, Minnie, Honorable Will.
And they will sleep forever on this hill.

ANICE BEALER   475

Now he belongs to Plum Grove's rotting dead
And he lies silently upon this hill.
And I remember many words he said
Before his brain was dust and tongue was still.
"See here, by-god, I tend my business here.
I have my land, I raise my grub to eat;
And I been here nigh onto seventy year.
I raised nine children, put them on their feet.
I never go to church—I do not pray.
See here, by-god, my church is in the woods.
On Sundays I get out and spend the day
In the green temples—God's cool solitudes.
See here, by-god, I'm just old Anice Bealer;
A damn good farmer and a cattle dealer."

476

"See here, by-god, you see my timothy meadows.
You see my tall green corn and rank potatoes.
You see how plump and sleek my cattle grow.
You see my peppers and my red tomatoes.
You could not chain old Anice in a town
If these few snags he has could gnaw the chain.
I want to be out where the sun shines down
On me in Spring a-plowing fields again.
See here, by-god, you see the horns of plenty
Each way you turn to granary, loft and stack.
I cheat no man—I save each copper penny.
See here, by-god, feel of this leather sack.
See here, by-god, no preacher's getting any.
My neighbors borrow, but they pay me back."

477

"I trust my neighbors—never take a note.
I know them that are honest as the day;
For in each breast beneath a ragged coat
There beats an honest heart of human clay.
See here, by-god, my neighbors are good men.
The words of these old men are good as gold.
And if we trade I never question when
I'll get my pay for land and cattle sold.
This is the way I live among my neighbors.
We try to live and let each other live.
When one is sick we help him with his labors.
We see-saw round and give and take and give.
And if I deal with men I do not know
I take a scrap of paper for to show."

478

"These temple hills and harvest fields of grain
Are all the heaven that I want for me.
For after death I'd love to plow again
And spend my Sundays out where I could see
Green fields, white skies— No heaven with bright faces
For me—gold streets and harps and white silk clothes.
I want this farm with its familiar places—
The singing creek, pine trees, and nesting crows.
I want the yellow sunlight on my corn,
I want to see June morning glories climb
Corn stalks and freshly blossom in the morn,
I want to hear winds hum some old lost rhyme.
And this is all the heaven that I crave;
And this is all I want beyond the grave."

479

"Last Wednesday morning when I went to shave
I got my razor, mug, and brush and paper.
Not one wind blowed—that paper cut a caper
Out of the house and to a Plum Grove grave.
And there it stopped beside my dead child's grave.
And then I went and got another paper.
See here, by-god, it cut another caper.
I growed so nervous that I could not shave.
See here, by-god, that is, I feel a token;
I'll soon be planted there beside my son.
And that before the land next spring is broken;
And that before the deep snows melt and run.
Now time goes by—I'm nigh on seventy-four.
I never seen a thing like that before."

480

"And when I'm gone I'll bet that you will see
My children then come back and fight and fuss
Over the gold I have left here with me—
I'm glad I will be dead to miss the muss.
For they will come right here to get the gold.
They'll come before my coffin has been made;
Before my face is shaved and body's cold.
I know they'll come before my body's laid
Down in the grave Bird Skinner digs for me.
And all they'll want's my money and my lands.
They'll plant no shrubs above my wife and me.
Sometimes they'll have reunions and shake hands
And eat their fine grub under some shade tree—
A man nigh seventy-four well understands."

481

"See here, by-god, I hate to leave this world.
I hate to leave and let earth be my doom.
I must be gone when black-oak leaves unfurl,
I must be gone when meadows are in blossom.
I must be gone when brassy cow-bells ring
In yellow blossoms of sweet eglantines.
I must be gone when house wrens nest and sing
And feed their young among porch creeper vines.
And not one of my nine kids will come back.
They'll say they've found an easier life in town.
Not one will come and keep a money sack
And do hard work when summer suns beam down.
Not one will come though these hills call them back.
They'll sell my farms when I am planted down."

482

"And all I hope is I don't live to see
My meadows broken by the plow next Spring,
Or circle saws a-going through my trees,
Or porch vines torn away where my wrens sing.
I hope if I am dead I can't remember
Just how much harm the plow will do my meadow,
Just how much harm the ax will do my timber.
It takes the time to grow tall trees, I know.
When I am dead if I remember well,
I think I would turn over in my grave.
See here, by-god, I'll be confined in hell
When people come to take all I have saved.
They'll have me foul down in this little hell.
By-god, a man is foul down in the grave."

483

I do not know how Anice Bealer died.
I was not there to see his last breath go.
I do not know if people laughed or cried,
But I do know he died when January snow
Covered his granary, his loft and stack,
And laid so lightly on the frozen ground.
I know his children came and then went back.
I know how winds blew loud with lonesome sound
And left oak limbs so sparingly of leaves.
I know how winds sang on the snowy moors
And blew wheat straws into the viney eaves
And swept the corn chaff off the granary floors.
And I do know that Anice Bealer lies
Under a sheet with pennies on his eyes.

484

And all I know is what the neighbors said
About his children when they all came back.
A few short breaths before the man was dead
They said one girl had stolen the gold sack
And nine were fussing over lands he had.
If he had come to life he would have said:
"Get out of here before I do go mad.
Now stop this fuss, for I shall soon be dead.
Please stop this fuss, for I shall soon be cold.
Now death has numbed my feet and tongue and hands.
Get out of here and take this sack of gold.
Get out of here and take my home and lands.
Get out of here, for I shall soon be cold.
Get out of here and take my sack of gold."

485

His heaven now may be green fields of corn
And yellow sun and clean white spacious skies,
And morning glories on a dewy morn.
And it may be the grave where-in he lies—
I do not know just what his heaven is
Since he is sleeping peaceful here below.
It may be silence and it may be bliss
Under the frozen earth and January snow.
But I do know his old mules neigh for him.
And I do know he's missed among his neighbors.
The winter wind sings a sweet dirge for him
But Anice Bealer's resting from his labors.
Surely he does not hear the lonesome sound
Of winter winds that swept the frozen ground.

486

The time moves swiftly on and never dies.
The snow has melted and the waters run
In little streamlets flashing in the sun.
The grass is green where Anice Bealer lies.
And high and white are changing April skies.
Black crows fly in the light of yellow sun.
Men go to work before the day's begun.
Men go to work, for time so swiftly flies.
And now the Bealer meadows are turned under.
The land is streaking with deep yellow cuts.
The crash of falling trees is like low thunder.
The ox cart and the rain are leaving ruts.
The tall horse weeds are growing round the shack.
The farm is calling, but no one comes back.

487

He would not give his flesh and blood to steel,
For he was young—he would not be a slave
And let his flesh and blood be turned to steel—
Just steel awhile and then a Plum Grove grave.
Think, live for ever on that silent hill—
Silent among the saint like and the knaves,
Silent among the other unmarked graves—
Out where it is so lonesome and so still.
He'd rather take his body out and kill
The flesh of his with his own hands than have
His body tortured down to death with steel
And then be buried in a pauper's grave.
He said, To hell with steel, and barred the door.
To hell with steel, he would return no more.

488

He said farewell to steel—a long farewell.
He said farewell, for he would not return—
It was all over and he had rebelled
To waste his body where the forge shops burn.
Farewell to all—the hammers in the rack;
The tongs and cleavers by the water hole;
The cinder cart and shovels on the track.
Farewell to furnaces so dark and cold—
It was all over now—he prayed to see
The time when all the sheds would turn to rust,
He prayed to see men going to the land
Before steel laid their bodies to the dust.
He said forever and a long farewell.
He said forever to his world of steel.

489

That afternoon before he left the mill
The crane hooks slipped, four tons of thin sheet steel
Came down and mashed his body to the floor—
They trucked him out like men do hogs they kill
Through well-fanned corridors and empty doors.
Tom Leadingham would speak of steel no more.
Tom is under the cover on the hill.
If he could speak, he'd speak to Sadie Blaine,
For him and Sadie had once lived together
And Sadie got his pay checks at the mill.
If he could speak, he would ask Sadie Blaine
To come and lie in bed with him again—
For he was lonely in his narrow cell
And she could lie and comfort him a spell.

490

The years go by, but Tom does not come back
In time to see the steel sheds turned to rust
And weeds grow tall enough to hide the track.
He does not know the steel mill men now dust.
He does not know of men gone to the lands.
They said farewell to steel—a long farewell.
And they are gone—he cannot shake their hands.
For friends of Tom's it is all over now.
Machines are silent and forge shops are cold,
And silent is the thunder of their strife.
And yet will flesh of men be bought and sold—
Sold to a hill at the dear price of life.
Life will be sold as long time does last,
Be sold and hidden in a past that's past.

491

The darkness hovers down upon the hill
Like a chicken hovers on her early brood.
White stars beam through green leaves where all lie still,
And on the April grass they leave a flood
Of silver light—some silver in their night!
The wind and grass sing in a playful mood.
They are unheard by those now sleeping under
A quilt of dirt and wind and sky and star.
These sleepers sleep full sound through April thunder—
Asleep where good and bad of Plum Grove are—
All sleeping now beneath the heavy door—
A jail to which no jailer keeps a key—
All sleeping now—the rich, the thief, the poor,
All sleeping in their small eternity!

492

Some say the night is kind to all young lovers
When they are fast asleep and out of mind;
But I prefer to walk above with lovers
Than trust those saying that the night is kind.
Life is too full of life at twenty-five!
The earth and stars and skies are great to me—
I know I'd rather be a man alive
Than have the black oak boards to cover me.
For days have come of rugged loveliness
And I have met such girls as Jean, Elizabeth—
The richest lips of all to mine now press.
And speaking secret things I waste my breath.
I want to live, since I know youth is kind.
I hate to lie low now and out of mind.

493

Here lies in Plum Grove earth Tennessee Bealer
She was the daughter-in-law of Anice Bealer.
She died too young of premature child-birth.
Her five young children saw her laid in earth.
They hauled her on a wagon to the hill
And there they prayed for her a lofty prayer.
They left her in the silence on the hill;
They left her sleeping with her baby there.
There are some things that I can still remember
The songs they sang—words of their lofty prayer—
Red roses on white snow in cold December—
I still remember five old women there—
One said: "Tennessee was sure a lady.
For she met Death a-trying to save her baby."

494

And Fonnis Bealer went on preaching "God"—
He soon grew tired living the single life.
He soon forgot his dead wife under sod
And Fonnis Bealer went to hunt a wife.
He found a woman on the streets of town.
He took her to his first bride's wedding bed.
And "God" became a notion in his head
When he was sleeping with his Lettie Brown.
And Lettie Brown became the Reverent's lady.
She ran Tennessee's children from their home.
She ran them all off but the youngest baby.
She told them now to go and find a home—
Reminding them, they were not born to her,
And she was boss and wife of Fonnis Bealer.

495

The oldest son, Rodney, was just a boy.
He found refuge in corn-fields of Illinois.
He husked corn for a farmer—slept at night
Under the autumn stars in a corn stack—
Rodney was used to Kentucky star-light
And he was used to sleeping in a shack.
The fever struck him like frost nips a weed—
They put him in a box and sent him back.
And now he's planted here, a Plum Grove seed—
Corn-fields may call, but he will not go back.
Rodney Bealer is sleeping by his mother.
Sassafras sprouts are growing by their side.
They're growing tall and shading out the clover.
And Fonnis walks on earth with his new bride—
Too busy to cut sprouts from her grave-side.

496

It was Tennessee Bealer's last request
That blue larkspurs be planted on her breast.
Rodney planted them there before the sprouts
Grew down and sank their roots into her breast—
He planted them above her taking rest.
The larkspurs grow in patches there-about,
For they have spread from under shade to sun.
They grow among the sank-field vines that run
And climb the sprouts to blossom in the sun!
The blue lark-spurs are pretty on her mound.
The wind bends them among the sank-field's hair.
The wind blows the blue petals to the ground
And shriveled down to death it leaves them there,
Where Rodney and his mother sleep full sound.

497

Here lies young Martha Boggs in Plum Grove earth.
She sacrificed her life for her child's birth.
She left two children with her worthless man.
And soon Sam Boggs wed to a worthless woman.
The roses bloom above where Martha lies,
And when the roses bloom the larkspur dies.
Sam has five children by his second bride.
And one is sleeping by his first bride's side.
May roses wet with dew stoop down to them;
Tall green sassafras sprouts root down to them.
But the wind cannot sing a song to them—
Their cozy rooms are too deep under ground.
Their night of rest may be too long for them.
It is the sweetest rest that they have found.

498

The house where Martha lived has gone to wrack.
The roses grow and blossom 'mong the briars.
The house is doomed and only Sam comes back;
He comes and crawls between the rusty wires.
This place has memories for old Sam Boggs.
Here stands the weather-beaten chimney stack.
The lizards sun upon the pile of logs.
Something to Sam the years keep calling back.
He can't forget the days with his first bride
He spent here-in this tumbled high-hill shack.
He searched for flowers she had planted there—
The bleeding-hearts she wore in her black hair.
He did not take death serious when she died,
But he is now in love with his first bride.

499

Who would believe that Shooting Charlie Paul
Was hauled out on this hill after a brawl?
Am Sickler shot him at the Hood-Run dance.
Am knew him better than to take a chance.
He was hemmed in—victim of circumstance.
He was stabbed twice with Charlie Paul's dull knife;
But he tore loose and at a frightful chance
He drove a bullet through Charlie Paul's lung.
Charlie Paul fell to death at twenty-one.
Charlie Paul had two notches on his gun.
Am Sickler went and served his year in pen
And Charlie Paul is sleeping under clay.
The key has turned that set Am free again.
Paul's sentence is forever and a day.
His prison is a jail-house made of clay.

500

"Fonnis" Bealer had to search for words to say
When he was speaking over Charlie's clay.
He did not say Charlie would rise someday:
He preached that Charlie Paul had gone to hell—
"In torment Charlie Paul has gone to dwell."
For Charlie Paul was fond of drink and gun.
Charlie was in his grave at twenty-one.
Reverent "Fons" said Charlie lived too fast
And Charlie's brain would decompose at last.
I know not if his brain is decomposed
And if his dust nourish roots of a rose.
But I do know that Charlie's prison bars
Remained forever closed beneath the stars.

501

"What is this, Mind, I hear, the sound of rain
Beating like fists down on my cold grave rock?
It keeps a-fallin like white spikes of rain
And regular as the ticking of a clock.
What is it, Mind, I ask? Why don't you tell?
What is it, Mind, I ask—I lie here-under—
I lie confined down in this narrow hell.
Sometimes the beating fists get loud as thunder.
I get too restless lying deep here-under!
Get close the earth and whisper to me, Mind.
Get down and whisper like the blades of corn.
Don't whisper loudly, for the tattling Wind
Will play a tune on Resurrection morn,
Words you have said on his sweet violin."

502

"I'll gather close and whisper to you, Dust,
Since you are part of me long laid away.
I feel it is my duty and I must
Whisper to you before Resurrection Day.
That is the Judge's gavel that you hear
Sounding above you like a ticking clock!
After you have slept here for many a-year,
A-soundin like rain beating on a rock!
The Jury sentences you for men you killed.
The Jury sentences you for your life-time!
Silence in the courtroom when a life is willed!
Do you remember, Dust, the penitentiary?
Ah, man can hold you, Dust, behind the bars,
And they can plant you down beneath the tree;
And they can hide you to the wind and stars,
But they can't keep your Mind from being free."

503

"But listen, Mind, so free and beautiful,
Since I am ugly in the house of clay,
You were once cunning dreams in this white skull
Now lying in a jail-house made of clay.
My Mind, I ask of you, does it look fair
For twelve small minds to make my destiny
A life imprisonment in the penitentiary?
I kilt men for America's stripes and stars.
I kilt men for her in the great World War.
There were no juries there to jail a man,
But those were days we fought it man to man.
But I came back and took a life or two
And I sleep under walls of heavy clay.
Ah, is it fair, my Mind—I'm asking you?
To be jailed till the Resurrection Day?"

504

"Lie still, my Dust, and sleep—you cannot wane.
Lie still, my Dust—I pray your sleep is sweet.
I am immortal, for I am the brain—
My Dust you're tempered in a different heat.
Lie still, my Dust, now hidden from the stars
And from the wind and from white floating skies.
Lie still and sleep—why dream of prison bars?
Why dream of anything beneath the stars,
Of silver wind, and trees, and floating skies?
Why dream of killing in America's wars?
Flesh of immortal Christ was crucified
And nailed by jury-men upon the cross.
Immortal minds remember how he died,
The common man remembers how he died—
The long-haired Nazarene nailed to the cross."

505

"Then I must lie beneath the roots of tree,
The dust of one nailed to a public cross,
And branded with, 'the penitentiary,'
Which meant to earth I was but little loss.
Eat up my dust, roots from the grave oak tree!
And give it to your leaves beneath the stars.
I want to live again in oak tree leaves
And tell the wind of penitentiaries.
I want to speak of killing men in wars—
I want to tell the wind—to tell the trees.
The tattling trees will tell the honey bees.
The honey bees will tell it to the clover.
The honey bees will whisper it to flowers
And they will laugh about these wars of ours."

506

"At last, my Dust, you sleep—you thin and pine.
What does it matter if you lie and rot?
What does it matter I ask, Dust of mine,
If you're remembered or you are forgot!
There is no difference to kill in war
Than kill a man you know in time of peace.
In peace one knows what he is killing for,
In war one kills because he's asked to kill;
It does not matter how it grains his will.
Lie still, my Dust, and sleep—now all is over.
Twelve jury-men are sleeping under clay
And honey bees are speaking to the clover—
I cannot understand just what they say.
Lie still and sleep, my Dust—the best is over!"

507

Murt Hensley found her Willie in the bed
With Howard Hall's widow, Missouri Hall.
She put a bullet through her Willie's head;
Five through the heart of old Missouri Hall—
She left them there unparted in the bed—
She put a white,sheet over Willie's head.
She knew how Willie frolicked out to see
Old strumpet, Howard Hall's widow Missouri,
In his best suit she bought with eggs and cream.
Now Willie sleeps where sprouts are growing tall.
Missouri sleeps at last by Howard Hall
And near their graves there flows a dwindling stream.
Howard and Missouri do not speak at all.

508

Here on the head of Sheaf lives Lemuel Raggs
Fond of plug horses, whiskey, and old hags.
Lem Raggs has never drawn a sober breath
Since his first wife, Symanthia Raggs, met death.
Some say Symanthia drank the jake-leg gin
And the Lord brought her to a fruitless end.
Some say that Lemuel left a keg of brandy
By his wife's bed before she had her baby;
They say Lem left the dipper there too handy—
Symanthia drank too much for her weak body.
Some say Symanthia bloated on sweet cider;
Some say that she was bitten by a spider.
Now I do know old Lemuel lives in rags
Since she is gone and drinks and sleeps with hags.

509

Now no one ever speaks of Myrtle Lane.
There is no need to ever speak of her.
No one will ever see her like again,
So many women were afraid of her.
She pulled a pistol on fair Dolly Crump,
She slapped the face of smart Symanthia Moore,
And called Tim Brannam's wife a stinking whore,
She shot old Preston Haily in the rump.
One night a chicken squalled and Oscar Dunn
Shot at the sound with his twelve-gauge shot gun.
Save for the chicken's cackling night was still
And Oscar Dunn went back and went to bed.
Next morning Oscar Dunn trailed up the hill
Blood-tracks and found Murt Lane a-lying dead.

510

Bill Haily found his wife down in the corn
One morning early with old Charlie Ball;
He thought she had gone down to weed the corn,
But Lydia harkened to a lusty call.
Bill Haily pulled his gun and that was all—
The heart stopped and breath left old Charlie Ball.
And Charlie sleeps where weeds are growing tall;
Pusley and careless hide white bones of his
And tall corn waves above his resting place;
The tall corn sings for him a song of bliss.
Winds ask the corn why Charlie came to this.
The tall corn speaks from Charlie's resting place:
"He harkened to 'Lid' Haily's lusty call—
The way of man and that is all—is all."

511
EASTER SUNDAY, APRIL 16TH
Why do you come to us this Easter morning
And slowly walk among our narrow beds?
Poet, I ask, why do you come this morning
Where yucca blades are wet in mourning,
Wet with the cool white tears of April rain?
The yucca blades now mourn departed dead
Though they lie in sweet peace and comforted.
Why did you come?—they cannot live again
And know the touch of gentle Easter rain.
They cannot live to feel the hurt of pain,
For everlastingly they must sleep here
Throughout the Springs and autumns of each year.
Poet, why do you come and walk alone
Among their graves? Birds sing and grass is green,
And one can see a pretty wind-flower scene—
Why come where men have turned to dust and stone!

512
Why do you ask me this—you Whispering Grass
As you stand up and drink the April rain?
And Grass from those that will not live again
You gather nourishment. The things that pass
Are food for you— Grass, is it your business
If I walk out amid fresh loveliness
Of Spring and watch you drink the April rain;
And watch white flowers waving in the wind?
Is it your business, Grass, I ask of you!
This Easter morn I walk among the dead,
Each pillowed well deep in his narrow bed.
My sires are sleeping here, you Whispering Grass,
And you partake of them—these men that pass!
Little of you—but still you do it, Grass!

513

Poet, you come among us sleeping here.
Don't be a fool and quarrel with the Grass,
For we give nourishment unto grass roots.
The strength of us is in the tender shoots.
The strength of us is in each sweet grass stem;
The strength of us is in each leaf and flower—
And now the Grass speaks of us while we dream
And tells on us a scandal every hour.
Poet, now will you listen to the Grass
Speak of the old that now have come to pass.
Poet, your sires are sleeping here among us,
And do you listen to Grass speak of them
Beneath where yucca blades hang tremulous
They lie, and the Grass scandalizes them.

514

Let the Grass speak of them and I shall write
A sonnet to commemorate their night—
The Dead have done all was their will to do.
They were no better nor no worse than you—
And if the shoe fits them then fits the shoe—
I'll write the truth—though truth won't always do.
The dead are dust—yet some have sallow faces.
I have come here to them this Easter morning.
I choose to come back here of all the places
Where rain-drenched yuccas bow in mourning.
I have come here to spend the day with them,
And let the Whispering Grass speak now of them,
And let the yuccas drip with rain and dew,
And wet my legs as I go wading through—
I have come here to spend the day with them.

515

Green Grass of Spring, what are you to the dead
And, April yuccas, why do you mourn them?
Each sleeps so soundly in his narrow bed,
And what is any stem of Grass to them?
And what are yuccas and red thorn to them!
They are no more than dog tracks in the mud,
They are no more than snake prints on the sand,
For earth has taken back their flesh and blood
And once again they have become the land;
And there beneath the low descending skies
The dead lie with worms slithering in their eyes.
But when the worms help decompose to clay
The flesh of those that lie beneath the thorn,
The worms are fed and then they go away.

516

You come to us—you walk above the ground.
Five feet beneath, my friend, we sleep full sound.
It is our turn to sleep and thus we sleep.
We sleep unmindful of the worms that creep.
We would love now to see the April green
That has come to the hills. We'd love to see
Just anything besides eternity—
It is too blank for our blurred eyes to see.
Sing, gruesome Poet—yes, sing this of us—
There's nothing else to sing but this of us.
You are too young to know our yesterday
When we were young as you—carefree and gay,
When we were young and careless boys at play—
And you will take your turn to sleep someday.

517

Now I come out to write about the dead.
I sit among stones where a brisk wind whines.
Of April rain I think we've had enough—
The whining wind has drained the water off
The yucca blades and grass and berry-vines.
I want to write—there's little to be said.
I'll have to teach this Collie to behave—
He's digging after mole into a grave.
I scold at Don and after this is done
I rise and walk in April wind and sun.
Too many lie here dead—how can I speak
Of all the dead and dust, I ask the wind.
How can I speak for all—they cannot speak
Through heavy walls—they're deaf and dumb and blind.

518

Here lies Kate Whittinghill beneath the green—
Her grave is flat and often is unseen.
They say Kate was as pretty as a flower
Before the fever killed Kate Whittinghill.
The old folks say Kate spent her idle hours
By Sandy River gathering wildwood flowers.
But here she lies at last, Kate Whittinghill—
The petals of a flower gone to decay.
Above Kate are the flowers in bloom today,
In April wind they stand in fresh array.
But poor Kate Whittinghill lies thereunder
And has slept soundly through the April thunder—
She does not see today white wildwood flowers
Adorning hills after April showers.

519

If Kate could speak, I think that she would say:
"Life was not fair with me—I went too soon.
I lie with eyes blinded to April moon
And to white clouds that float across at noon
The big blue bowl of April wind and sky.
If I could speak, I would—perhaps I'd cry.
Life was before me clean as any flower,
And I went clean to meet my life, but I
Was stricken by the water in a stream.
I drank of water crystal in the gleam
Of sun—blue water in a mountain stream—
Though pretty waters, typhoid germs were there.
And now I lie where the white headstones gleam,
Near-by where I drank water from this stream."

520

"Oh, I would love to walk on earth today
Beneath white spreading sails of windy skies,
And I would love to hear the soft wind cries
And see white blossoms on the hills today.
I know of old fields where wind flowers grow;
I know of rich ravines where grows the thyme
And wildrose vines the wind beats like a rhyme.
These were the scenes I knew once on a time.
I went there with a boy named Charlie Lee,
And Charlie would sit down and write a rhyme.
And now I'd love to ask where's Charlie Lee?
Where are the rhymes he wrote and threw away?
Are his rhymes gone? Is Charlie under clay?"

521

"If I were free today, I think I'd go
To one brush pasture field where flowers blow
In April wind—this field I used to know—
Wind flowers were so pretty in the wind—
I used to go there with poor Kate Baldwin.
And there blue violets were fine to see
After they had been drenched by April rain
And then warmed by the April sun again,
Bending their stiff necks so impatiently;
Violets blue and soft and velvety—
And there we heard wood cranes laugh merrily.
But now I sleep, and where is Kate Baldwin?
"Kate's grave is next to yours, Kate Whittinghill,
You both are sleeping, sleeping on the hill.
You sleep the bed beside the bed Kate's in—
You, and Kate Baldwin are sleeping silently."

522

Eighteen was mighty young for Clem to die,
But then he died before Pete Wimpler's gun.
Pete said he did it accidentally—
Court evidence proved that Clem Malwell won
The fight and then Pete pulled his gun on Clem.
And now Clem fights no more, but he lies still
And Pete goes free of prison bars to kill.
Who married Lill the girl Clem chose to wed?
Pete Wimpler married Lill, since Clem was dead.
What did life mean?—Clem had not lived one score
Of years until his youth met fatal doom.
Clem was an oak bud bursting into bloom.
That bloom is dust—now dust forevermore.

523

Seth Laxter is a farm boy sleeping here
So silently now moldering into clay—
He has lain here will be ten years this May.
Seth cut his knee—blood poison cut him down
Like frosts cut down a weed in early autumn
Where frosts bite first along a Sandy bottom.
Perhaps Seth would have married Mildred Jayne,
Though Mildred Jayne, they say, loved Herbert Lane.
Seth Laxter had not gone far in book rules—
He did not give a damn for all book rules—
Seth knew his farm, his mules and farming tools.
The body of Seth Laxter did possess
Fine qualities of strength and ruggedness.
It was a shame Death took such youth away,
Converting him into a pile of clay.

524

If Seth Laxter could speak, I think he'd say:
"Have my grass fields grown up with sprouts again?
How does my grass look in this April rain?
And are my fences downed by fallen trees?
And have the redbuds bloomed out on the hill?
Is my grass smothering under chestnut leaves
That blew down to the yard from chestnut hill?
And are my apple trees in bud to bloom?
And have you ever heard the whippoorwill?
I would love to go home and plow this Spring
And hear the red birds fluting from the wing.
And have my mules now grown too old for plowing,
And have my farming tools been set aside?
And friend, if there is anyway of knowing,
Has Herbert Lane yet taken Mildred bride?"

525

If one could speak: "Your fields grow sprouts again.
Shades cause your grass to spindle in the rain.
By fallen trees your fence is broken down
In many places—your barn has weathered brown.
Seth Laxter, these are things you hate to hear
Beneath the grass—you moldering into clay.
This Spring the redbuds wear a scarlet gown.
Your apple buds are bursting into bloom.
Your mules grew old for working—met their doom—
And they are white bones on the pasture hill.
On evenings now we hear the whippoorwill.
It sings above where you are lying still.
Your farming tools well-worn are set aside,
  And Herbert Lane took Mildred Jayne his bride."

526

Over the dead (a thousand here below)
The roses drip of dew and Spring winds blow—
Over some graves a century old, I know,
Petals fall from the rose when the winds blow.
Green yucca blades stand stiffly in the wind;
Red thorns sway lazily now out and in.
It's time enough for summer to begin.
Gather a petal, you—you living one,
  And hold it with your hand before the sun
  And you will note how thin and beautiful
It is—then think that petal in one day
Will crumble swiftly into sure decay.
Like petals of the rose you will decay
  And winds will blow your shriveled dust away.

527

The moon and stars come in the white night sky.
Abe Lester does not see, since he's asleep.
The black tops of the pine trees sigh and sigh.
Abe Lester does not hear, since he's asleep.
Down in the nether world of void and deep
Abe Lester does not hear the April wind
Play "Havoc" on a green-grass violin—
Walls of the house he's sleeping in are thick.
Abe Lester will not hear—will never hear,
Regardless how long Abe is sleeping here.
Abe Lester will not hear the corn-field songs,
Nor will he guide again his plow along.
Abe Lester's in the house where he belongs,
A dangerous man to folks he lived among.

528

They laid her here too young to have a name,
An unripe seed in this depository.
Here sleep the good and bad and rich and poor,
The sinister, wife, the maid, the wretch and whore;
The soldier, farmer, merchant and the thief;
Eternity for them all will not be brief,
From buds of Spring till autumn's fallen leaf—
They laid her here a seed that will not sprout.
And what was done this unborn should be killed?
The preacher said she died, for 'God so willed.'
She died because it was another's will—
Her mother carrying water up the hill;
A load too heavy and her mother fell—
And one unnamed is sleeping on this hill.

529

Lie still and rest, my friends, and call rest good.
Lie still and sleep and I shall spend this mood.
Why do you have regret? You should not have.
You idly sleeping in a country grave!
Life has its shifts— Death is a shift for life.
And you are taking yours—and I shall be
A-taking my shift of eternity
Someday. But now my shift is breathing-life,
And I am free to run on feet of clay.
I'm free to do the things you cannot do.
Lie there, contented Dust—for once, Dust, you
Were free to do things once I couldn't do
When I was still unborn. This is my day—
This chance to breathe and run on feet of clay.

530

Above you, Dust—these flowers are sweet to smell.
Above you, Dust—yuccas blow in the wind.
Above you, Dust—I stand and wish you well.
I think: "Oh, well, a poet will someday
Come to my grave and stand and wish me well—
Me sleeping then like you down in my hell!"
But until then, dear Dust, I do assure
My word to you, I shall laugh loud and long
And dance on feet of clay and sing my song;
For sleeping Dust that shift will come to me
When I shall share the darkness of your night
And one small space in dark eternity.
For thus I see the shadows of my night—
Shadows I'll share of my forthcoming night.

531

Here lies Bert Hall; under the turf and sun
And waves of sweet green grass lies old Bert Hall.
He came to rest after his day was done;
Gave up the ax and sledge and plow and maul—
Here lies the hardest working man of all.
He was devout; each Sunday old Bert prayed
And gave the church one-tenth of all he made,
With ax and plow and sledge and maul and sweat.
At Death he gave them all—wonder if they'll forget
Like children will grow foolish and forget
When parents leave to them inheritance
Of gold, that spoils their hands and kills their chance
Of making life and loving life to live.
Ah, now the church remembers old Bert Hall,
His name is on a small plate on the wall.

532

Here lies Toad Hall beneath white April rain;
Here lies Toad Hall beneath the April green—
And since his death no one has ever seen
A man to fill Toad Hall's likeness again.
He was a grave-digger. With his broad-ax
He smoothed rough walls of half the graves now here.
His age was near half of one century.
And then they brought Toad here in Spring of year
To sleep. Just five feet tall and hair was red—
Large feet and hands, small head, and shaggy brows—
This was the Toad they left among the dead.
They sold his mules and put away his plows,
For Toad lived with his mother on the hill.
Had he lived on, he'd been a bachelor still.

533

They brought him here at last, old Andy Withe.
He sold his hand a thousand times and more
In Binghamtown where he was keeping store.
But now we guess he weighs on different scales.
We proffer now he has no need for gold,
Since there is little to be bought and sold
Down in the grave. Then why does he need gold?
I've heard the old men say he paid a whore
To service him and bought her clothes to wear.
He let his children and his wife go bare.
I've heard the old folks say he stole from them
Before they found him out around the store.
They were the folks that made the gold for him
To buy flesh and put clothes on a whore.

534

Here lies Rose Baldwin in this rose-wreathed bed.
Rose Baldwin died of bleeding at child-birth.
And she lies here among the pioneer dead—
No chance to shun her shame she came to earth.
A preacher took advantage of her mind.
She was "a little off" the neighbors said.
That's why she sleeps today among the dead.
Her brothers searched, but they could never find
The scoundrel that betrayed Rose Baldwin's youth.
He goes scot-free to betray other youth.
It would not look so bad if Rose had been
Sensible, but he betrayed this foolish girl.
Him preaching to her people of their sins!
The petals of a weakling flower lie curled.

535

Here lies Bill Tongs in this depository.
They brought him back dead from the World War glory.
His brothers looked at him when he came back
And if it were Bill Tongs they could not tell.
Part of his flesh was gone—the rest was black.
First he was laid to rest near where he fell
Beside the Marne. His kin asked for him back
So he may lie in earth beside his sires.
Bill was shot down near-by the River Marne—
Machine gun bullets riddled his strong lungs.
His mother did not dream of this when he was born.
She had ambitions for her son Bill Tongs.
They brought him back from France wrapped in "Old Glory"—
Insolvent man for an old depository.

536

If now Bill Tongs could speak he'd surely say:
"I'd hate like hell to send a son to war
Not knowing what my son was fighting for.
Who knows today what we were fighting for?
Who knows just what we have fought and died for?
We gave our heritage throughout the years—
(Well given if my country needed me)
We gave our heritage as did our sires.
We gave our blood to make our people free.
And war is not a game of chess men play.
But war robs nations of supreme manhood.
War should not be forgotten in one day,
For war is darkness, hell, and war takes blood—
War dooms a future heritage to clay.

537

Here lies the man that said he'd not return
Alive if he must go beyond the seas
And do strange fighting in strange countries.
His word was good—he never did return
Until they brought him back a box of clay;
And now they left him here a hidden urn
Of dust to rest forever in a quiet way.
Like other men, Tom Long stood facing fire.
Like other men, Tom Long had tried to live.
Like other men, Tom met the fate of gun,
With other men he fell near-by Verdun.
Maybe he won his life by giving life,
But now another man has wed his wife,
Another man is father to his son.

538

Bill Antis crept into his narrow bed.
Now Antis sleeps under an April moon—
And now he sleeps, there's nothing to be said.
Bill Antis sleeps—his sleep will not break soon.
The wind is calm tonight where Antis sleeps.
It does not even stir green vines above.
The dew slides down green blades and then drips off.
White stars come in the pale-gray sky above.
Bill Antis sleeps—of life he had enough,
He lived too long—at last he ran a bluff
With his own self. Said he: "Bill Antis, you,
Are not so old—you are just eighty-four."
But something said: "Your life is nearly through,
Old Bill—you dare step out and close the door
And leave this game of life." He closed the door.
He lies beneath the sod forevermore.

539

He does not hear the tremulous cadence slow
Of wind among the leaves and dripping dew.
He does not hear—the boards are breaking through
His box, he does not hear the violin
Of leaves and wind and notes of rain there-in.
He does not hear nightwinds beat down the world
Like blowing bellows lone thin hollowness,
Like early frosts sting autumn leaves to curl,
This man lies deaf to all sounds in the world.
Lon Martin has not heard one single word,
One blowing wind, one sad note of the rain;
And for one century Lon Martin's lain
Deep in the earth that gave his body growth.
Death makes agreements with people at birth.
Someday he knows they'll compensate the earth.

540

Not far away sky meets the moonlit land.
And on this field the moldering headstones gleam;
Blue dreamers lie beneath—each in his dream.
Above is twilight beauty of the land.
Green twilight beauty spreads like a green sail
A-spreading softly over hallow ground,
Spreads slow above where lies old German Kale—
Above the cell that confines him at last.
Unlike the other cells old German found,
The cell of earth where he must sleep full sound
Was narrow and it did not have a door—
Eternal darkness and sad notes of rain
Breaking above the dust of German's brain,
Beating where German sleeps forevermore.

CLIDE JARVIS   541

"Ah, Death, you play with me—these things I miss:
The wind and sun and earth, stars and the rain
And sky. I miss the lips I used to kiss—
Lips once so warm and pretty in their day;
And think you turned those precious lips to clay!
You turned them back to clay and me to clay.
Life is a swindler. Death, you are a cheat.
Life brought me here and gave me brain and feet
And hands and a strong body built of clay,
And eyes to see the beauty of a rose,
And nose to smell the fragrance of a rose.
Life smiled on me and I did love this life."
But Death came by and complimented me
Until I climbed into his two-horse surrey
And Death and I drove his horses in a hurry.

JOHN SHELTON   542

"I'm sorry that I did not live my life.
I settled down to a one-woman life.
I should have known more women than this one.
I should have drunk more licker and more gin.
I should have lived and let them call it sin.
For now it is too late—too late to live,
When one is confined to the mortal's dust—
For what is licker when a man is dust?
And what are kisses when a man is dust?
Now dead, I'm faithful to a woman's trust.
Go taste of life before your passion leaves you,
Before your lips grow old and dirt to kiss;
Ah, know of life before this Death deceives you,
For if you don't you'll not know what you miss."

LIMA WHITTINGHILL 543

"And this at last—I ask, why I was born.
And this at last—O Resurrection Morn!
I've heard of you— You do not come, I fear.
I have slept here forever and one year.
When do you come? I ask— Or do you come?
My blood is brittle and my brain is dumb.
My flesh has long been dust, my eyes are blurred.
It has been long since any words I've heard
Come to these ears of dust; it has been long
Since I have heard winds blowing cross the fields;
And long since passion in this flesh has stirred—
Never since my young body's been interred.
Ah, Life, I see you are a joke at last—
Once living dust and then forever past."

TINY LITTERAL 544

"Ah, Life, why did you play with me for years,
Then take this thing called breath away from me?
You took my eyes that see, my drums that hear,
My hands that touch and lips that kiss from me.
'I did not do this temple of strong clay.
I would keep you forever and forever.
Death drove his horses to my gate one day
And called for you. My Dust, he took your breath.
It was not I to take you—it was Death.
Death came to get you, he was in a hurry—
Death driving two black horses in a surrey.
He drove to the front gate and asked for you.
You went with him—you lost your ears and eyes;
You lost your hands that touch and lips that kiss.
I did not play with you—Death played with you.
Sorry for you—so many things you'll miss.'"

545

Here lies a poet under phlox and thyme
And blades of yucca strong against the wind,
And men now say: "In his day and his time
With words of power this poet spun his rhyme,
And now his verse is old and out of mind
Since he was poet once upon a time."
Here lies a poet and he hates to lie
Beneath the wind and sun and grass of Spring;
Here lies a poet and he hates to lie
When in the poplar trees the red birds sing;
He hates to lie beneath the autumn skies
Descending and the drizzling autumn rain
Beating like fists upon his quilt of clay.
He hates to sleep beneath the light of day—
Sleep with his hands now crossed in a quiet way.

546

I am this poet's mind and I speak thus
Unto my Dust, this hidden part of me:
My Dust, it's strange how Death has parted us
And each must go now in his separate way.
What of it all, my Dust, can you tell me?
Would it be better if we should not be?
Would it be better if we were in clay,
Left there unborn and never draw a breath?
Or is it better, Dust of mine, we came
To earth and bore a name and lost a name
And left our dust collateral to this name?
What does it matter, Dust—we left behind
Collateral for our dust of futile rhymes—
Ah, far superior to silver and gold—
Collateral to stand by when we are cold!

547

I am the Dust and I speak back to you.
I cannot answer anything you say.
The things you ask they do not matter now;
They are not facts as blossoms on a bough.
The things you ask I cannot grasp somehow.
Now I ask you, where is the girl I love?
Now does she sleep—is her dust thin and pine?
Or is the girl I love a lass alive,
And is this girl I love far less divine
Or more divine than I thought that she was
When I walked by her side a man alive?
These things are now left to the tattling wind.
And will you tell to me, eternal Mind,
The things I ask of her I left behind?

548

Ah, yes, the girl you love is less divine
Than she told you when you were man alive.
The girl you love is not so thin and pine,
For she sleeps by an old school mate of mine.
They do not sleep together under clay,
But they sleep limb to limb fresh and alive;
And she was sleeping by him in your day;
And she was telling you she was divine.
Ah, many nights her lips had sipped of wine
And she laid limb to limb with men unknown.
You were too fond of her and she was vain.
My Dust, if you had cost her body pain,
Her love for you would not have been so vain—
A way to treat some vanity in women.

549

And what about my rhymes—are they all dead?
Or do you think a dozen are still read?
I did not give the people what they wanted,
I gave the people rhymes that my moods haunted
Deep in the heart of me to feel and write—
I gave the people rhymes of day and night,
Of flowers, rivers, birds, and men and trees,
Of sky and wind and stars and moon and bees—
I do not know if these are things they wanted.
I do not care if these are things they wanted.
But I do know these are the things that haunted
Me—the verse I left for men to read,
Since I am sleeping soundly with the dead,
Since I lie here at peace and comforted.

550

I said the girl you loved was not divine,
That she slept by an old school mate of mine;
Not on the kind of bed you use today,
But single bed deep in a house of clay.
And now I say your verse is never read,
Since you are sleeping soundly with the dead.
Why should men care for poetry on bees
And sky, and wind, and rain, and moon and trees?
Men do not see the things the poet sees.
Be still, my Dust, beneath this drip of rain.
Let poems cease and girls be undivine.
Why dream of days that will not come again?
Why dream of girls that say they are divine?
Be still, my Dust, and sleep—you thin and pine.
Remember, your lips tasted richer wine
Than lips of her who said she was divine.

551

America, here sleeps the dust of you!
Deep in the bosom of your earth they lie;
Blue Dreamers now—this once-tried dust of you!
Earth, they have gone into the clay of you;
Beneath the clay, the grass, and trees of you—
They have gone there to sleep one night and day.
The yellow harvest moon is riding through
White floating clouds upon the June night sky,
The silver winds of June are blowing through
The grave-yard grasses where these dreamers lie.
Among the dewy grass the night winds sigh;
They sigh unmindful of the sleeping dead;
Down in their graves beside the copperhead—
America! America! Here is your dead.

552

"America, we sleep—Blue Dreamers now,
We sleep America—the dust of you.
We are men from the foundry and the plow,
Men from ore mines, coal mines and hilly farms;
We are men builders of railroads and cities—
American and builders of the nation.
And now we sleep where lonesome winds hum ditties—
The dust that cleared your land and built your cities.
And our wives sleep—strong mothers of the land;
They worked beside us, helped to clear the land
And build the homes and drive the frontier west;
They bore our sons for us to carry on,
They sleep beside of us and sleep is best.
America, we sleep—Blue Dreamers now;
Home from the foundry, mines, log-woods and plow!

553

"America, why don't you speak for us!
America, why don't you speak to us!
Above our beds the leaves hang tremulous
And gossip to the silver sheets of wind.
Now speak to us, for we are left behind
And you push on, America—and on.
Speak out for us—let poets rise and sing,
But not of butterflies and white-moth wing;
But let them sing of earth and men of power,
And let them sing of seasons and the flower—
To hell with singers' sentimental songs,
Let them go sing for men where they belong.
Give us a singer that will sing for us—
The truth of us—then listen to his song
For we must sleep—and our sleep shall be long!"

554

"I sing for you, Blue Dreamers of the dust,
I try my best to wake you sleeping under
The dirt and wind and tree and grass and fern—
Oh don't you hear the bass notes of my thunder!
I sing for you an autumn monotone.
Ah, don't you hear me drenching your grave-fern
And scrubbing, scrubbing on your lichen stones!
And don't you hear me drumming on your roof
And I ooze through your leaky velvet roof?
I am the wind, I speak to you and laugh.
Dear dead, I write your wordless epitaph."
Ah, yes, they speak to you—the wind and water;
The lightning, thunder, wind and earth and storm—
They sing for you, dear dead, in your hereafter;
They sing to you, dear dead, in your hereafter!

555

Who built America?—now I ask you.
Who cut the forests, plowed the rooty hills?
Who spanned the rivers and who built the towns?
America—the pioneers built you!
Or they destroyed you! Their stubborn wills
Help conquer you, help cut your forests down.
The oxen and the horse help conquer you,
And they sleep with their masters under clay—
(Kentucky, mother of horses in her day)
And no one dreams that they lived yesterday.
These conquerors now are dust—they are all dust,
And tall beech trees grow where their dusts are lain;
Tall nettles grow above and die again
In white caressing of the autumn rain.
Dusts of these pioneers now did their shares;
Blue dreamers now—America's "Conquerors!"

556

What do you say, pioneers—who speaks for you?
Blue-bellied lizards speak for you. I see
Them crawl above you on the cedar tree
And they sun on your gray stones in the grass;
They seem to try to tell men when they pass
Some one lies here. The blacksnake speaks for you;
He writes your epitaph across your graves
Where sawbriars cluster and the thin grass waves.
The gray owl comes at night and hoots a hymn
For them—his pulpit is a cedar limb.
The toad frogs hop among the stones at night,
And katydids come to sing lonely here.
They have come here to sing in the starlight
Over forgotten graves of pioneers!

557

Do you not hear the drums of falling rain;
The tap-tap of the rain on the dead leaves!
And if you hear the tap-tap of this rain,
Do you feel like that you could march again!
The falling rain is like a blowing fife—
What man is there who hates a blowing fife!
And don't you love the heavy drums of thunder,
And does it wake you since you're sleeping under,
And make you want to rise and march again!
The drums of thunder never sound retreat;
It is a charge the drums of thunder beat.
Now would you march to thunder or the rain
If you could rise up from the dust again;
Proud warrior's dust, if you could rise again!

TISH MEADOWS   558

I sleep beneath the earth-scarred battle ground;
The English and the Indians were my foe.
Now I have slept here many years below,
Where wind and water and the trees make sound.
America goes on because I sleep
And others sleep—we died to make her go.
Corn will grow over us and ripen brown;
Wheat will grow over us year after year;
Each year a coat of new leaves will drift down;
Farmers will pass, not knowing who sleeps here.
What does it matter who is sleeping here?
For death is death just anyway we die;
And when we died, we were fighting for
The land you keep today—something to have;
America, for you we took the grave!

WILLIAM THOMAS   559

Blow over me and blow, you worlds of wind,
Blow over me and drift the leaf and straw,
Blow over me and leave the earth behind,
The early autumn freeze and April thaw.
Fall down on me, you torrents of white rain,
Fall down on me in torrents of disaster,
Tear up the earth—do it again. Again.
You cattle, tramp around to make it nastier
Since winter freeze has come into the pasture,
Where sires of mine are spreading out the fodder.
Mix snow, manure, and dirt into a slime
Beneath where winds now sing a lonesome rhyme
And snow flows over me—dung-inked water—
These are the things that I am sleeping under;
Awaiting to wake with snakes in the Spring thunder!

SUE PITTS   560

This silly girl now sleeps, and may she have
Rest from her toil and sweet peace in the grave.
Life in the hills was hard for her—too hard for her;
At last the grave for her was good for her,
For in the grave at last she has found rest.
The primrose now is blooming from her breast.
Men took advantage of her fruitless mind;
Got her with child and then left her behind
To live the best she could with her poor kin.
Three different charcoal burners now did this.
Each time she gave her baby to her kin.
Better for her that she is sleeping in
The earth. The cold, cold earth to one is bliss,
When Life betrays one with a dirty kiss!

BUNION MADDOX   561

"At last, my Laura, we are taking rest
Out on the hill we wore out with the plow.
Our rest is time-forever—that is best,
To lie in our own earth worn by our plow.
Our twenty children lie here in our world
Out on our farm where we grew up and married—
Lie here beneath corn tassels now unfurled
Our children lie together now and buried.
Sweet Laura Vance, you were a pretty girl,
And I remember still the day we wed:
It was when percoon blossoms first unfurled,
Before the primrose blossoms garland'd red
The pasture rocks down on our old home place.
But Laura, now we lie without a trace
To show where we are left among the dead."

LAURA MADDOX   562

"Bunion, I sleep by you where all is still—
Out on this summer hill where all is still,
Save drowsy lullings of the beetles and
The crickets that hug close the dewy land,
And lonesome calling of the whippoorwill.
The plows and hoes we used have turned to rust;
The fields we cleared have grown in sprouts and weeds—
The fields are far too poor to furnish needs
Of people now moved there since we are dust.
I sleep by you among our children buried—
Our twenty children now are taking rest.
I know you are their father—I'm their mother.
We shared our lives together—that was best.
And now we sleep—the best for us is over!"

EPHRIAM BOONE 563

Wake up, Ephriam—don't you hear the call
Of Spring and don't you hear the cardinals sing!
Wake up—throw off the shackles of this death,
Breathe deep of April wind—take you a breath!
Go out and work your fields from Spring till fall.
Why do you sleep when you have heard the call?
Now don't you hear the working cattle bawl?
And don't you hear the crows cry with a caw
About the time Spring winds begin to thaw
The hungry weed-fields of the early Spring.
Ephriam, don't you hear the cardinals sing
Down in Kentuck's tall naked yellow poplars?
A little sun and bright warm rains have come;
The pheasants sit out on the hill and drum.
Wake up, Ephriam—why do you sleep and sleep?
W'y don't you know the sap of Spring has come!

EMANUEL NORTON 564

Do not disturb me with the plow and hoe,
Nor by your singing of that "Old Black Joe!"
For I lie in the corn-field's lonesome sound,
Safe from the plow, though it wears through the ground
Deeper and deeper as the ground is plowed
Each year. Oh, don't disturb me with your crowd
Of red-faced jolly huskers in the corn
Singing and working on an autumn morn
When frost is white upon the blades of fodder.
And don't disturb me by your wild geese flying
And autumn wind and dead leaves flying after.
Color is in the wind—color and laughter!
Now I sleep here—I'm not content with dying;
I'm not content with what you call hereafter!

TWOBIAS HOLBROOK 565

When I was once a man and strong alive
I hitched my cattle to the cutter plow—
I plowed up roots and tore them all to hell;
For when I plowed my land I plowed it well.
When I was once a man and strong alive,
I plowed the earth; but see what I am now.
Today I am a man down in the earth,
Patched up in garments far too fine to wear;
I am a piece of dust of little worth
And my fine clothes have rotted now thread-bare.
I'd love to rise and greet my farm today,
And till my fields—improve my meadow lands;
It is too late when a man understands—
For that is when he's sleeping under clay.

PRESS HYLTON 566

Seems like there is a creaking sound I hear—
The heavy axles grinding at the wagon hub;
It is a heavy heavy sound I hear—
The axles grinding and the check lines rub.
My friends, it is my kin—they're tired of here;
It is my own blood-kin—they're westward bound;
They're going on to seek a better ground;
They're tired of living here year after year!
Houses are thick as snow birds round dead weeds,
And farms are cut and scarred by wire and rail.
My own blood kin is moving to the west
And I am left at one end of the trail.
But they'll return to drink of lonesome water;
It's only a golden set of sun they're after!

DOLLIE BRUCE 567

She was worse than a blood-hound bitch in heat.
At night she went into the woods with men,
Sometimes with one, sometimes with five and ten.
As hungry dogs fight for their bitch in heat,
Men fought for her with strong intent to kill.
Where are they now—they're sleeping on the hill.
Yes, Dollie Bruce—she knew a thousand men.
Not one of them sleeps here today beside her,
They met her once then took no pride in her.
The earth is friend to her—she finds repose
Beneath the daisy, phlox and woodland rose.
The earth is kind, these flowers do suffice.
The moral is: (I speak it not for whores)
A bitch that eats dung once will eat it twice!

568

"Throw down your rifle now—throw down your knife,
You will not need your rifle anymore.
He was too quick for you—he took your life,
Now lie you there and sleep forevermore!"
"We rise for him to fight with gun and sword;
We take the life that took his life—my word."
"Down through the blood of many generations
Among earth figures of the hills and hollows
Let rifles bark and let them clinch and fight,
Let them take brother's blood and meet the night,
And let them fight and kill and take a rest
And seek the barricade of earth's deep breast!"
Rifles have thinned men of each generation.
No Law can tame men of the hills and hollows.

WINSTON CAMPBELL 569

I loved the water—loved to swim and float,
I loved to swim with face up to the skies,
I loved to get blue water in my eyes.
One day when I was fishing from a boat,
The boat upset—my hip boots pulled me under.
They weighted me till I could never rise—
No more to swim with face up to the skies.
I wonder if the youth go there today
And swim as we swam in the long ago—
Go there and splash through whitecaps, waves and foam.
I wonder if those youth do dive below
And get the bottom gravel from the river.
And do the willows in the wind still quiver?
Strong swimming youth—ah, may they live forever.
Go brave the current of the stream forever!

570

"Blue water slashes on the banks today
As water slashed there years and years agone,
The youth and old go there to swim today
And in blue water swim and dive and play—
They have forgotten those in years agone.
There-on their backs they watch the floating skies
Till wind blows water white-caps in their eyes,
They watch the martins cut across the blue,
The shikepokes circle and the kildees too—
The same goes on today as years agone:
The night wind's and the water's monotone,
The soft edge water slapping at a stone,
Clean bodies plowing through the blue, blue water,
With willow leaves and sticks a-swirling after.

ELIZABETH GRAVES 571

Elizabeth Graves lies here—a jewel rare,
She was among the fairest of the fair.
Her hair was black and curled as rag-weeds curl
After they have been bitten by a frost
And winter winds have blown and stripped them bare—
Her skin like poplar leaves that still do hang
After a frost was bleached—her violet eyes
Were of a richer blue than the deep skies.
She was more shapely than the slender birch;
Her fingers pointed like the leaves of birch—
A jewel rare; for one could search and search
And one could never find one like Elizabeth.
Rare-jeweled was the dust of her in life;
Rare-jeweled was the dust of her in death.

INA CALLIHAN 572

Ina Callihan died after her child's birth;
Ina Callihan lies here beneath the earth.
The Doctor did not come—the hour was late;
The place was back so far and desolate.
Pay was uncertain, for the folks were poor.
Now Ina Callihan will never more
Walk out and pluck plum blossoms from the boughs
And go barefooted out to hunt the cows.
Now Ina Callihan lies under sod
And not again will Ina pray to God
For good deliverance of a child in birth.
Though her last baby born was one of seven,
And her man Dick did wed next year again,
Dick's second wife has given birth to eleven!

MAUD CLEMMENS   573

My bed is under primose and sawbriar,
Around my lichen stones trail the woodbine;
And I am sure that many girls less fair
Would wish a bed now just as soft as mine.
For they get up and go afield by light
Of day to hoe before the change of moon,
And they come in to eat good food at noon;
Then back to fork the mow in afternoon
Under the downpour of the sun in June—
The downpour of a golden heat in June.
And they lie on straw beds and watch the moon
At night— a bed of straw is hard, I know—
And I sleep in a velvet bed below.
I sleep beneath the silver stars of June,
The sky and silver wind and golden moon.

574

"Now you may have your velvet bed below
And you may lie under the rose and briar,
We hope you love your quiet cool bed below,
The velvet dirt below since you retire.
But we prefer a bed of straw in June,
And we prefer to breathe the wind in June
Than to lie in your bed of earth in June—
Lie there so still under the golden moon.
Yes, we go out to chop field-weeds in June
And hoe our corn before a change of moon,
We fork the mow in the hot afternoon,
We go beneath the silver stars of June.
Sun-kissed, we go out with our farmboy lovers,
We slip away from fathers and our mothers,
And by your grave we've stopped to spoon and spoon,
Beneath the silver stars and golden moon,
Our brown lips met the brown lips of our lovers."

BOYD STEEL 575

They do not know about you now, Boyd Steel.
Life is all over, Boyd, and you have found
Peace in this thing called Death and in the ground.
No more you'll take your sack and slip to steal
A pig or chicken, turkey, goose, or lamb—
Sometimes they say you carried off a sheep.
It is all over now and Boyd, you sleep.
And when you died one said: "Who gives a damn
To hear that old Boyd Steel has met his doom!
His hot board didn't work—a chicken squalled—
Four shots fired at the roost—"Boyd jumped the broom!"
And now he sleeps and he will not awake,
To take his sack and go the rounds again.
"Squawkers!"—He didn't get an even break!

VIRGINIA BARR 576

Under the drip, drip of the silver water
Dripping from pretty leaves of fern and poplar,
Under the music of winds blowing after,
Sleeps one, maker of music—Virginia Barr.
She may have caught the music in the wind,
She may have caught the cornbird's reckless flute
And way he trills his flute from young birch shoot.
She may have caught the pine tops' violin.
And when the voice of wind and birds was mute
And stillness settled to the earth like leaves,
She may have caught the sweet fine spirit of
The low harp music in the wind that grieves
And organ pipes of blue, blue falling water.
Under the drip, drip of the silver rain,
I know she's dead—that's all I know of her;
Only sweet songs died in the dust of her!

KATHERINE DUNN   577

Yes, I speak through these weeds—I'm Katherine Dunn!
I have lain here, my friends, for ninety years.
Here by my side my daughter lies—Grace Dunn,
Here by my side lies Willis Dunn, my son.
We sleep forever here throughout the years—
Not married in my life to anyone.
I lived with Ferris Hare—he got my daughter!
I lived with Martin Hill—he got my son,
I lived with Cauldwell Spence—he got me neither.
My children bore my maiden name of Dunn.
I ask you, friends, if I have lost or won?
Cows tramp above our heads and farmers plow;
Who lives through ninety years to gossip now!

MAURICE FINLEY   578

Under the weeds I lie— I speak to you:
The roots of weeds and dirt I'm speaking through—
I ask you, living, what is life to you?
Do you love life and do you battle well—
Step in the fight of life and fight like hell?
Instead, my friends, are you afraid of life—
Enough afraid of life to lose your life?
Ah, let me speak to you: Go meet your life,
For you are young today; why do you fear?
Go meet your life, for soon the time draws near
For you to sleep like me year after year.
Listen, my friend, when you are lying under,
You will not hear the songs you've often heard;
You will not hear from low notes of Spring thunder
To finer notes of cricket, beetle, bird!

MARCUS PHELPS   579

I hate to leave the world, for I have found
Such joy in life— So many things to love:
The sky, the wind and dead leaves on the ground
And wild geese flying through the clouds above.
I've loved the color of the autumn leaves,
And color of the frozen corn-field stones;
And I have loved a winter wind that grieves
And dwindling autumn water's monotone.
Earth is too great to lose—earth is too vast!
Life is too great to lose—life is too vast!
I hate to part with life and things I love;
I hate to leave the earth and skies above.
And life must pass, but surely Earth will last.
All life must end—the ending must be vast!

580

Under the roots of sycamore and thyme;
Under the lull of summer winds and rhyme
Of beetle cricket and the whispering leaf
That one hears in the dewy grass at night
When one's alone under the white starlight,
Lies dust of one part red child and part white.
It never knew of day—it knows of night.
Its mother gave it birth and broke its neck
And said: "To hell with birth of Indian blood
Against my will—it is no harm to kill."
Red men had captured her—forced her to yield;
And now one of their blood lies here concealed
Beneath the roots of sycamore and thyme
Where kildees sing across the pasture field!

INTERLUDES

(I)

I've come for rest in this green solitude
Where lengthy nettles vine beneath beech wood;
I've come to rest where wind and woodland rose
Kiss on the steep banks where blue water flows;
And I have come to rest where white starlight
Gleams peacefully over the dark hills at night;
I've come here for rest and I do know why
There's peace in the wind, the leaves, and the sky—
Peace in blue water and wild woodland rose;
Peace in talking leaves when the night wind blows.
I'm seeking rest and peace—balm for this pain.
My flesh has grown tired, my nerves and my brain.
The peace I am seeking comes gentle as rain,
Comes gentle and soothing as white Spring rain.

(II)

In this green world one finds much endless play
Of wind and leaves and blue light of the day.
One finds much joy in the barking of squirrels;
And in white moths that flit on frailest wings
One finds some recompense when a bird sings.
One finds love for a rose when it unfurls
Its petals first to wind and sun and shade;
One finds love for the working honey bees,
These day-long workers on the black-gum trees
And the thin petals of the woodland rose.
One has a love for Nature's sing-song glade
Where songs by birds and bees and winds are made,
That tune to swaying tree-tops in the wind,
Like Titl's "Serenade" played on a violin.

583

(III)

The bees are caressing the clover tops red,
The wild rose is lifting its pink thorny head.
The dove is cooing on a branch of the pine,
And deep in glades where sun cannot shine
Crickets are humming of sawbriar and pine,
Crickets are claiming this land I call mine.
The wind is a-weaving the tops of the trees,
The wind is turning silver the poplar leaves,
The wind blows over the clover and grieves.
In the hole of an oak the bull-bat day-dreams,
Forgetting dark nights and his terrifying screams.
On cool bed of earth in green solitude
The blacksnake entwines with his fair young love.
Over them roll the white night clouds above.

JACOB KOUNS 584

Cold Harbor's where I fell to fight no more,
And now I lie upon a muddy floor.
A log-chain shot was what that mowed me down,
It mowed me like a sickle mows a weed.
And now I lie, my flesh has ceased to bleed;
My flesh has ceased to be—it's dust instead.
If you disturb my dust you will find here,
Shreds of my uniform perhaps, and hair
And bone. If you will dig into my grave
You'll find my uniform retains its blue;
You'll find the wind will change that color too.
I do not know if we have won or lost;
I know that I have helped to pay the cost
Of war—I leave one son and my young wife.
At age of twenty-four I gave my life.

JOHN KOUNS 585

Cold Harbor's where I laid my rifle down.
I gave my rifle there to fight no more.
Cold Harbor's where I laid my young life down
And I'm left to sleep on this muddy floor.
Mine is a house of clay, and you will find
My room is velvet dark and full of worms
And bugs that hop like fleas among the worms.
And here among my bones and hair you'll find
Some tatters of my uniform still gray,
Gray as it were the day I marched away.
Now who has won the fight I do not know,
Since I am sleeping, sleeping here below.
And who has lost the fight I'd like to know,
Since I am sleeping, southern-dust below.

586

If John could speak today surely he'd say:
We sleep, my Brother, where the dirt breaks through
The roofs of our small houses made of clay.
We sleep, my Brother, blind to light of day,
We sleep, Brother, forever and a day.
I'm sleeping in my gray—you in your blue;
You killed at twenty-four, I at twenty-two.
What does it matter now, the Gray and Blue!
We sleep, my Brother, now to flower no more,
Our dust is resting on the muddy floor.
What is Cold Harbor to our blood-kin now,
And what is Gettysburg and all the rest!
I ask, What are these things to living now
And to a clay heart in a Brother's breast!

587

Ah, John, my Brother, now I speak to you:
You know defeat and I know victory.
We know the roots of grass, the roots of tree,
Down in this final earth of you and me.
This is defeat and this is victory.
We were the same in flesh and spirit too;
Only you wore the gray, I wore the blue.
Brother of mine, you fought for stripes and bars;
Brother of mine, I fought for stripes and stars.
What does it matter now that I have won;
What does it matter now that you have lost;
In flesh and blood and spirit we were one—
And for such kinship war we've paid the cost--
(Our part of cost). The cost is never paid,
Not even when we in our graves are laid.

VOICE 588

Now Blue and Gray, you sleep in the same clay,
Beneath the tufts of poison-vines you rest.
Do you both dream that you will rise someday
Or sleep forever—which will be the best?
Why did you fight—what is this thing called war?
Brothers, what did you spill your rich blood for?
Yes one of you did win—the other lost,
But in the end, even the winner lost.
You gave your blood—blood is such heavy cost!
Where is that line called Mason-Dixon line?
A silly line to set one blood apart,
To sever northern oak and southern pine.
The Mason-Dixon line runs through my heart.
Tell me, how can it set one blood apart?
Stays in my head: "Was silly from the start!"

589

THOMAS KOUNS: JACOB KOUNS' GRANDSON

Yes, I marched on the poppy fields in Flanders
And I marched on the shell-torn land of France;
I found my life in Flanders only chance—
And gas found me and I was doomed in France.
My dust is now at peace with Flanders dead—
I sleep beneath where poppies toss their heads;
Beneath roots that sink in our shallow beds.
Never again the Army Band will pep
New life into our dragging, dragging step.
Again, again the bugles will resound
Retreat for us—the soldiers underground!
We cannot hear—why do the buglers call?
Why not leave us to rest and that be all!
No use to call, for we cannot arise;
Holes in our bodies and dirt in our eyes!

590

When he marched on the poppy fields of Flanders,
When he marched on the shell-torn land of France,
Two ghosts, tall ghosts, kept step with him in Flanders,
Two ghosts, tall ghosts, kept step with him in France.
One on each side they marched by him in Flanders,
Went marching, marching, marching endlessly.
One on each side, they saw him laid in Flanders,
They marched away together there—those three;
And one tall ghost was dressed in Northern blue,
And one tall ghost was dressed in Southern gray,
Beside a youth in khaki they went marching,
Beneath the stars and stripes they marched away.
Down through all times those three go marching, marching,
Go marching, marching, marching endlessly.

TIM WINTHROP   591

Under a husky harvest moon Tim Winthrop sleeps,
He has come in from fields to rest at last.
Life to Tim Winthrop now is in the past,
Under a yellow harvest moon Tim Winthrop sleeps.
The oxen too that pulled the cutter plow
And broke the stubborn roots on new-ground hill,
They sleep beneath the roots of tall young trees;
The cutter plow and cattle's hoofs are still.
Tim's wife Symanthia sleeps here-by his side,
She was sixteen when she became his bride.
Under the dirt and moon she sleeps by Tim,
Through life, in death, she sleeps beside of him.
Their sixteen children sleep somewhere about;
Surely, the century's blown their candles out.

592

Do you hear creaking of the big ox cart
Over the Kentucky wilderness road?
Ah, don't you hear the creaking heavy load
And cattle panting under the heavy load?
And can't you see the party as it comes,
The party of Stewart, Culver, and Winslow;
Everyman, Crump, Winthrop, Boone, Chitwold,
    Thombs—
This pioneer party of the long ago?
Why did they come—what kind of blood were they?
They sought new homes under a quieter sky,
These men and women wrought of finest clay—
And they believed in God and they did pray.
Would their descendants welcome them today,
This old dust sleeping in Kentucky clay?

POND EARLMORE   593

He dreams not of the lovers he has known,
Nor does he dream of fruitful fields and skies,
Since over him soft drifts of snow have blown;
Since snow sheets and the dirt sheets blind his eyes.
His loves have gone perhaps to other lovers;
Perhaps they went and since have died away.
Since to the frozen earth Pond is a brother,
Since his strong flesh returns to shoe-make clay.
His Lucy Clarke has gone to Denver Wray;
His Lillian Meade has gone to Chester Bright;
His Eileen Phipps is sleeping under clay
Near where his Winfred Fields has met her night.
He loved them all, but never cherished one.
Now old and dead, their little lives are run.

594

RAHOON McCLEANNAHAN

Who lies beneath this dismal autumn rain?
Who lies beneath to never flower again?
Pretty Rahoon McCleannahan lies here.
Her flesh was autumn brown, her oak-black hair
Fell to her waist. Few women could compare
To fair Rahoon—a jewel rich and rare!
Her shapely feet and hands, her fine curved lips,
Her body shapely as a white larkspur.
And now where is this jewel rich and rare!
Under the red leaves and the autumn rain;
Under the bare trees and the dismal skies
Pretty Rahoon McCleannahan now lies.
Under the wind and stars and autumn moon;
Under the wind now kissing autumn corn,
Lies one—color of corn, pretty Rahoon!

BURKE CHITWOOD   595

Shovel him under—let the strings be mute!
Shovel him under—let his violin
Be set aside—and let his silver flute
Cease fluting silver notes to pretty wind.
It is all over for Burke Chitwood now—
The violin, the flute, the wooden plow;
No more will he flute to the wind at night
Beneath the yellow moon and white starlight;
Nor will Burke Chitwood play his violin
To lonesome tunes of tree tops in the wind.
Under a yellow moon and white starlight
And wind among the trees lies Chitwood now;
Under the harvest moon's soft yellow light,
Free from the violin, the flute, and plow.

KNAT HORNBUCKLE   596

Shovel him under to the stars and moon
And sun—shovel him under to all light.
He has not loved the light—he loved the night.
Now rest has come to him so sure and soon.
His eyes are blinded to the yellow moon.
The scent of corn is naught to his black nostrils;
His lips are dead unto the sense of touch;
His ears are deaf to songs of whippoorwills;
He lies in silence on a bee-glade hill.
He cannot smell the fragrance of the rose,
Where his wife and her new prime lover goes.
Near by they pluck the rose and kiss and kiss.
In Knat Hornbuckle's youth what did he miss?
He sacrificed his youth to come to this!
She dreams not of her husband here below
Who gave the wealth her other men now kiss!

"TIGER" BLEVINS 597

His guts hunger no more for nourishment;
His lips will parch no more for thirst of drink;
His local Law will not seek banishment
For future years—to him—people now think
Of him and speak of him, the life he led.
Someday they'll show his mound among the dead
To men unborn—now "Tiger" Blevins lies
Under a mass of weeds and floating skies.
And some folks love his name and some despise.
He leaves no single seed to grow his kind;
He gave his wild seed to the prostitute.
There was no harvest—neither took the loot
Now he has long been dead and out of mind.
The mound where "Tiger" lies is hard to find.

DAVE BLAKE 598

He stood alone and watched the passing crowd,
He was deformed of limb but sound at heart,
His life was silent as a passing cloud,
He came to earth and played the jester's part—
For Dave Blake laughed and laughed at everything.
When old friends died he laughed and went away;
Sometimes his guts went empty and he laughed;
He laughed and never had a word to say;
His flesh went bare of cloth and he laughed then;
He laughed and laughed among the sour-dough men.
More feeble grew his limbs, short grew his breath,
And he went laughing to the arms of Death.
Men went to see him on his burial day;
His clothes were new, a smile was on his lips;
They looked at him and laughed and went away.

599

"Earth is as kind to Dave as any man;
Kind to Dave Blake as president or king—
The gentle rain falls on him in the Spring;
Green grass grows from his dust same as the more
Ambitious dust—and birds alight to sing
On stiff green briars now springing from his bosom.
(Under the skin all men are just the same,
Some women say.) At death men are all clay,
We know, and all the difference is the name.
The serious and the jesters are the same.
All dead men's dust is rich to feed the blossom
(Much richer than the ordinary clay)
Of larkspur, rose, yucca, fern and jonquil
And sawbriar nestled on the sunburnt hill."

VOICE   600

Dust of America, we lie here still
Beneath the skin of you and ribs of you,
We lie beneath this battered winter hill
Where sleet and snow for many months have lain.
America, under the ribs of you
We lie and feel the water seeping through
Your skin—we hear the lonesome winter winds
Blow low and hard above our frozen mounds
And swirl the dead leaves on the frozen ground—
And we have heard the lonesome winter winds
Play through the barren tree-tops like violins—
And we have heard beneath a sheet of snow
Roots of the violets whispering low
About a better day of sunny Spring
When birds alight on blooming boughs to sing—
And we are cold as stone in beds below.

LEONARD SEATON 601

Here lies the tiller of a one-horse farm
With beauty in his brain and strength in his arm.
He built his log shack in a walnut grove
He farmed a white-ash and a dogwood cove.
He grew fat barns of wheat and corn and rye
And he was generous to men going by.
He plowed his uplands with a span of mules
And rooted up ten thousand wild fern stools.
He picked a guitar and sang to the stars
And served as soldier in two Indian wars.
He spun a few rhymes—they all were lost
Like he is now lost to the great wide world.
He's now a sleeping flower—with petal curled
Under the dead leaves of a silent world.

BERTICE McMEANS 602

I used the wooden plow—steel hurt the ground.
I used a log-beam plow the cattle pulled
    Through beech-tree roots and stumps and green-briar
        stools.
I believed in cattle and brown loamy ground,
And I loved frosty mornings when the sound
Of chestnuts dripped like rain from velvet burrs;
I loved brown autumn fields and stacks of grain;
I loved the windless autumn rain and stirs
Of autumn winds among the golden tops
Of oaks from September until November—
And these are scenes I wish I could remember.
I loved to saunter off among my crops
Of golden wheat and fresh buff-colored corn
And breathe the crisp air of the autumn morn.

VIRGINIA POAGE 603

Do you not hear the creaking wagon hub,
The panting mules—the sliding of the box?
Do you not hear the heavy check lines rub
The harness and the wagon wheels strike rocks?
That is Virginia Poage they now haul here
Over the dead leaves of the current year.
And there they stand—farmers under the trees!
Do you see them—under the sassafras trees,
Pointing to cloudless skies—trees bare of leaves!
And do you smell fresh yellow dirt heaped high
Under the trees on this day of September?
One thinks this is a day one should remember:
Virginia Poage now coming here to lie
Where wild birds and dead leaves are flying by;
This is the day that many shall remember!

PEARL HAMLIN 604

She will not hear the rhythm of the wind
Playing in tree tops like a violin,
She will not hear the monotone of water
Lapping at night along the Sandy River,
She will not hear the Falls incessant laughter;
She cannot hear since she has died forever!
She does not hear his voice when day is done
And he sings from the field at set of sun.
(Her country lad with life and honest air
Has grown to love another just as fair)
She does not see the red leaves drifting over;
Nor does she see the high clouds floating over;
Nor does she feel a sharpness in the wind
That brings us frost and clouds raveled and thinned.
Pearl Hamlin lies—the best for her is over!

605

BERNICE COLLINGSWORTH

There is no use to speak the truth of her,
Let her bones rest under the grass and thyme.
Now is no time for truth—she does not hear
After she has lain here year after year.
Much can be said of her; but let the dead
Rest now in tongueless peace and comforted.
These women know much as they need to know
Of her now dead—this one beneath the ground
Where drips of autumn leaves come slowly down,
Come gentle as the rain with ghost-like sound.
Their husbands loved fair Bernice Collingsworth—
And now these women call it well and good
That fair Bernice must sleep beneath the earth— .
This menace to their little neighborhood.

CONNIE PEYTON   606

The dead leaves drift where Connie Peyton lies
Under the autumn earth and windy skies.
Dead leaves wind-swirl and settle on her mound—
Color of leaves that bed the autumn ground.
Connie has come to rest from harvest fields
And no one knows her beauty earth conceals.
The light of stars was in sweet Connie's eyes;
Her skin was color of the sun-kissed leaf—
It is a pity that her days were brief.
Now Connie Peyton lies—sweet Connie lies
Under a heap of dirt and change of skies.
The dead leaves drift under the windy skies.
Above this youth of beauty earth concealed;
The wind blows over where sweet Connie lies,
Above her mound out on this autumn field.

INA JENKINS 607

Ina Jenkins from the fields has come to this:
The fever cut her down and she lies here
A sister to the earth, and over her
The autumn leaves blow withered brown and sere.
The autumn sun had browned her like the leaf—
She worked beneath the sweltering autumn sun
Till corn was cut and autumn work was done
And multicolored leaves blotched barren ground,
And winds whistled through trees with lonesome sound—
Then Ina Jenkins was laid in her mound.
She danced all night went home through morning rain;
Through cold December rain that drizzled down
Upon the fallow fields and leaves turned brown.
She danced that night—she never danced again!

EARTH SPEAKS 608

"And you come back to us, you Jesse Stuart;
We welcome you, our son, to bosom clay.
We welcome Jesse Stuart, your brain and heart;
We welcome you forever and a day,
Since you lie here, rough Bard, and take your rest.
Your pen is stilled, your voice is stilled and done;
Decomposing of your flesh has now begun.
Above your head wreathe friendly stems of grass:
Above your head the snake and stranger pass;
Beneath the roots of grass the friendly worm
Has slithered through your box into your warm
Decaying flesh to do it little harm.
We welcome you, our son, you Jesse Stuart;
We welcome you, Bard of the rustic art."

GRASS SPEAKS 609

"What did the Earth say to you, sleeping Dust?
Did Earth say worms had penetrated through
Your oak-board box and entered into you?
Goddamn a slithering filthy worm
That slithers through your sleeping dust yet warm.
I hate a worm that feeds on roots of me;
White worms that fatten on the roots of me;
A worm that gnaws through oak boards unto you.
These worms will speak of you, my fertile friend,
And they will fatten on you to the end.
I am the grass—my roots sink down to you;
And you are warm, I feel, with roots of me—
You with the black, the brown, cream-colored worms;
You rotting, rotting to eternity."

EARTH SPEAKS 610

"You Jesse Stuart, lie close against my ribs;
You feel eternal pulsing of my heart
Like water pressing a thin rhine of earth.
You lie with me, you Bard of rustic worth.
The clouds you loved are floating over you;
White clouds now roll across the windless blue
Of Heaven and the stars look down on you.
And now eternal organs of the wind
Harmoniously play with the violin
Of barren trees among the wind at night.
You do not hear, your little race is run;
The white-heat passion of your brain is done.
Dark moods eternal now you cease to have.
Since you lie in a wormy Plum Grove grave."

611

Now Earth, I care naught for your grave and worms;
Not for the grave and its eternity—
There is no need to care: these things must be.
Earth, I have come to play my little part
Among the lowly folks, for I belong
To them—it is for them I sing my song;
It is for them I give my rustic art.
And what is song—why does one sing and sing—
His rustic art behind the handles of a plow?
But may I ask, why do the cornbirds sing
Among Spring blossoms on a cherry bough?
Now let time fly like wild birds over me,
When I am sleeping, sleeping eternally.

612

And when at last the cold, cold earth has found me
And I am one of millions deaf to sound,
I am no better then than those around me,
The millions gone before and underground
Beneath where leaves and grass hang tremulous
And a million living feet throng over us!
I am no better than the millions were;
They have gone back to earth and so must I,
To sleep eternally year after year
Beneath the dirt and stars and wind and sky.
After I've lived and spent my little life,
From burst of bud until the turn of leaf;
After I've lived to sing my little song,
Life will be good—life will not be too brief.

613

Dying may not be so with me, Great Earth.
I dread to think it is—dying is change
I hope—back to a childhood or new birth;
Back to new life—to something fine and strange.
I've loved the Earth: I hate to lose the Earth,
The tree and bud, flower and leaf there-on;
The mist, the day, the dark and dusk and dawn.
I hate to lose the friendships I have made
With forms of flesh the graves of Earth destroy;
I hate to lose this life when I have played
With joy of life more than the average boy.
I am in love with life—I love to live
One of the light and time, the dirt and sky,
And one of wind and rain—I hate to give
My life—I hate to think at death we die.

614

I am no better than those gone before.
Let me think death is process and a change
And I shall live again—be something strange.
Let me think anything; for no one knows,
And all we choose to think perhaps is vain.
But I do know I've come—come not to stay,
My body is a living house of clay,
It must go back as men's have gone before
To Earth's jail-house behind the heavy doors.
The sentence there is long just for one crime
For birth and life—and we are crucified
When we are born and when our flesh has died.
We're brought into immeasurable space and time;
Earth is our jail-house and who holds the key
Unlocking space and time and eternity!

BERTICE EVANS   615

I walked on winter pavements cold and gray
In many far-off towns, for all my life
I was a tramp— feeble and in the way;
And with a dream that life was all a strife,
And other dreams that I could never realize,
I quickly put an end to my own life.
A tramp has dreams, but many men despise
A tramp with dreams on pavements cold and gray—
A tramp that's old and in the people's way.
And now I sleep, my friends—I sleep today.
My little dreams were never realized,
They died with me—same as men's farms will die
When they are dead. And now, my friends, I lie
With men who scornfully passed me by.

TUG OLIVER   616

I plowed these fields—I pushed the forest back;
Followed the forest when I pushed it back.
I raised my sixteen children in a shack,
I paid my honest debts—and here I lie
Among my sixteen children and their wives,
Their husbands and their children's children.
We spent our days trailing the cutter plows;
We killed the copperheads in waist-high fern;
In head-high oats and crabgrass in the corn
We pushed the forest back—it grew again
In second growth for our blood yet unborn.
We cleared the new-ground hills and plowed them well;
Our cutter plows did tear them all to hell.
But now our cattle cutter plows are rust;
And we—my wife and children—we are dust!

617

"The mold-board plow turns furrows over us
Where jeweled blades of rye hang tremulous.
The soil is thin and ruts are coming in
The fields; the black oat roots and leaves are gone
And all that's here is yellow clay and stone.
Over these barren hills a lonesome wind
Is blowing and the crows fly down and caw.
Over these graves a train of hungry crows
Will fly when April winds begin to thaw
The fields and children cut corn stalks with hoes.
No one knows where we lie in clay and stone;
No one knows where our dust has long been gone—
Gone with the plow, the weed, the tree, the years—
To sleep eternally—dust of pioneers!"

HOG MULLINS 618

Under the dirt by-hell I sleep at last;
Under the dirt by-hell I am confined—
Mad at myself—why did I live too fast?
Under the dirt I lie and out of mind.
What in the hell is work and what is life!
By-hell I lived—I put the tree line back;
I helped build furnaces and make the steel
For tea-rails, spikes, and slabs of railroad cars.
I helped to build this nation— I did wield
The saw, the ax, the sledge the pick and spade.
Now look at me—I sleep beneath the stars.
I sleep by-hell under the drizzling rain!
I sleep by-hell—life will not come again!

FON WILLIAMS 619

The fields I furrowed once have grown again
In blackberry briars and poplar trees and sprouts!
The fields I furrowed once have been farmed thin
And streaks of gulley wash are setting in,
And waves of tall horse weeds grow there about
The house that will not shelter me again.
I can't return to use my cutter plow
And tear the roots of tall trees all to hell;
No, I cannot return to ax and plow,
And there are many men to use them now.
No, I cannot return to plow again.
It is all over now and so I sleep
Under a harvest moon and void and deep;
Under a harvest moon I sleep and sleep!

BRYAN TULLEY 620

The river slashed along the brinks that day
And I did love the endless monotone,
Sitting beneath the willows on a stone.
Birds circled in the blue light of the day
Above the monotone of surging water,
And wind in willows and leaves blowing after.
I swam into this monotone of water,
Picking up leaves when winds blew through the willows.
When I was found, my face was cold and fair
And drifts of weeds were tousled in my hair.
Between my teeth I clinched a willow leaf
And in my hands death-gripped a willow stem.
Now I sleep in the land in peace and dream.
The land takes back my body strong and fair,
A drift of roots is growing in my hair!

CHESTER BLAIR

621

I lived my life and I did write some books!
I loved clean paper and my name in print.
It is all over now—where are my books?
They're dead as I and all my life is spent!
What is dream-stuff I speak—how can one bear
Clean paper and one's name in cold, cold print?
My friend, how can you let your days be spent
To give the best you have to die forever!
Forget your work and live—forget forever!
For words are cold when written on a stone;
Book words turn yellow as corn in the wind—
The best is not to play with words, my friend.
Where is the time I spent to write and write?
It's gone—gone—gone—and I live in this night!

622

Shovel them under, Earth—drink back their blood!
Shovel them under—they belong to you!
These pioneers of this vast neighborhood,
Shovel them under—bring them back to you!
You are the Earth and they are dust of you!
Why did you breed them strong and weak and wise,
And why did you not let them live forever?
Why let the worms now slither through their eyes
And cell them in a place that they despise?
Shovel them under, Earth, and feed them rain!
Earth, let the lightning rent your trees asunder,
Tear up their graves—do it over again.
Beat down the grass and make the tall trees wonder,
Moisten them with the silver drizzling rain,
Shovel them under, Earth! Again! Again!

LEW CUNNINGHAM 623

My friend, here is the tree they swung me to—
This black-oak tree with winds a-blowing through
The leaves that color now each swaying bough.
This is the place I gave my final bow
To life and then passed on to quieter clay—
The yellow clay I sleep beneath today.
I killed my wife—she would not live with me.
I stabbed her at her father's house one night.
Her blood splashed out—I carried it on me
To rock-cliff dens and den in hollow tree.
I slept at day, I searched for food at night,
I ate the grains of golden autumn corn,
I prayed for hell, I cursed "why was I born!"

624

I saw them bury her, for I was in
A locust thicket on a hill near them.
I crouched down low, I had a fear of them—
A fear of leaves that rustled in the wind.
I heard them sing for her—songs in her praise,
I heard them pray for her their lofty prayers.
I knew my time to live was numbered days,
My throat would be in strangling hands of theirs.
For days hard golden corn was sweet to taste,
The dry oak leaves made me a feather bed—
Better to sleep on leaves than with the dead!
Better to lie couched in a red-fox den
Away from searching eyes of the mob-men—
Better than swinging to a black-oak limb!

625

I saw them bury her and I loved her.
Why did I plunge a knife into her heart
And have to run and battle with the night?
Why am I now afraid of whip and stir
Of wind and autumn leaf? Ah, from the start
Another man loved her. I live with night
That he may not have her—that I may sleep
Only a hill away from her—my wife.
And now she sleeps because I took her life!
We'll sleep together—yet, one hill apart,
They'll take my life because I stabbed her heart.
I have not tried to get so far away,
For soon—soon I'll be sleeping under clay—
I put off dying though from day to day.

626

"A man came running, running down the hill,
His beard was long, his clothes were full of holes;
I saw him running running down the hill.
I saw him lose one of his old shoe soles.
And he went up the hill. I was afraid.
I knowed he was the man that kilt his wife.
The men soon come following tracks he made,
With baying hounds that smelled the tracks he made;
And when they passed I heard one curse his life.
They crossed the hollow and I was afraid.
They treed him up a low persimmon tree,
They brought the ragged stranger back by me
And he was weak to walk—I heard one cry:
'It is tomorrow, Killer, that you die!'"

627

After the hood had dimmed his living eyes
And noose was placed about his slender throat,
After the Killer whom the crowd despised
Was swinging dying on limb of an oak,
His own blood kin came there to take him down—
He was their clay and he was dear to them.
And on the hill beyond—not far away
From where his wife was lain, they laid his clay
To rest—and now the leaves swirl over him
In autumn and the green grass grows in Spring,
And birds alight near-by his grave to sing.
Many, many a child remembers still
The ragged bearded man that ran the hill—
The man that stabbed his good wife to the heart
To sleep in death—only a hill apart.

628

"Why do you stay, old woman—why stay here?
Why do you stay when you are ninety-four?
Life for you cannot be so many years
And you will sleep beneath a heavy door.
Wild phlox and thyme will cover then your bed;
A gray stone for your feet—one for your head,
And you will be one of the sleeping dead.
How can you stay, old woman, ninety-four,
When your own kin have slept for many years?
And they now sleep beneath a heavy door,
Beneath the thyme, the wild bull-grass and phlox;
Between the marking stones of old field rocks.
Why don't you go, old woman—why stay here?
Your breath is weary to your feeble lungs,
And life is weary to you living still,
Since your dear kin are sleeping on the hill!"

629

Ah, now, young friend,—here's why I'm staying here--
Not long till I'll be sleeping by my Dear.
He lies upon the hill—has lain for years,
And I stay close his dust and wait to die.
I have no relatives who live near-by,
And I stay close the sleeping of my Dear!
And of our twelve I am the one now left,
The rest are sleeping under thyme and phlox—
Sleeping, sleeping under the cold grave rocks!
My Dear and me—we raised our ten strong children,
We raised them grown and saw our ten-strong married.
And now, young friend, that's why I'm staying here
To be close my dead dust upon the hill—
My dust that will lie there forever still.
Soon I'll be sleeping by dust of my Dear!

RAG TUSSEY   630

Here is the railroad trestle where I died.
I still can feel the noose about my neck,
I still can hear the way the people cried,
And called me names before they broke my neck!
They tied the rope around an oak cross-tie,
They tied the rope securely so I'd die,
They let me fall down through to break my neck.
After my neck was broken and my heart
Had ceased to beat, they hauled my cold clay out
To sleep—to sleep just anywhere about.
After the jeering crowd had had their way,
After they spit on me and saw me die,
They went their way and had few words to say,
For I was dead and ready for the clay.

631

Why did they hang Rag Tussey in a trestle?
Rag Tussey and Tom Wilburn tried to wrestle,
Rag Tussey shot Tom Wilburn in the heart—
He shot him down in cold blood while at play
And in his grave Tom Wilburn lies today.
Rag Tussey scooped for Tom a shallow grave
And buried Tom under a drift of leaves.
The neighbors thought Tom Wilburn left his home.
They searched for him, but all their search was vain.
They smelled his scent in winds that touched his leaves,
They kissed his leaves and then for him they grieved.
Rag Tussey's hound dogs got the scent of him
And then Rag Tussey's hound dogs went for him.
Tom was Rag's neighbor and his bosom friend,
Could he let hound dogs eat him in the end!

632

"What did you do, Rag Tussey, with dead Tom?
What did you do with him the way he smelled?
What did you do with Tom the man you killed?"
"I'll tell you men what I done with Tom Wilburn—
I carried him each night to a new place.
The night was dark I couldn't see Tom's face.
Each night I scooped a new earth grave for him.
I carried him—a dead man on my back,
I smelled the human flesh that I had killed,
And when winds blew I had a fear of him;
Carrying the man I killed alone at night,
Burying him before the morning moon shone bright,
I scooped new graves and buried him each night.
And when I scooped each grave I had a fear
That on some night Tom Wilburn would appear
To me—not as a man, but as a light."

633

How did they find Tom Wilburn, old Rag Tussey?
"I kept him hidden through dark of the moon.
In light of moon—one night was light as day—
Church people saw me by light of the moon,
Carrying a dead man by light of the moon—
Under the trees in moonlight light as day;
And they could smell the scent of flesh I killed.
And when they saw me I threw down Tom's clay.
I had grown used to him—I did not fear;
As once I feared the wind among the trees—
A wind that stirred the leaves dead on the ground
And stirred the green leaves with a whispering sound.
New dirt had helped to kill the scent of him;
And flesh had now begun to fall from him."

634

ELIZABETH HARKREADER

Now she lies here—Elizabeth Harkreader;
She lies between the two tall men she married.
The first was Alec Thombs. When he was buried,
"Liz" married John—a better man to feed her.
Alec would play his fiddle on Sale Days
When there was not a bite at home to eat.
The people said Alec had funny ways—
His mind run on old tunes and dancing feet.
But John Harkreader was a man to work;
He was a good provider for Elizabeth.
Alec and John now sleep by her in death.
She had two sons by Alec—nine by John,
And seven of these sons now sleep upon
The hill by John and Alec and Elizabeth.
Two husbands and their wife now sleep in death.

CHARLIE BLAIN   635

Charlie lies here. For many years he's lain
Beneath the sunlight, sleet and snow and rain.
He has lain here beneath green growing grass
And yucca blades and honeysuckle vines;
He has lain here where people seldom pass
And where day-long the winds sigh through the pines.
He sleeps beneath low-hanging winter skies
And trains of hungry crows that send their cries
Down to the frosted barren winter lands.
Charlie drank heavily and he lived too fast;
Out in the cold, his body could not last.
And now he sleeps beneath sunlight and rain
And sleet and snow. The men loved Charlie Blain—
They will not see old Charlie's like again.

EMMIT ALLEN   636

I do not hear the pounding horses' hoofs
Over the dusty roads of Spring again,
I do not hear the patter on the roof
The night-long patter of December rain.
I do not hear the fiddle for the dance,
Nor do I hear heels cracking on the floor;
For I sleep here a man of circumstance—
I lie beneath Earth's heavy jail-house door.
I went too young, I would have married soon.
If one's life is a day, I went at noon.
Where is Sue Cartwell—the girl I loved?
Answer me, Wind: Where are my friends? I ask.
Now where are Monnie, Bill and Pearl and Joe?
"Monnie and Bill and Pearl now sleep below—
And Sue the one you loved has married Joe."

TOM JUSTICE 637

Tom Justice left his farm for quieter rest.
Earth drank him back and loved the taste of him.
Tom Justice takes a rest and that is best.
He sleeps—the farm can go to waste for him.
Under the yellow moon Tom Justice lies;
The arms of hills hold him against Earth's breast
And time goes on and on and never dies.
But Tom was man and he is taking rest.
"What is this life—what is it all about?
Why work like hell—follow the cutter plow?
Why have to face the world—be down and out,
Better if one had never seen a plow."
"Tom Justice, you lie still and take your rest.
Better you worked like hell, following the plow.
Lie there, you working man—you are the best,
For what to hell are all the rich men now!"

638

Listen! Do you not hear the seething rain!
Listen! Do you not hear paws of the mole—
Look at the ground a-bursting round his hole!
And watch the soft dirt drinking up the rain!
These things disturb a quilt that will not tear.
Look at the roots of grass and briars and trees!
Look at the heavy ruts the wagons wear
And gully wash—far deeper streaks than these!
Always, always—repair is blowing over,
Such as the weeds and grass and leaves and clover.
Always, always—just anyone can find
The greatest needle woman—Lady Wind.
Trees are her needles and sky is her shade
And all her patches are so neatly made!

"JUDGE" WINTHROP 639

"I hear a pounding on my narrow bed—
A pounding, pounding running through my head.
What is this pounding I would love to know
Beating down on my grave like heavy rain!
What is this pounding I hear here below—
I hear it till it shakes my eyes and brain!"
"That is your gavel, Judge Winthrop, you hear;
The one you used for order in the room—
The one you used when many met their doom.
You'll hear it, Judge, many, many a-year.
Remember men you sentenced to the pen;
Hard-working men—honest in daily toil!
They made a drink these tillers of the soil;
You got their drink and sent them to the pen!
Now lie there, Judge, this is your final doom—
The gavel, Judge—it's order in the room!"

DAVE BARNES 640

"I was a jailer once, I held the key—
I held the key all times and barred the doors.
Now I'm in jail, a key was turned on me—
A key that locks Earth's heavy jail-house doors.
And now who holds the keys that keep me here;
And will he ever come to set us free?"
"Lie there and sleep now on your dirty floor
And let your hip-bones cut into the dirt—
You were a jailer once afraid of work!
Lie there and sleep beneath the heavy door,
Lie there forever—damn your dust to hell!
A jailer once and you kept men confined,
Now you lie there at ease—you just as well
As be forever quarreling with the wind."

641

Here she sleeps under a thin blue moon.
Soundly she sleeps under the summer breeze,
Where lightning bugs are flitting through the trees.
Soundly she sleeps under the thin blue moon!
Lid Wingbright spent her life on wasted farms.
She spent it in the corn-fields with the hoe.
In winter when the ground was white with snow
She sat beside the fire and knitted socks,
But now her grave is marked with two field rocks.
Lid died with her twelfth baby in her arms.
Lid Wingbright sleeps upon this wasted farm
With her twelfth baby pillowed on her arm.
Under a thin blue moon they take their rest,
Under the lightning bugs and trees they rest;
And under breeze a-blowin through the trees,
And under stars they rest—and that is best!

642

Here lies Paul Wingbright—Lid Wingbright's Paul.
Do you remember seeing the cattle haul
Him to the grave? The snow lay on the ground.
The earth was cold and still—only the sound
Of wind and running water could be heard,
And plaintive chirruping of hungry bird.
Over the cream-white snow on sassafras sled,
Ike Mealer's cattle pulled Paul to the dead.
Do you remember the yellow heap of clay
Fresh from the hole we put Paul in that day?
Remember how we shoveled this man under?
And how we bowed our heads in prayer and wonder;
And how we kicked the snow and went away?
Not one of us had any words to say.

643

Who was Wingbright—the man we buried here?
Ah, don't you know? To you he was old Paul—
Just old man Paul Wingbright and that was all.
Now let me tell you, friend, about Wingbright:
He was a man compounded of the finest clay
There was on earth. And in Paul Wingbright's day
He helped to push the forest on and pave the way;
He helped to blast the cliffs and make the roads;
He drove the oxen with their heavy loads;
He helped to make cross-ties for these railroads,
And drive the spikes that hold down rails of steel.
Now that was Paul Wingbright. He sleeps today,
But not a single stone does mark him here—
His name is on old records left somewhere.
Unknown, unnamed, here sleeps earth's finest clay.

644

And where are Lid's and Paul's twelve children now?
The twelfth is dust and on its mother's arms.
And Bill and Wid and Steave follow the plow
On slopes of their Kentucky mountain farms.
And Jim and Ike now sleep beside the Seine;
They'll not return to their Kentucky hills again.
And Don fell at this Old Ike Mealer's Brawl—
And no one knows this day who stabbed Young Paul.
Young Lid and Kate live somewhere in the West,
And Maud and Grace live somewhere in the North.
Good flesh to leave the hills—it is not best;
For what is all the money in the North
To folks with hearts contented in their breast?
What is the North, the East, the South, the West;
And bloody Seine to them—and all the rest?

645

The sun and moon and stars now shine on them:
The sun at day; the moon and stars at night.
But what is light to them—I ask my friend;
And what is wind and what is anything
From winter leaf to blossom in the Spring?
It is all night to them and night is end.
The gray stones in the grass are naught to them
And petals of their thorny grave-side rose.
And blades of grass above are naught to them
And songs of crickets, birds, and wind and rose.
The creamy colored belly of the snake
That writhes amid dew-jeweled grass at night
Is more consoling to them in their night
And more caressing to them in their tombs,
Than mass of parasitic blackberry blooms.

646

Under a yellow harvest moon they sleep—
Thousands of dreamers under the evening sky;
Under the moon eternally they sleep—
"The fling they had at life" has been laid by.
The tilted moon rides high above them here;
Above the field stones at their head and feet
The moon rides high above these pioneers
Where their rich dust with the thin earth did meet.
Ride high above them, moon! Ride high and laugh!
Blow over, winds, and write the epitaph.
Blow over, winds, blue dreamers here below
And sing for them a song of long ago—
Sing melodies for them they used to know,
Sing: "Nellie Was A Lady," "Old Black Joe."

647

Ride high above where they have met defeat
Beneath the golden wheat and talking corn;
Ride high above them, moon—the fields of wheat
And spacious fields of tall green talking corn;
Come down, you silver spears of silver rain,
And tear the earth where these dreamers have lain
So long they have become a part of stone.
Blow over them, high winds, and make your moan.
Blow over, winds, and tell it to the trees—
Swirl down on them, you brown late-summer leaves.
And hide them, early ripening autumn corn!
Harden the ground above them, autumn sun!
Hold these blue dreamers, since their race is run,
Under the leaves, the snow or anything;
The corn, the wheat, the green grass of the Spring.

648

Who cares—you torrents fall hard as you may
And beat into a pulp the earth's hard clay.
Blare forth earth's bedded rock unto the sun!
Tear up the earth and let wide rivers run
Into a muddy sea. Make the earth new.
Tear up the dust of all the sleeping old;
Tear it to shreds and cleanse of human stain;
Filter with gushing torrents of new rain,
Or freeze like stone until it crumbles cold.
Let earth be new, let all the old be past
And let the stormy heavens overcast
The world into a darkness. Let this night
Be jeweled by new stars and different night.
Let us have new earth, new life, new death;
Give us new everything and a clean breath.

649

Under a thin blue moon these dreamers lie,
Under the moon with faces to the sky.
Maybe their spirits stalk and winds have swept
Them out among the briars and under trees—
Maybe they swept them to their destinies.
Last night an owl sat on a snag and wept
For them; a jar-fly sang of discontent;
The whippoorwill wailed forth his discontent;
But corn-field beetles lulled a deep lament.
But still they sleep—builders of destinies,
Beneath the stars, under the roots and trees;
Beneath the grass, under the summer breeze—
And sleep, you builders of the nation! sleep!
Our heritage from you we hope to keep—
Builders of destiny. We pray your sleep
Is rest for you—forever kind and deep!

650

Blare forth, you brazen trumpets of the wind,
And bellow loud, you guts of marching thunder!
Split wide the earth, you whips of lightning, in
The rain-cloud heavens—split the earth wide!
Belch up her dirty vomit from inside!
Show this small earth that you can hurt her pride!
Heavens, throw down your torrents of white rain
And clean the earth. Do this again. Again.
Moisten the lips of dreamers in the earth—
Blue dreamers with dirt lips and blurred eyes,
Blue dreamers with the worms in paradise.
Blare forth, wind trumpets! thunders roll!
Beat down, you savage rains, so white and cold!
Beat out the written footprints from this scroll!
The earth is new no more—the earth is old!

Preface
    for after
        Death

651

I have lain down to sleep—I close my eyes;
I close my eyes to darkness and the night—
To weed fields, corn-fields and the starry night;
To brown leaves in the wind, to gray moonlight.
I've closed my eyes to every living thing;
To wild birds in the skies, to leaves that wave;
I've closed my eyes to streams that leap in Spring
And cut and scar across old warriors' graves.
My eyes are closed to harvest fields and plows
And shacks that dream in gourd-vines and the rain;
Hill pasture fields spotted with stumps and cows;
Brown stubble fields with little stacks of grain.
And think, my eyes will be forever closed
To all of these, since I have found repose.

652

My ears are deaf to winds against the ground
That whine through briars and weeds and then grow still.
My ears are deaf to water's lonely sound,
Where water leaps the rocks upon the hill.
My ears are deaf to all the tunes I made;
My ears are deaf to winds among the trees;
To winds among the frost-white fodder blades;
To sounds of rabbits' feet upon dead leaves.
My ears are deaf to whippoorwill and lark;
My ears are deaf to willows in the wind;
And deaf to bass strings on an oak limb harp—
Earth's quilt's too deep for music to sink in.
I do not hear cool drippings of the rain
Nor feel grave clouds a-falling on my brain.

653

I shall not feel cool water on my shoulder;
I shall not touch the dead leaves with my feet
Since I lie under dirt and root and boulder;
Since I lie under such a heavy sheet.
I do not feel the wind against my face;
I do not feel wild plum roots pierce my heart—
I must be stone down in this silent place
When green-briar roots have pushed my lips apart.
I have not put my feet against dead leaves
Nor back against the earth to watch the skies;
I have not touched the rough bark on the trees;
Nor cool rain dripping down into my eyes.
My brain can't grasp the vastness of this night;
My brain can't sense the darkness or the light.

654

My body strong as any black-jack tree
Has gone back to Kentucky mountain clay.
The sun and stars and moon now shine on me.
Under this dirt I dream I'll rise someday.
I hope the same blood will flow through these veins;
I hope my bones will give rebirth to flesh
Once mine—but now rich dirt. I hope this brain
Again grows active in this living head
And wild plum roots are severed from this heart
When I have risen from my narrow bed
And torn the tufts of grass and briars apart
And come to earth to earn my daily bread;
Come back to earth to play a different part.

655

Since I am dead, I shall speak back to you.
Don Davidson, eternity is night.
It is one long dark night—no light breaks through
The thick walls of the grave. I have no sight,
For coffin worms have slithered out my eyes,
And my eye-sockets are two deep dark holes.
And my jaw-bones protrude above the skin.
My finger bones are shining white and cold.
The black boards of my box are breaking in.
Oh, Don, eternity's too long to wait,
Down in this nether world so desolate
Where worms have left me dust and stench and bone—
Where worms crawl through my straight black hair;
In life they would have had no business there.

656

Don Davidson, I walked on top of earth.
My guts went empty and my flesh went bare.
I wrote of sadness and I wrote of mirth,
I was a poet and I did not care.
I was not greedy for small things in life;
Don Davidson, you know I write the truth.
I stood an oak—winds cut me like a knife;
Don Davidson, you know I write the truth.
It is all right if poets come and look;
My earth is six feet long and two feet wide.
The books I wrote are dusty, and this book
A yellow manuscript long laid aside
Upon the wall-plate of an old log-house—
Its lone admirer is a brown wood-mouse.

657

Don Davidson, I know you are a man.
And unafraid you've gone to meet your life.
You are one poet in a world of men,
You've marched to beating drum and shrilling fife.
Once, Davidson, I went to you with lays;
I read you plow-boy lays no man had heard;
I read you lays of my kin's rustic ways;
I read old tunes to you like a fluting bird.
And you did like the shrill notes of my fife;
You liked the splits I wove into my baskets;
And you did like the way I sang of life;
You liked the black boards that I used in caskets.
Proud poet of the rustic life you heard,
Me make the low notes of a corn-field bird.

658

Don Davidson, since I am left to lie
Under the cold earth for so many years
When the white moon floats up the summer sky
And shines down on my grave red-brush and briars,
There's something then I shall speak back to you:
I'd like to ask you if my Jean Elizabeth
Is living with another lover now;
If mountain Lydia Doore now sleeps beneath
The rose bush or the thorn; and if my plow
Is rusting in the field. Don Davidson,
I spent life freely and I went too young,
Without a wreath for some small glory won.
I went before my best of songs were sung.
This eternity's long for me to wait;
Eternity's so dark and desolate.

659

Since I am dead and Davidson you read
These rugged lines you carved in crumbling stone,
Remember now I'm sleeping with the dead;
Remember now I'm dust and stench and bone.
I was a man who hated silly stuff—
Don't let men make a moon-god out of me,
When I am dead and they can run a bluff
And tell about the fool I was at tea.
Don't let them sentimentalize this man.
I've lived the things that I have said and done.
And I did not belong to clique and clan
And I was unafraid to gut and bone.
These words won't live when I'm a rotted man,
For rain and time will blur the page of stone.

660

And now I shall speak back to my own hills
And say farewell to them—these hills I love;
Farewell to hills of phlox and daffodils;
To rugged hills and flying clouds above;
To hills broad-shouldered and the deep ravines;
And sky-blue mountain water leaping rocks.
Farewell to rock-cliff ribs and scrawny pines;
Farewell to stubble fields and fodder shocks—
These are my own Kentucky streams and hills.
Kentucky's womb gave blood and flesh of mine
Where men still unafraid will shoot to kill;
Where men still clear the dirt of briar and bush;
Where strong men clear earth and use bull-tongue
    plows;
And make their bread by the sweat of their brows.

661

Farewell to Springtime in Kentucky hills;
Farewell to dogwood blossoms and percoon;
To blood-root in the wind and daffodils;
To wild plum blossoms and white April moon.
Farewell to walnut trees beside the river;
Farewell to April's sky-blue singing brooks;
Farewell to young thin April leaves that quiver;
Farewell to white clouds mirrored in the brooks.
Farewell to Spring wheat waving in the wind
And rank potatoes bursting from the ground;
Farewell to shower-clouds watery-thinned
And to the far-off cow bell's lonely sound.
Farewell to April and bright bull-tongue plows;
Farewell to green pastures and spotted cows.

662

I hate to leave Springtime among the hills
Of dark Kentucky and her solitudes;
I love her blood-roots and her daffodils;
I love fern-shaded water in beech woods,
And midnight singing of the whippoorwill,
And thin-pipe music from the lean swamp frogs.
I love dark silence on a wooded hill
And mushrooms growing on old rotted logs.
I love the fox-fire growing on wet leaves.
To all of these, think, I must say good-by,
To my Kentucky and my strong oak trees;
To April night and the white starry sky.
I say farewell to these—farewell is long.
There may not be a new life and new song.

663

I say farewell to Springtime and the rose.
It is all over now—Springtime has gone
And I am gone. How quickly the time goes
And I have come and gone to my long home
And left behind my log-shack in the rain,
And butter-cups and ferns along the streams,
And leafy black-gums growing by the lane.
It all goes back to memories and dreams:
Thin black-oak leaves, wood-smoke from burning
    brush;
May-apples growing by a rotted log;
Thin-fluted notes from a brown spotted thrush
And long barks from a far-off running dog.
Farewell to Spring—season of growth and sun;
Farewell to Spring—season of youth and fun.

664

I hate to sleep and let the summer pass—
Lie dead and let the summers go and come.
But I must lie beneath the summer grass
While generations of men go and come.
And I shall say farewell to summer rose—
The ramble rose that arches a front gate.
And I shall say farewell to wind that blows;
Farewell to winds that stir the sprouts and corn.
And I have loved the high dry summer days;
Brown stacks of oats, clean harvest fields and stubble;
And I have loved green landscapes in the haze;
And pasture streams the ferns and willows trouble.
Oh, I have loved the summer next to Spring;
These lazy days with birds on whirring wings.

665

Oh, I have said farewell to many things—
To hills I love and people there among;
Farewell to winters, autumns and to Springs;
Farewell to loves I had when I was young.
Now I must say farewell to summer days;
Farewell to fields of wheat and oats and corn;
To yellow sunlight and the purple haze
And morning glories fresh among the corn.
Farewell to martins gathering for the south
And drift across the windy skies like leaves;
Farewell to white old hills in summer drouth;
Farewell to leaf-bare fruit-red apple trees.
Farewell to music of the corn-top wind
That plays with tall crab-grass a violin.

666

Summer has faded from the mortal eyes.
Summer has gone and leaves have flown and trees
Are wind-bent silhouettes on windy skies.
Summer has gone—the blood-red shoe-make leaves
Drift on September's low-lipped dwindling streams.
Summer is gone—the old grain fields are fallow
And trains of crows black as wet chestnut burrs
Fly over painted fields of red and yellow.
And I must say farewell to summer now.
Farewell to briars and sprouts and pale green rye;
Farewell to sheds and rakes and bull-tongue plows;
Farewell to all between the dirt and sky;
Farewell to summer, for it quickly goes,
Faster than yellow fields are searched by crows.

667

Farewell to autumn's melody of words,
Harp music for the tree-tops in the wind
And heavens filled with flying leaves and birds,
For now the leafy trees are getting thinned.
The autumn water is not fit to drink.
Lean cattle eat spice-wood and mulberry sprouts,
For grass is green and brown and black as ink.
The crows fly down and follow cows about
And daub their tough toes into warm cow dung,
And peck and caw and wipe their bills and caw,
And fill their craws and poke their necks and crane—
And then they fly away across the pastures.
Farewell, wise bird—the wisest of the wise.
Go on and eat cow dung with opened eyes.

668

Farewell to highland pink and Scottish thistle;
Farewell to purple blossoms of iron weeds;
Farewell to woods rain-washed clean as a whistle
And shoe-make leaves now red enough to bleed.
Farewell to the sweet smell of autumn woods—
The rich sweet smell of golden leaves and flowers.
To days that did excite poetic moods
When I with gun and book did waste the hours.
Farewell to autumn and brown stacks of grain
And fields of frosted weeds where rabbits nest;
Farewell to cool gray days with windless rain;
Farewell to autumn scenes I loved the best—
To high ridge roads with pinks among brown rocks;
To green-briar hills and valleys filled with phlox.

669

I love these brown Kentucky autumn hills.
I've earned my bread from them with hoe and plow.
And there I sang my lays like whippoorwills
And gray-corn birds; but I have left them now.
I left the gray moon-rise and gold sunset;
I left this land dark-gray and desolate.
I left my rugged lands; I must forget
The log-shack and the rusty square-wire gate.
I did not want to go, but I have gone,
Back to the warm womb of this Mother dirt.
I'd rather stay above and write in stone
That crumbles—plow my fields and sow and work.
I am not fond of this eternity—
The grave worms and the roots of a plum tree.

670

Farewell to naked briars and rag-weed stems
And dwindling streams reflecting trees and skies;
Farewell to wind and grave-yard grasses' hymns.
To these I close my ears and blind my eyes.
I hate to sleep and let the autumn pass
Over my bones and never speak to me.
I hate to be deaf to the sound of grass
And wind, and blind to red and yellow tree.
But I must say farewell—if I could rise
I would arise and go back to my shack
And drink of water that's reflecting skies
And dig my hands into a loam that's black.
My eyes and ears and brain are empty shells
And I am nothing speaking back farewells.

671

The seasons are unto the life of man.
In Spring man is a hidden piece of clod.
This clod is given breath by a birth plan,
It lives a life and then lies under sod.
Springtime is youth to man, clean silver hour;
Springtime is life to man, he plows the loam.
Springtime is love to man, he takes his flower
And sometimes settles down to make a home.
Springtime, and gather roses in your May;
Gather your roses while you two are young,
For Springtime roses only bloom today.
In Springtime days the sweetest songs are sung;
The songs are sung—immoral, good, or nice;
Remember Springtime days will not come twice.

672

In summer man goes forth to work the soil
With mattocks, spades and bull-tongue plows and hoes.
He goes to make a living by his toil;
Goes forth to work before the summer goes.
In summer man goes forth, eager and strong;
Masculine flower in his mature bloom;
The time to make his bread and sing his song,
For winter brings white-sheeted hills and gloom.
Man, go and work, for winter night is coming!
Look at the winter trains of hungry crows!
Man, go—the yellow summer sun is shining
And you will reap part of this grain you sow.
Go forth, soil man—it's time to work and sow!
Go forth! Don't leave a weed in any row!

673

When autumn comes, man's going down the hill.
It is the season when the leaves turn brown—
The season man cannot revive his will;
He's reached the hilltop and he must start down.
He sees his work that he has left behind.
The Springtime and the summer's work are there;
Brown stacks of grain fresh-colored in the wind—
The bins of corn made by his rough plow-share.
His flesh shall wither like these autumn leaves;
His bones grow ashy and his skin turn brown;
And autumn winds shall strip his flesh from bones
And winter winds shall blow his white bones down.
But over him these winter winds shall moan
When leaves and dirt have claimed him for their own.

674

Ah, winter man, a naked forlorn tree,
You stand the winds that cut you like a knife;
You've come with none or some philosophy;
You have come now to meet the end of life.
You strong oak tree, stand out and bare the blast!
Stand unafraid of destinies that come!
Sledge-hammer tree, whip back unto the last,
For when the winter calls she beats her drum.
When winter comes, the mountain world is still
Save creaking timber and ice-slushing streams.
Man lies there-by at the foot of the hill.
An old man lies there-by and dreams his dreams;
An old man sleeps there-by so cold and still;
An old man sleeps at the foot of the hill.

675

And now I speak, my friends—what is a book?
To put life in this book I give some life.
And now, dear friends, draw out my life and look
And you will find a shell of rusty strife.
A book is hell—why does one write a book?
Why does one write and write and leave one's food?
The answer is: Why do the stars give light?
Why does the body's heart keep pumping blood?
A book is hell—there's nothing to a book;
But yet one hates to give words to the wind.
And in a book I never saw a brook,
I never heard a wind-grass tambourine.
A book is word-stuff to be sold and bought;
For men to feed and profit on one's thoughts.

676

No Sir, I never tried to write a book.
My pencil traced the sounds of high winds blowing
And sketched a willow-aggravated brook
And made some pictures of the green grass growing;
Word-drew a peddler in a thread-bare suit;
Word-drew a new moon piece of cleared ground;
It pictured oak-brown leaves and red plum fruit;
White windy skies and water's lonely sound.
The hand that touched the pencil and the brain
That told the hand to shove the pencil on,
Did not write this for profit, loss and gain.
They wrote before my body's food was gone.
For words are slow to buy a poet bread.
Sometimes his words will sell when he is dead.

677

Don Davidson, if I have stolen words
To write in books, you must erase my name;
For words to me were big as skies to birds
And rhymes beat in my head hot as a flame.
Don Davidson, I did not ask them come.
But I sat by the plow and wrote them down.
I rhymed them to the slow beat of a drum
And to the whirs of dead leaves drifting down.
Why should I steal my words from books, I ask?
I carried brains and baskets filled with words;
I spun my rhymes—(To me it was no task)—
Words were to me I've said as skies to birds.
If ever I stole words from some dead poet,
Since I am dead I do not want to know it.

678

Maybe there is the sound of windless rain,
The steady thump of rain on my grave rock;
I have no way to tell with this dead brain
The sound of rain that's ticking like a clock.
Though flesh is close related to the time;
(My ears are deaf to any ticking sound)
Though life is close related to the rhyme;
What chance has one now lying under ground?
And then to think each comes and takes his turn.
Each man's a god and each is crucified—
Each goes back to the dirt and grass and fern
After the temple of his flesh has died.
Each comes and goes and each must go alone;
Each life is dirt and time and rhyme and stone.

679

There is no more to say when I have lain
So long I have become a part of clay
And wild plum roots grow down to pierce my brain,
And roots of ferns have pinned me down to stay.
Better if I had fallen on some hill
With face upturned to high white floating skies;
Better if I had lain there cold and still
Till ants and crows had eaten out my eyes
And hounds had pulled the carrion from my bones.
Better than lying here to never rise
Under the weight of earth and trees and stones.
Better to lie out where the night wind cries
And hound dogs bark and growl when one is dead
Than to lie pinched-up in a narrow bed.

680

The winds are kind to white bones on a hill.
The black snakes love to coil among white bones;
White bones are foot-rest for the whippoorwill;
White bones are a clean kind of pretty stones.
And dust of one is quick growth for the weeds,
For round a pile of bones the weeds grow tall;
They get the kind of nourishment they need—
These barricades wherein the snakes may crawl.
Then let my bones lie open to the wind;
My dust give quick growth to the roots of weeds;
Let my eyes' socket-rims turn to the skies;
Let wind and weeds play the sweet violin.
This is the mountain requiem my dust needs
When on the surface of some hill it lies.

681

If I could now come back I would not come,
For my Kentucky hills have made a change.
The hill-man's heart stirs not to fife and drum;
His hunting grounds have grown to something strange.
It is all strange—white boards replace the black.
There is no cutter plow nor hunting horn
Nor farewell-summers growing near the shack;
There are no morning glories in the corn.
The Showmen cried: "The hills-men need a change.
We'll send their young to school and iron them out."
And if they need a change they got a change
To strawlings that the wind could blow about.
When their good work was done, our life was lost.
And now men are the same from coast to coast.

682

My trees have fallen to the saw and ax.
And now my hunting grounds are open fields.
The dirty Showmen gave my people facts.
The old were stubborn, but the young did yield.
And now there are no possums, minks and coons
And foxes in the bare Kentucky hills;
And few oak leaves to play against the moon—
Nor any midnight singing whippoorwills.
And I would rather sleep than to come back;
Lie through eternity and never rise
Than see white frames replace the mountain shacks
And find trees gone from under windy skies.
I'll take eternity though it be black
And I be blinded with worms in my eyes.

683

The sweetest music that I ever heard
Was autumn tree-top music in the wind
When clinging dead leaves fluttered like wild birds
And reached the bass notes on a violin.
And in some rainy season of that year
When I heard the slow beat of autumn rain,
It made me think an enemy was near.
(A rain war-drum would fire this mortal brain)
(To this far drum men lightly marched on leaves)
And there was music in the quail's wild calls,
And in the lizards scaling black-oak trees;
There's low coarse music when the blacksnake crawls
And loud shrill music in the barking hound
And streams of water running underground.

684

I always loved Kentucky's lonesome water,
And when I went away I wanted to return.
Just something to Kentucky's lonesome water
Makes me remember and my burnt heart burn—
(Cool silver water under beech and fern)
A stream curved more than a dry-blade of fodder,
It is enough to make one soon return
From things he went into a far world after.
So many times I craned my neck to drink
When I lay down on leaves by lonesome water
And pushed the drooping ferns back from the brink
And I drank from this fodder-blade of water.
And lonesome water is so sweet to drink,
And I was proud to hear its welcome laughter!

685

I loved the earth—I loved to dig the dirt.
The earth was mine and I belonged to earth.
I loved to put my hands in dirt and work.
It's noble to work down against the earth.
I did know men who feared an honest toil;
Parasitic men who lived without a reason;
Their hands were clean, they were afraid of soil;
They did not plant and harvest in a season.
I loved to work with earth, for in this end
It may be I have gone to meet the night.
The night is kind (night cometh as a friend)
When one lies down too tired to work and fight.
Eternity is long—it is the end.
I shall lie here with earth, my bosom friend.

686

I had to leave the earth and woods there-on;
I had to leave my mules and bull-tongue plow;
Their trace chains rattling at the early dawn
When I rode out across the fields to plow.
Without the crack of whip my mules would pull
The bull-tongue plow to furrow new-ground earth;
The plow would hitch on every green-briar stool,
For green-briar stools are tough in new-ground earth.
Now who will keep my mules since they are old
And men got from their bodies the best work;
As "plugs" in Greenup soon they will be sold
For skins and bodies to enrich the earth.
If I were a man alive, they'd not be sold
For green-back paper and cankering gold.

687

Don Davidson, think after you have read
These words that I have spoken back to you
That someday you will be one of the dead,
Be dead so long the dirt will soon spill through
The thin planks of your box and you will crave
The sunlight and the wind and things you love.
You'll find that Hell is sleeping in a grave
When moon and stars are in the sky above.
Remember you will be as I am now.
You will not hear the music in the wind.
You will not get to use a bull-tongue plow.
Don Davidson, you will lie there confined;
Lie deaf to all the cricket sounds above.
When dead, you'll know what I am speaking of.

688

Don Davidson, you walk on earth today.
The earth is yours and you belong to earth.
Remember Davidson, some things I say,
Since I speak back to you—the actual worth
Of man's not what he takes but all he gives.
I see this now, since I am in the grave.
Happier is he who works and barely lives
And does not get the things he'd like to have.
Power of happiness belongs to him—
(Not comfort, now), happiness is bliss.
"The dead take to the graves in their clutched fingers
That which they gave away." (Memory lingers)
I ask if life at last comes not to this?

689

There were some things in life I learned to heed.
That knowledge was not carried out in baskets.
Some blossoms spring from the rough useless weed.
And rotten flesh is buried in fine caskets.
I learned it did not take a Ph.D.
To walk between the handles of a plow.
I bartered cash and life and time to have
The greatest cheat on earth—my own degree.
I learned that money was the root of evils
And it would send me worthless to the grave.
I found the Saintly Saints were very Devils
Living behind cord-wood stacks of common lies
And snooping round in search of paradise.

690

I know I do not need a Ph.D.
To throw the fodder over to the cows
And to interpret wind in the pine tree
And to sit by and watch the cattle browse.
Degrees are things to have on parlor walls,
This written scroll that shows what one can do.
Degrees would make good bedding for cow stalls;
They surely would be richer than manure.
Oh, it is strange how people run a bluff
And put themselves above the things they are.
They look upon unlettered men with scoff,
These chosen intellectuals striving for
To drop ten pole-beans down a craw-dad hole
And give to charity—God bless their souls!

691

Now when that uninvited Guest appears
And drives his two-horse surrey to your gate,
You will drop in beside of him with fears
Of where you go and fears of being late.
But he will take the lines and slap the rumps
Of his black horses and the wheels will roll
Into the night by leaps and bounds and jumps
Until these horses are beyond control.
And where you go (remember as you read)
Is surely beyond all mass of space,
Where time is vain and millions lie asleep.
And when you go (remember to take heed)
There's not a sweet word-woven woman's world.
You'll be a Voyager upon the deep.

692

Someday your spirit may stalk back among
The hills you loved and peer behind closed doors
Of gourd-vine shacks you knew when you were young.
In that yard you may find old-fashioned flowers
And apple trees with swings made of trace chains.
And you may find paths trodden to the well,
Woodhouse, corn-crib, smoke-house and the draw-bars
(Yard paths worn bare enough for feet to tell)
And in the heavens the white swarms of stars
May shine above the place where your remains
Lie on the place—and your spirit walks and grieves
And smells the wild phlox wet with cool June dew
And listens to the silver-fluttering leaves,
And thinks of her—the dearest one you knew.

693

The stars will shine forever over you,
But they will never reach down to your face;
And the dead leaves will hover over you
Not knowing it is your last resting place.
In summer, burdock leaves will flap and wave
And shoe-make sprouts will grow and spit red leaves
That will lodge on a net, brown love-vine weaves
And webs that spiders weave above your grave.
You will not care for rhymes and gold leaves when
You lie in this place I am speaking of.
I don't think you will know about them then,
And I don't think that you will dream of love
When you lie blind to drifting skies above.
Out of the womb of woman at your birth.
At death you go back to the womb of earth.

694

The moon is darkened and the cloud-dimmed sun
Won't rise to greet you Don Davidson.
This is the end—your race in life is run.
I do not know if you have lost or won.
But do you think it matters, won or lost?
You hate to hear men cheep about "a chance."
It's up to one to run and pay the cost.
To win or lose, there's no big difference!
But run, you'd say, regardless how you run.
It won't be long until the mourners go
About the streets and grinding will be low
(A beauty seer spoke of this long ago)
And songs of birds and crickets be a burden,
And light will fade: the moon and stars and sun—
Now let me say "Farewell," Don Davidson.

695

This pasture land is filled with blackberry blossoms;
There-under lies the dust of generations;
Rich dust with blackberry blooms sprung from their
    bosoms!
Rich sleeping dust, the builders of the nation!
They sleep—their houses are a-tumbling down.
The worm-rail fences built by them are rotten.
The fields they tilled grow green with sprouts again
While they lie in their graves and are forgotten.
A yellow wind is spilled in briars above them.
Cobwebs are woven with a thread-like sound
In these tall weeds the spiders make their home.
Spiders may whistle to these men they love them.
The moles may write the same in mellow mounds
While the new crop of youth turn back new loam.

696

I do belong to these men of the past.
I am one of a sleeping generation.
(We all go to weed roots and dust at last)
I may not have been a builder of the nation.
But I was just one of a hundred millions,
Lover of earth and trees and blackberry blossoms,
And a one-horse scrap of land, Don Davidson.
But now the blackberry roots grow in my bosom.
My fields wait for the plow and weeds are growing.
They soon will be too tall to turn them under.
Cow birds swarm to my fields for April sowing.
Blacksnakes crawl out after the first loud thunder.
Don Davidson, I speak: Go take the plow,
And peace will come from tangled grass and wind.

697

I told my mother when the years had crept
If she were living and I had grown still,
I must not sleep where my two brothers slept
Beneath the pine trees on a pasture hill.
That place is far away and desolate,
Where cow bell sounds are muffled by the grass;
Where blunt-tail copperheads lie still and wait
To swallow toads and rabbits as they pass.
I'd like to sleep by them, but not sleep there.
And I am glad that I am left to lie
In Plum Grove many long and lonesome year
Under the stars of a Kentucky sky.
Kentucky black-oak boards now cover me
And I sleep at Plum Grove eternally.

698

To Martha Hylton: My Mother.
My rest has come and I speak back to you
Of days we worked under the grilling sun.
Black loam and burley was a fact to you
And goose-neck hoes a-gleaming in the sun.
Hot burley loam that worked between our toes
And smell of green tobacco in long rows
Were facts and how you'd stop to light your pipe.
Oh, I remember how you'd stop to wipe
Rain-drops of sweat that stuck above your eyes.
Sometimes you'd stop and listen to bird cries.
I worked beside of you, my mountain mother.
How great it was to work beside of you!
Too strong to be a flower, my mountain mother!
How safe I felt to die beside of you!

699

I shall not pluck the farewell-summer blooms
And give them to my Mountain Lydia Doore;
For farewell summers now bloom at our tombs
And shed their petals by our narrow door.
I gave farewell-summers to Elizabeth;
And phlox, blue-beggar-lice and goldenrod.
My Elizabeth was loved by Lester Withe
And Lester lies near-by under the sod.
He would extend his hand to my Elizabeth
If it were not for his strong heavy door;
And I would not be mad at Lester Withe,
For if I could I'd greet my Lydia Doore.
I know that Lester Withe loved my Elizabeth
But I was only fond of Lydia Doore.

700

The trees grow tall from flesh and blood of me.
White-farewell-summers bloom from my Elizabeth;
These things are fair for living eyes to see
But living eyes could never see who lies beneath.
I do not know where Lydia Doore is lain
And who lies by my Mountain Lydia Doore.
One cannot know when roots grow in the brain.
Dark sockets cannot see through the grave door.
I cannot kiss four lips when mine are dust.
I must lie here to dream no pleasant dreams.
I must lie here and break no lover's trust;
Long as the sun shines on the rugged hill;
Long as the mountain water flows in streams;
I shall lie here to dream forever still.

701

Winter of earth, your green has turned to gray;
Winter of earth, your hair is getting thinned.
Ah, frozen earth, you have no life today;
Your guts are empty and your sides cave in.
The white December moon rides high and laughs.
The trees point their stiff fingers to the moon.
The moon says he will write earth's epitaph
Across the starry sky with a golden pen.
"Remember Moon, this poet never sees
Nor even hears nor knows—this poet lies.
And once he loved a white moon in the trees
And wrote dirt epitaphs for windy skies.
Don't write for sickly earth, but write for him
And pin it to his grave with a white-oak limb."

702

A white oak leaf the early frost has curled
Is my experience, Donald Davidson,
When I think of myself in the past world.
A wreath of green corn-blades was all I won.
And Davidson, I found some merchant men
Like hogs for corn, lived for profit and gain.
They were white maggots in a rotted hen
And tramp them in the mud they'd rise again.
Our laws were, most of all, the greatest cheat.
One could not tear them and the gold apart.
All politician friendship was a cheat.
Some preachers had white skins and dirty hearts.
I went into the world and met defeat
But on that scene I tried to play a part.

"Oh, take a rest," I know the wind has said.
"Lie still," the ferns have said, "there is a reason."
Muscles are lifeless in a body dead—
A body dead and corn sprung from its bosom.
"Lie there," a gray stone said, "the best is over."
"I'll pin you down," oak limbs have said to me.
"I'll make a quilt for you," said the green clover
"If I don't spindle under this shade tree."
"I love dirt lips," the green briar roots did say,
"I love the heart and ribs and slimy eyes."
"Now, I shall hold you down," said the warm clay.
"I'll hold you down so you can never rise."
Now if there is a Resurrection Day
I shall be one that's taken by surprise.

THE END

ACKNOWLEDGMENTS

The reprinting of *Man With a Bull-Tongue Plow* was made possible by the generous support of these friends of the Jesse Stuart Foundation. Their gifts also provided more than 300 copies of the book to school and public libraries across Appalachia.

Anonymous
Anonymous
Marian Adkins
Sandra Aldrich
Thomas A. Allemang
Dr. Ronald L. Baker
Bob & Liz Barnett
Billy Best
Vicky Borders
Evelyn S. Boyd
Louis J. Boyd
Donald E. Burke
G. Alan Burnett
Curt & Betty Cassell
Jean L. Charles
Susan Chiles
Kerry JoAnn Clendenen
Carlos W. Colon
Judy Colvin
Rick & Gerri Coski
Lois Coy
Jerry Crouch
Helen R. Deese
Linda Scott DeRosier
Jack D. Ellis

Naulayne & Michael Enders
Allen & Nancy Englebright
Marcia G. Flannery
James & Helen Fout
James M. Gifford
Charles & Peggy Gilley
Mary & Duane Gilliam
Lorene D. Goff
Wade Hall, Ph.D.
Mortimer B. Hersch, Jr.
J.R. Hersh
Charlie & Jan Holbrook
Jonathan Jeffrey
Ernestine Jennings
William J. Jessie
Harry W. Johnson
Loyal Jones
Bill & Eleanor Kersey
Judith F. Kidwell & James O. Schlicht
Carl & Buzzy Leming
Ann R. Looney
Dr. Robert Love & Ms. Kathy Leadingham
Bill Lloyd

Priscilla Lynd, M.D.
Ginny & Jim Marsh
Mary L. Martin
Journey & Alex McAndrews
Nancy T. McClelland
Donald & Ruby Miller
Mary Ellen Miller
Mary Moeller
David L. Moritz
Mr. & Mrs. Harrell Murrey
Dr. Marshall Myers
Joan M. Nichols
Jane & William Nine
Wayne Onkst
David R. Palmore
Edwina Pendarvis
Janey & Mike Perdue
Doris Price
Jeanine Provencal
Mr. & Mrs. H. Anthony Raiche
Gary Reffett
Dr. Cathy Roberts

Dianna A. Ross
Craig Evan Royce
Jeff & Lori Schroeder
Stephen & Nancy Shy
John Roger Simon
David J. & Lori A. Slagel
Fay Smith
Dale C. Smith
E. Vernon Smith, M.D.
Mr. & Mrs. Fred H. Smith
Harry L. Smith
John H. & Elizabeth S. Spurlock
Marilyn H. Steele & Rebecca and Steve
Stultz Pharmacy, Inc.
Ivan & Deanna Tribe
John & Wanda Lee Vaughn
Ruby Lewis Vencill
Ivry Bussey Ward
Joe S. Wheeler, M.D.
Colonel Charles Dahmon Whitt
Charles Woodruff

Mrs. Robert Yancey, Jr.

Some friends made their gifts to support *Man With a Bull-Tongue Plow* in memory of loved ones:

Janice Folden Burnett
Richard Carroll
Carolyn Carey Childers
Clara Moore Clark
Gene Landrum

Alma Roberts
Joe H. Shy
William G. "Bill" Smith
Wilbert "Bud" Ward
Opal Williams

Isabell Woodruff

Some friends made their gifts to support *Man With a Bull-Tongue Plow* in honor of loved ones:

Mackenzie Victoria Royce
John Slagel

ORIGINAL REVIEW
by Merton S. Yewdale,
Editor at E.P. Dutton & Co., Inc. of New York:

MAN WITH A BULL-TONGUE PLOW
by Jesse Hilton Stuart
No. 34949 • February 1, 1934

I would publish this book. It is a long poem written by a Kentucky mountain farmer, and I believe that it is one of the greatest works of poetry that has come out of the American soil. It consists of 703 sonnets; but the author does not adhere strictly to the sonnet form. This presents two problems: first, that the very freedom from the strict metrical form of the sonnet avoids monotony and holds the reader's interest; second, the constant violation of the sonnet form would no doubt be a serious hindrance to traditional and classical scholars. For my own part I believe that the author's freedom adds to the spontaneity and power of his work.

In the poem he says that he is 25 years old and helps his father cultivate their Kentucky mountain farm. He explains that he has written this long poem (which is really a novel in verse) by snatching moments from his great bull-tongue plow and sitting in the soil with his paper and pencil recording the poetic lines that surged through him. He writes about the things in Nature that he loves: the dirt, the plow, the horses, the flowers, the trees, the sky, the seasons, the lizards, the bees, the snakes. Then he writes about the mountain people, both men and women, whose lives he either knows about or imagines. He describes their appearance, he tells who and what they were—whether saints or sinners—and he presents memorable portraits that are so vivid that they almost come up to your eyes. His usual mood is serious and wistful and at times tragic. Like all mountain people he has no conscious humor. He likes to tell about the tragedies in the lives of the mountain people and he writes about the living and the dead. As a matter of fact, he writes more often about those who are dead and they seem very near to him. This can be explained by something that Miss Jean Thomas told me: she said that the mountain burying ground is always near where the people live, and on summer afternoons the women frequently take their work with them and congregate in the cemetery to visit there while they finish the work. Apparently the mountain people have a feeling that their dead are not far away from them. This is particularly true of the present author.

Sometimes he becomes a little obscene and vulgar; but it is almost always when he is in an angry mood and is describing somebody whom he detests for having done something mean and contemptible. He hates crafty people, especially when they are from the cities. He describes how he once went to work in Nashville and what a terribly hard and unhappy time he had trying to get used to the suffocation of city life, especially when he had been used to the free life amid the free air of the Kentucky mountains. One thing he does which I have never noticed in any other poet: he writes about certain people who are dead as though they themselves were speaking in death. He writes of himself as though he were dead and setting down his own account of his state and of his thoughts.

His style is rugged, full of vitality, heavy with the feelings and similes and metaphors of Nature. He has a powerful force for making you feel the things of Nature in Kentucky; he writes so vividly that you can smell the Kentucky earth which he describes; and you can see vividly every person he portrays in this peculiar and eccentric gallery of Kentucky mountaineers.

Actually he did not write this work: it wrote itself and he was merely the bard through whom the words surged and found an outlet. There is nothing studied or self-conscious or artificial about the man. He is truly simple and has the innocence of Nature. Yet, like Robert Burns, he writes barefacedly of his own love affairs with the mountain girls and he writes with equal frankness of the love affairs of other mountain men and women. He writes many unforgettable lines:

> And when I found the cow on autumn morn
> I drove her up and stood on the warm leaves
> Where she had lain to get my cold feet warm.
> Cold feet and cattle are dear memories—

In writing about himself in the grace he said:

> Then who will know if I were saint or knave?
> And who will know I have a resting place?
> For there will be no markers at my grave.
> The wild rose roots will grow into my face.

Once he was describing how he was writing a poem in the Kentucky shack at night:

> I wrote about a mouse and brown oat stack,
> The room was mighty cold and damp and damp.
> I threw the poem out into the rain,
> Its destiny was darkness and the rain.

The poet seems to live in a place called Plum Grove in Greenup, Kentucky. Obviously he has read the works of a great many poets. I would guess that they were Chaucer, Burns, and Poe. But it is not unlikely that he is acquainted with the works of Housman, Masefield, Frost, and Masters. His work shows a little of the influence of all of these men. Yet, fundamentally, it is highly original and characteristically American. Like Poe and Hawthorne, Jesse Stuart has a deep streak of melancholy, and he rather likes to write about desolation and death. Furthermore, he has not a scrap of humor nor does he write his best lines when the subject is pleasant. He is essentially tragic and he has a curious belief that the finest literary work is done when a man is under the influence of his own inspiration. He has no thought of great financial reward. He wrote this book because it poured out of him and because he loved to set down the words, the sound of which give him such great pleasure. He is a true poet and in my judgment one of the greatest poetic forces that has developed in modern America.

If I were to compare this poem with a modern work of music I should select "Sacre du Printemps," by Stravinsky, the greatest Russian realist composer. The composition describes the bursting of Nature in spring, not emphasizing joyousness but all the ecstacies and delights and pains and secrets and odors of creation and procreation. This man is truly the rustic bard of Kentucky. At no time during the reading of this long poem did I lose interest.

It is like reading a novel or even a history of an interesting group of people. The way to read the poem is to forget the strict sonnet form and merely pay attention to what the poet writes. If you keep in mind the strict metrical form of the sonnet you will certainly be bothered by the liberties which he has taken; furthermore you will not get the full effect of his thought if you try to carry along the consciousness of a line perfect for scansion. All artificial medium even metrical form, must be put into the background, and the poetic lines themselves allowed to come straight into the mind and heart of the reader. Otherwise it will seem to be but an amorphous work, crude, coarse, rhapsodical, and at times overheated. Very refined and overcultured people will not like this work. But I think that such men as Dreiser, Masefield, Frost and Housman will like it in spite of its amorphous ruggedness. It is filled with sensuality—not the sensuality of human beings, but of Nature. The things of the farmyard are spoken of freely and frankly, and the poet writes of the most intimate things with the naivete and spontaneity of a truly innocent person. Apparently he lives and writes as though he were not an individual person but a true extension of Nature, perhaps a kind of hot, dark-colored flower that was still attached to a thriving bush.

This work had moved me deeply, and though I have just finished reading it I could turn to the first page and begin to read it all over. Some of the lines are so fertile and lusty that you really like to linger over them before reading on. Furthermore, some of the lines thrust up such startling poetic images that you simply cannot go on reading without pausing for a second. Now and then there is a quiet intensity when he describes some of the inevitabilities of Nature. Then he sometimes lashes out against human beings who live scoundrelly and contemptible lives among their fellowmen. When you consider the comparative narrowness of this poet's life and then reflect how long and how rich a work he has been able to write, you will realize that this is truly a great work. It should be published and, except that it will have to the copyread for punctuation and capitalization, I would not change the text. To try to make all the sonnets perfectly metrical would ruin much of the man's work. To tone down some of the obscene passages (there are only a few) seems to me to be unnecessary. It would be like a farmer cleaning out his barnyard before he invited some friends to look at the calves. Somehow the few obscenities in this work do not seem to be conventionally obscene. I would publish the entire manuscript as it stands. I firmly believe that there will be some critics who will pronounce this one of the greatest poetical works that ever came out of America.

MBY:DM